SAINTS, DEMONS,
AND $ASSE$$S$

Gary Holloway

S AINTS, DEMONS, AND ASSES

Southern Preacher Anecdotes

INDIANA UNIVERSITY PRESS
Bloomington and Indianapolis

Manufactured in the United States of America

Library of Congress Cataloging-in-Publication Data

Holloway, Gary
    Saints, demons, and asses : Southern preacher anecdotes / Gary
Holloway
      p. cm.
    Bibliography: p.
    Includes index.
    ISBN 0-253-32841-1. —ISBN 0-253-20528-X (pbk.)
    1. Churches of Christ—Southern States—Clergy—Anec-
dotes. 2. Wit and humor—Religious aspects—Churches of
Christ. 3. Southern States—Religious life and customs. I. Title.
BX7077.Z8A25   1989
398'.352—dc 19   88–46036

1 2 3 4 5 93 92 91 90 89

To Deb,
who loves me when I'm
a saint, a demon, or even an ass.

CONTENTS

PREFACE

This book is designed to be enjoyed on several levels.

Those who read it for entertainment will find some of the funniest stories they have ever read. I wish I could take credit for the humor, but I cannot. These stories spring from a deep reservoir of laughter found in the nature of religion itself.

Scholars of American religion will discover in these pages a neglected resource for their studies: oral tradition. Most of us have been content to rely on written, published sources, which certainly are used in this study. Oral lore, however, can give some insights that written sources by their very nature cannot. The differences between oral and written evidence are discussed in detail in this book.

This volume also provides folklorists with more grist for their mill. Folklore studies are still something of a mystery to most people. There is a misconception that folklore is only found in ancient myths, fairy tales, or yarns told in the backwoods. Instead, this book makes it clear that we all participate in folklore. Upon reading these stories, some of you may say, "I've heard these before." Indeed, you have. You may have even told some of them. All of which makes you something of an amateur folklorist. I hope this book prompts you to listen more closely the next time you hear a preacher story, maybe even tape it or write it down. If you want to share your stories with someone who studies these things, I, for one, would be happy to hear from you.

Many people assisted in the production of this book. Those who provided oral anecdotes, particularly O. B. Perkins of Kentucky, gave cheerfully and willingly of their time. I also want to thank three of my teachers who provided encouragement and criticism: John Burrison of Georgia State University, and Fred Craddock and Robert Detweiler of Emory University.

Saints, demons,
and Asses

I.

INTRODUCTION

People love stories. Even in a society overwhelmed by a variety of entertainment media, a good story can still hold an audience. However the word "story" itself is ambiguous, since both oral and written narratives are stories. Stories, then, can be told in several media and can be changed from one medium to another.

Walter Ong argues that a change from an oral culture to a writing one entails a change of thought forms. Writing restructures consciousness. To support his argument, he compares oral and written narratives, both historical and fictional. Ong lists several methodologies used to compare orality and literacy: literary history, new criticism, Russian formalism, structuralism, deconstruction, speech-act theory, and reader-response theory.[1]

And Ong himself admits, "Study of the contrast between orality and literacy is largely unfinished business";[2] therefore various methodologies and texts must be utilized to explore this contrast. Most of the methodologies listed above begin with written texts and are only secondarily concerned with oral presentations. Two methodologies begin with oral presentations. Speech-act theory concerns itself with all oral presentations, but structuralism, as practiced by Lévi–Strauss and others, concentrates on long traditional narratives—myths and folktales.

With the exception of structuralism, these methods do not deal with the traditional nature of certain oral narratives, and structuralism deals only with longer traditional narratives. By contrast, this study will attempt to confirm Ong's thesis by focusing on traditional oral texts—folklore—using the comparative method common in folklore studies. The particular texts in view are brief personal narratives: anecdotes. Thus this study will show that the change from oral to written anecdotes affects the style and function of those anecdotes. A change in medium is a change in message.

The anecdotes in this comparison will be anecdotes of Church of Christ preachers. To lay a groundwork for this comparison, we will first discuss the discipline of folklore, the nature of anecdotes, and the peculiar aspects of the Church of Christ that affect this study.

FOLKLORE AND ANECDOTES

The field of folklore studies the oral, customary, and material traditions of a people.[3] It focuses on what is handed down from generation to generation in a culture, by informal, non-literary means. Unfortunately, in our highly literate American culture, "folklore" carries with it the connotation of "uneducated" or "backwoods." Another misconception of folklore is brought on by popular presentations of certain "folk heroes" (Paul Bunyan, for example). Stories of these heroes are often creative literary productions and not traditional tales; they therefore are not genuine folklore but what Richard Dorson calls "fakelore."[4] Folklore then is not only what happens in rural areas or what is told in literary or cinematic tall tales. Folklore is an integral part of the life and conversation of all human beings, including literate, urban sophisticates.

To clarify this universality of folklore, one must realize that human beings simultaneously participate in different types of culture. There is elite culture that produces and appreciates good novels, classical music, and modern art. Normative or popular culture is seen in most television shows, movies, and popular writing. Folk culture is expressed in the telling of jokes, following of superstitions and other means. Modern Americans belong to all three types of culture—elite, normative, and folk.[5] Every time one tells or hears a traditional joke or story, one participates in folklore and becomes part of the folk.

Anecdotes thus are folklore not because they belong to a particular "backward" group in society, but because they express the traditional (as contrasted with the elite or popular) element in a culture. Anecdotes are classified as oral folklore; however there is some disagreement among folklorists as to what genre of oral folklore anecdotes represent.

Some place the anecdote as a short personal legend (legend meaning an oral narrative believed to be true by teller and audience).[6] These narratives feature a historical person, usually someone accepted as a hero by the audience, and serve to explain a facet of the hero's life or character. Although many anecdotes fit under the legend heading, others, in which the main character is not a historical person, do not.

Anecdotes are similar in many ways to folktales, fictional stories told primarily to entertain. Some anecdotes have formulaic phrasing, characters, storylines, and functions similar to folktales. Most anecdotes are shorter than folktales, however, and many anecdotes are told to illustrate, not just to entertain.[7] Anecdotes as a group, then, cannot be classified as short folktales.

Like proverbs, another oral folklore genre, some anecdotes are used to make a point, to pass on wisdom. Could anecdotes, then, be simply longer proverbs? No, because the anecdote always tells a story, no matter how brief, while a proverb has no story or characterization.[8]

Most anecdotes are humorous, so some folklorists classify them with jests or jokes. In this view the anecdote is a short form of the *Schwank* or humorous story.[9] There are several difficulties in this view. Not all anecdotes are humorous, and even those that are may have a serious point,[10] so one cannot lump all anecdotes together as jests. Also, most anecdotes are attached to historical persons, but most jokes have fictitious characters. Along the same lines, anecdotes usually claim to have "really happened," while jokes rarely make this claim.[11] So, although most anecdotes are humorous narratives, they exhibit characteristics quite different from the typical joke.

Where then should anecdotes be classified? Most do fit the genre of legend. Even though most anecdotes are humorous and most legends serious, the connection of an anecdote with a historical person makes it legendary. Anecdotes can be defined as "brief, oral, traditional, usually humorous stories about historical characters that are believed to be true by the teller and the audience." "Oral" and "traditional" separate anecdotes from non-folk material. "Believed to be true" distinguishes anecdotes from folktales. "Stories" means they are not proverbs. "About historical characters" and "believed" separate them from jokes. This definition does have difficulty, however, accounting for anecdotes in which the characters are not named. In those cases the line between humorous story and anecdote is blurred. It may be that these stories began as jokes, were expanded into humorous stories by the addition of stock characters, and eventually will become full anecdotes by attaching themselves to historical persons.[12] In any case, a few anonymous preacher stories in which the informant knew it "really happened" to a preacher, but did not know the preacher's name, will be included in this study. If they are not fully anecdotal according to the definition above, they may be in the process of becoming so.

FOLKLORE AND HISTORY

Anecdotes, then, are folklore, but as legends they are stories believed to be true. Are they true? In other words, are these stories accurate oral accounts of historical events? What is the relation of folklore to oral history?

For the folklorist, "oral" is the important word in oral history, since orality is a mark of true folklore. However, not all oral productions are folk; they must also be traditional in form and transmission to be folklore. Not all oral history is folklore, but only oral traditional history.[13]

"Oral traditional history is a record of what a people consider important to themselves."[14] Nontraditional oral history comes from an individual who shares a personal memory of an historical event. Oral traditional history is shared by many tellers and is passed from one generation to another; it is shaped by the common outlook of a particular society. For example, people who fought in a war will tell their history from a particular slant, depending on which side they fought. Oral traditional history usually contains the repetition, formulas, and other oral patterns of folklore.

As traditional history is passed down orally, the characters in the stories tend to become more idealized, the heroes better, the villains worse. "An aura of legend envelopes the core of fact"[15] and it becomes increasingly difficult to separate the historical from the nonhistorical.

Anecdotes are oral, traditional, and claim to be historical. Are they? Did the preacher stories in this study "really happen?" That is difficult to answer. In some cases there might be enough corroborative historical evidence to establish the likelihood of a story being historical. In others, the different versions and the stock characters of the story make historicity improbable. The historicity of these particular stories is outside the scope of this study. That is not to say that this study has no bearing on history. "What the folk choose to remember is itself a historical datum"[16] and an important one. The themes, contexts, and functions of these preacher stories shed light on the history of the Church of Christ, the South, and American culture as a whole.

This study then will focus on the oral, traditional, process shown in the preacher anecdotes, not on their historicity. Historical or not, these stories are about historical persons and possess enough verisimilitude to be told as true. This is a study of those tellings.

The Folk Group: Churches of Christ

Those who tell the preacher tales in this study are all part of an indigenous American religious movement known as Churches of Christ, one of three large religious groups that grew out of a nineteenth century movement toward Christian unity on the American frontier. This section will focus on the history and characteristics of the Churches of Christ that most affect the preacher stories.[17]

The church was actually the result of two religious movements on the American frontier. The first was led by Barton W. Stone (1772–1844), a Presbyterian preacher in Kentucky. Stone presided over the largest camp meeting ever held on the frontier. From ten to twenty-five thousand people gathered at Cane Ridge, Kentucky, in August 1801. At this and similar meetings, thousands reacted to the preaching by uncontrollably jerking, running, dancing, or laughing. These "bodily agitations" (as Stone styled them) were similar to audience reactions to preaching in certain Pentecostal or Holiness churches today.

Not long after the Cane Ridge revival, Stone and other Presbyterian revival leaders broke away from their presbytery and formed the Springfield Presbytery. Within a year these men decided to follow the Bible as their only creed and to forsake the "traditions of men." Finding no authority for a presbytery, they published in June, 1804, "The Last Will and Testament of the Springfield Presbytery." This document rejected the idea of an ordained (and theologically educated) clergy. A church could choose any man to preach. It also pointed all Christians to the Bible as the only guide in religious matters.

The second movement was led by Thomas Campbell (1763–1854) and his son Alexander (1788–1866). These two were Scotch–Irish Presbyterian ministers who migrated to America from Ireland in 1807 and 1809. Though Presbyterian like Stone, their preaching style was quite different. Both had studied at the University of Glasgow and were deeply influenced by the Enlightenment, especially the philosophy of John Locke. Their preaching was more rational and called for a more reasoned response than the preaching of Stone.

The Campbells thought the division that plagued American churches on the frontier (they settled in western Pennsylvania) resulted from the churches' abandonment of "primitive Christianity." They advocated a return to the Biblical pattern for the church and felt that reliance on the Bible alone would produce unity among the churches.

In 1811, the Campbells formed a church in Brush Run, Pennsylvania. After studying the Bible, Alexander became convinced that only adults should be baptized. He was baptized, most of the Brush Run Church followed his example, and the Brush Run Church joined the Redstone Baptist Association. The Campbell movement was affiliated with the Baptists until 1827.

The preaching of unity based solely on the Bible (what these men called "the simple gospel") was quite popular on the frontier. Evangelists in the Campbell movement, like the enormously successful revivalist Walter Scott, began to preach an objective plan of salvation (as opposed to the subjective, emotional preaching of other frontier revivalists). As a result, thousands of people joined the movement and dozens of churches sprang up in Pennsylvania, Ohio, and Kentucky.

At the same time the movement was growing, it was also becoming more distinguishable from other religious groups. Besides being a preacher and publisher, Alexander Campbell was known as a fierce debater. He debated atheists on the existence of God, Catholics on the truth of Protestantism, Presbyterians on adult baptism, and Baptists on the use of the Old Testament. These debates not only clarified the differences between the Campbell movement and these denominations, but also showed the similarity between the Campbells and the Stone movement.

Consequently, in January, 1832, at Lexington, Kentucky, representatives of the two groups agreed to a merger. This united group, known as Disciples of Christ or Christians, continued to grow dramatically. Eventually, however, the group split and the more conservative branch, located mainly in the South, became known as the Churches of Christ.

This historical background has several implications for one preaching in the Churches of Christ. The church began as a "Back to the Bible" movement. A preacher in the church would be expected to continue that emphasis on Scripture.

The early preachers in the movement taught that Scripture can be understood by anyone. Thus, there is no need for a formal theology; such doctrinal teaching would be divisive and sectarian. If the Bible is taught, the individual can clearly see its doctrine (hence "the Bible should be our only creed"). As an example of this bias against formal theology, when Alexander Campbell began Bethany College in West Virginia, the charter called for the Bible to be the primary textbook. Another clause in the charter forbad the establishment of a theological professorship.

Since the Bible could be clearly understood by common people, there was no need for a professional clergy. Ministers in the church were not formally ordained, indeed the term "Reverend" was considered immodest, since anyone could preach. No formal education was necessary for preaching; after all, Paul and Peter never went to seminary. A preacher, then, was anyone who proclaimed the Word of the Bible; he had no authority over the church. At least, in theory he had no authority. In reality those who expounded the Bible had a great deal of control over the church. Preachers, although not formally ordained, were recognized as the spiritual leaders in the church. Church colleges, while not seminaries, did train many of these preachers and so the colleges, too, had great influence in the movement.

The focus of the movement on the Bible alone also led these preachers to reject all modern-day miracles. Direct operation of the Holy Spirit on the hearts of sinners was also a rejected doctrine. In this respect the rationalism of the Campbell movement overcame the subjectivity of the early camp meetings of the Stone movement.

This biblicism eventually led to a split in the movement. Although the Civil War was the major cause of this division, there were also theological reasons. Some Churches of Christ began to use musical instruments to accompany their singing in worship. In the early years of the movement, instrumental music was not used in the churches. Some members, especially some preachers, objected that instruments were not specifically mentioned in Scripture and so their use was not authorized. Others argued that the silence of Scripture permitted instruments. Eventually the movement split with most of the Northern churches (known as Christian Churches or Disciples of Christ) using an instrument and most Southern churches (known as Churches of Christ) not using an instrument. The stories in this study are all about non-instrumental Churches of Christ.

This particular view of biblical authority also led most Church of Christ members to conclude that they were the only group that had restored the New Testament church. The early preachers strongly believed the movement was not a denomination. Since they followed the Bible alone, they were simply part of the church spoken of in the New Testament, not a part of a "human denomination." The belligerent attitude toward other religious groups carried over into sermons. "Denomination" became a pejorative term.

Throughout this section, phrases like "most Church of Christ members believe" have been used repeatedly. The reason one cannot be more definite is that Churches of Christ have no formal creed. There is no central church authority; each congregation is independent. For this reason the plural "Churches of Christ" is used interchangeably with "Church of Christ."

In summary, Church of Christ history and dogma affect the Church of Christ preaching displayed in the anecdotes. Generally, pioneer Church of Christ preachers were biblicists, critical of other churches ("denominations"), theologically uneducated, but extremely dedicated to the task of preaching. A modern preacher in the Churches of Christ, to be faithful to the teachings of these pioneer preachers, would need to preach sermons full of Scripture, that are clearly understood. He would be against formal ordination and see no real need for a theological education (beyond knowing "what the Bible says"). He would take great pains to show the Churches of Christ are not a "denomination" and that those in denominations misunderstand the Bible.

WRITTEN AND ORAL ANECDOTES

Oral anecdotes are obviously folklore since they are oral and traditional in form and transmission. But in what sense can written anecdotes be folklore? In the strict sense, written stories cannot be folklore because they are not oral and do not exist in different versions; writing fixes the text of the story. Written anecdotes are not folklore, but can be representations of an oral folklore performance. In other words, anecdotes found in printed biographies are not folklore, but are the use of folklore in literature.[18]

In comparing oral anecdotes—folklore—with their use in written biographies, one must first establish that these biographies really incorporate folk materials. Just because a biography describes a colorful, backwoods preacher does not mean it uses folklore. Folksy is not necessarily folk. How then can one identify literary material that has a folklore base? Richard Dorson gives three tests of folklore in literature: biographical evidence, internal evidence, and corroborative evidence.[19]

Biographical evidence refers to encounters the authors of the texts in question may have had with oral lore. In this study, the question would be "What evidence is there that the authors of these preacher biographies had direct contact with oral storytelling situations?" The degree of contact differs from author to author, but in general, these authors had heard many oral stories about the subjects of their books. One specifically states he is relating a traditional story he had heard, even naming the source.[20] Others mention that several oral stories are told about the preachers they write about.[21] Even when no specific references are made to oral lore, the participation of these authors in the same church as their subjects (all of the authors of biographies of preachers in this study are members of the Church of Christ) means they are part of the storytelling folk culture of the church. It is unlikely that these authors could be in the church for years and not hear preacher stories.

The settings of the alleged folk materials in a work form part of the internal evidence of the use of folklore. If stories are set in plausible storytelling situations and if other scenes of folklife in the work are consistent with what is known of the culture in question, then the author probably used folklore. In the biographies of preachers, the anecdotes are rarely set in a storytelling situation. This may be because anecdotes themselves, unlike folktales, are usually told in interpersonal conversation and not in a more formal performance setting. The scenes of frontier folklife in the biographies are consistent with folk custom on the frontier.[22] The internal evidence of the biographies, then, gives some support to their use of oral anecdotes.

To argue successfully the use of folk materials in the biographies, one must also give corroborative evidence, that is, show that the anecdotes have an independent oral, traditional life. Chapter 4 of this study gives parallel oral and written anecdotes, showing that in some cases it is certain that the authors of the biographies used folklore. Even when the written stories have no direct parallels, they are consistent with the themes of oral stories. In some cases the written anecdotes reflect the types and motifs of earlier oral stories.

Written biographies of Church of Christ preachers thus use oral anecdotes. These oral stories are used to give biographical information and to provide local color. When biographers use oral stories they must transfer them from the oral to the written medium. This transference produces changes in both the form and the function of the stories. These changes will be discussed in chapters 5 and 6 of this study.

Not only do written biographies use oral sources, but oral tellers also repeat written stories. A particular teller of anecdotes may read a certain preacher anecdote, then tell it orally, having forgotten the written source. In certain of the parallel written and oral stories discussed in chapter 4, this seems to be the case. Are these oral stories with a written base folklore? Yes, if they are transmitted orally and are not simply conscious verbatim quotations of the written text.

Folklore, then, is always oral and traditional in transmission.

The oral preacher anecdotes are folklore; the written preacher anecdotes use folklore. This study compares the two groups.

COLLECTION AND ANALYSIS
OF THE ANECDOTES

The written anecdotes used in this study were culled from fourteen printed biographies of Church of Christ preachers published between 1847 and 1970. The passages containing these anecdotes are reproduced verbatim. Each biography is written by a member of the Church of Christ.

The oral anecdotes were collected using standard folklore field procedures. They are transcribed verbatim from tape recorded interviews with seven informants conducted between 1985 and 1986.

This study will compare the oral and written anecdotes on the basis of the three levels of folklore analysis described by Alan Dundes: text, texture, and context.[23]

First the texts of the anecdotes will be given, text meaning a version of single telling of an oral story or the use of an oral story in a biography. Chapter 2 will present texts of written anecdotes, grouping them according to theme. Chapter 3 will present oral texts in the same manner. In chapter 4, similar oral and written texts will be compared.

Next, the texture of language of the oral and written stories will be compared. Chapter 5 will deal with the linguistic features of the oral stories—rhyme, stress, pitch, tone, etc., and compare them with parallel linguistic features in the written stories—punctuation, allusions, etc. The chapter will demonstrate how writing changes the texture of the oral stories.

Two ways of comparing the texts and texture of folklore are put forward by Claude Lévi-Strauss and Vladimir Propp. In his work with myths, Lévi-Strauss discovered they all display a structure of unresolved binary opposites ("high"-"low," "east"-"west," "raw"-"cooked"). He reduced these binary opposites into a shorthand form of symbols, allowing easy comparison of myths.[24] Propp, by working with folktales, found that the characters in the tales serve stable, constant, functions. These functions of the characters form the fundamental components of the tale and, with other elements of the tale, they can be symbolically used to analyze and compare tales.[25] Though the systems of these two men differ, they are helpful in the comparison of folklore. Anecdotes, however, are quite different from myths and folktales.[26] The brevity of the typical anecdote makes the development of binary opposites and characters impossible. So a system of symbols will not be used to compare these oral and written anecdotes.[27]

Finally, the context of the stories will be explored. Oral context is the social situation that occurs between the narrator and the audience. Context in the biographies refers to how the anecdotes are framed in the story. Both oral and literary contexts affect the texture of the stories, so context will be a consideration in chapter 5. Chapter 6 will deal with the functions of the stories; these functions will be discovered based on an analysis of a number of contexts. Function deals with the meaning of the anecdotes to the folk group. Therefore, in addition to the context analysis mentioned above, chapter 6 will also present interview material in which the folk (in this case the tellers of the oral anecdotes) give the function of meaning of their stories.[28]

In summary, anecdotes are folklore—short, traditional, oral stories believed to be true (though their historicity can be questioned). The anecdotes in this study are all concerned with preachers in the Church of Christ, a religious group whose characteristics mark the anecdotes. Besides the oral anecdotes, this study will consider their use in written, published biographies of Church of Christ preachers. Oral and written anecdotes will be compared on the basis of texts, language style, and function in order to demonstrate how the shift from oral to written form changes thought.

II.

WRITTEN ANECDOTES

Following the time that the initial leaders of the Restoration Movement died, it became customary to enshrine the works of prominent preachers in a biography, usually published shortly after their death. All of the stories here come from biographies written by members of the movement; most are not by professional historians. Their tone is extremely hagiographic. In spite of these limitations, they do present anecdotes of certain preachers that were in common use soon after their deaths.

There are two general types of anecdotes here: serious moral exempla and humorous facetiae.[1] Under those categories I have arranged the stories by topic, either by the setting (sermon, debate, baptism) or the subject (providence, cleverness, et al.). When the stories fit Aarne's[2] type numbers or Thompson's[3] motif numbers, this is indicated; however, no attempt is made to create new type or motif numbers to fit stories not covered by them.

SERIOUS ANECDOTES

Special Providences

Life for preachers in the nineteenth and early twentieth centuries was much more dangerous than for preachers today. Frontier preachers faced the dangers all faced back then: wild animals, Indians, bad weather and other calamities. Being itinerants, they did not enjoy the safety of settled towns. In addition to these troubles, preachers faced financial troubles, especially in the Churches of Christ in which there was no central authority to set salaries. Preachers also faced moral dangers, challenges to the sincerity of their mission.

No wonder, then, these early preachers express a strong faith in God to protect them. Sometimes this protection took an unusual form. Church of Christ preachers did not believe in miracles—these had ceased in the first century—but they did describe unusual occurrences as the providence (sometimes "special providence") of God.[4]

Protection from accident

Travel for these preachers was hazardous. They traveled on foot, on horseback, by carriage, or by train. Each had its own dangers. Mrs. T. B. Larimore tells of a close call she and her husband had when traveling by train:

[1]

We had the usual experiences that evangelists and their traveling companions have. During one meeting we would have all the comforts and most of the luxuries of life, while the next meeting might find us in surroundings rather primitive. But we liked the life and the work we each had to do, Mr. Larimore preaching, I taking care of him. One incident of our travels is worthy of mention, perhaps, because it bears a lesson in its bosom. We planned in the spring of 1921 to start East the first of June; but, as the time drew nearer, we noticed that June 1 was Wednesday. We always did our traveling between Sundays, and fearing we could not reach Nashville before the next Sunday, if we did not start earlier than Wednesday, we moved the day of our departure forward two days, beginning the journey Monday, May 30—Memorial Day—though some inconvenience is attached to starting on a holiday. Part of our trip took us through the Royal Gorge, and at Pueblo, Colorado, we changed from the Denver and R. G. to the Missouri Pacific train. The two trains stood on parallel tracks about forty minutes while the change was made. Just *two days* later, at the same hour, the trains were again standing parallel while the necessary changes were being made. Suddenly and without warning a mighty avalanche of water, rushing down the Royal Gorge with the

speed of an express train, broke over them. Those in the
coaches were penned as in a trap, those outside were caught
up by the mighty force of the water, hurled against the trains
and other objects, and their lives crushed out. Some were
deeply buried in the mud that settled many feet deep in low
places. Had we adhered to our original plan we should have
been in the train or walking about the station at Pueblo at the
identical hour the tragedy took place. That experience made
us more sensible of the guarding, guiding hand of Providence.[5]

Note that this is one of "the usual experiences that evangelists
have." In fact, similar missed train or boat stories are told of
other preachers. Donald E. Byrne, Jr., tells of Anson Green, an
American Methodist preacher who in a visit to England misses
a doomed train because of the slowness of his tailor.[6] These
stories contain Thompson's motif V541, "Man prevented from
passage in a ship which later sinks."

This was not Larimore's only brush with death. Another biographer, after remarking that Larimore believed in special providence, tells how he survived another train wreck:

[2]

One very dark night he was returning home from Memphis,
Tennessee. A cyclone had carried away the railroad bridge at
Tuscumbia, Alabama, and well nigh destroyed the town.
Many houses were swept away, several people were killed
and a great many others were seriously injured. The train he
was on, not knowing of the destruction, plunged into the
swollen stream where the bridge was blown away, while running at full speed. He went under the raging current, from
which he emerged and by some means unknown to him,
crossed the stream. He was thoroughly wet, and wholly unconscious as to how he got out of the wreck and across the
creek. When he came to himself, he was leaning against a
telegraph pole on the bank of the stream. Someone, he never
knew whom, kindly pulled off his boots, drained the water
out of them and put them on again for him. He walked to
Florence, five miles, through the darkness and the mud.[7]

Here Larimore does not avoid the train wreck, but does somehow avoid injury (after all, he can walk five miles after the accident).

If this were not enough, Larimore experienced another accident, this time in a horse-drawn carriage:

[3]

At another time, he was in a carriage on his way to an
appointment in Middle Tennessee, in company with one of
the school boys. Passing around the base of a mountain, the
horses took fright, wheeled suddenly to the right and leaped
over a precipice twenty feet high into a creek. The school-boy
escaped the fall by quickly leaping out of the carriage; but *he*
went over into the creek with the horses and carriage. He was
entangled among the horses, harness and shattered carriage,
and his feet were fastened by something at the bottom of the creek.
Suddenly his feet were released, he knew not how, and he
swam to the bank; but his boots were left in the wreck. The
school-boy who was with him went into the creek and suc-
ceeded in getting the boots; but they were completely torn to
pieces and utterly worthless. The carriage was entirely ruined;
the horses reached the opposite bank of the creek with a piece
of it as large as an ordinary door shutter across their backs!
How he ever escaped unhurt was a mystery. He was in the
water, under the horses, his feet fast at the bottom of the
creek, when *somehow* his boots were torn to pieces and his
feet released. He says—*"The Lord delivered me."*[8]

No wonder the man believed God was with him.

With the dangers of travel, it is surprising there are not more
stories of this type. Perhaps the church's stand against modern
day miracles made preachers reticent to relate such stories.

Cured of sickness

Traveling and preaching out of doors made preachers vulnerable to all kinds of illnesses. Cures of these ailments were
not ascribed to the miraculous power of God but to God's providential care. That the distinction was a fine one is shown by this
story of Barton W. Stone. Stone had been preaching for many
days in the open air. As a result, his lungs became inflamed, he
developed a violent cough, spitting blood, and felt himself "fast

descending to the tomb."[9] His physician forbad him to speak; however:

[4]

When a camp-meeting was pitched "in a shady grove near Paris," Stone, undaunted, was there. A Presbyterian preacher launched there a formidable opposition to the Revival and the doctrines which had given it life. This opponent broke up the meeting in the grove, and led the crowd a mile to town to "worship in a house that could not contain half the people." Here another opponent was "put forward," who "lengthily addressed the people in iceberg style." Stone forgot his physical weakness in his reaction to this frigid threat. Deliberately at the first pause he led the group in a prayer, marked by the old Revival spirit. "Some of the preachers jumped out of a window back of the pulpit and left." The atmosphere was suddenly warmed. Awakened sinners demanded the attention of Stone. The Revival was on again. He labored. He perspired excessively. His physician found him and remonstrated. Stone, however, "rose next morning relieved from the disease." Stone believed that the heat of the Revival renewed under opposition was for him a physical curative.[10]

Though this recovery was not as "miraculous" as that experienced by preachers of other churches,[11] to Stone it was an example of God's providing for his servants.

Helped financially

Most Church of Christ preachers were constantly in financial difficulty. There was no central church authority to pay them, so they were dependent on local congregations for their support. Unfortunately, these churches promised little to the preachers and often delivered even less. Many preachers turned to farming or other businesses to support themselves. A few became independently wealthy, but many more scratched out a meager living. In this situation, some quit preaching, but others decided to trust God and not humans to provide for them.

The story below illustrates how preachers struggled inwardly with the question of whom to trust for their living. James A. Harding was a preacher who had taught school to support his

family, but had finally given in to the call to spend all his time
in preaching:

[5]

One day Mr. Hodgkins, a wealthy banker friend, called him
in. "Jimmy, I understand you are preaching continually
now," he said. "I cannot preach, but I can make money. That
is my gift. You can preach, but evangelizing as you do and
where you do, you will not receive much money. So just let
me know when you need any money, and I will be glad to
let you have it."

"Some time afterward," Harding related, "I saw that I
would need about twenty-five dollars in a few days, and I
saw no prospects of getting it except by availing myself of
this brother's offer. So I went to him and asked for that
amount, saying I hoped to return it in sixty days. He opened
his checkbook at once."

"Do you not need fifty?" he asked. "I would as soon write
this check for fifty."

I told him twenty-five would be enough. He wrote the check
for that amount and refused my note. He said, "If it suits you
to hand it back, all right; if not, all right. But if you need more
be sure to let me know. It gives me more pleasure to let you
have it, than it does you to receive it."

Numbers of times I went to him for money and he always
let me have it with pleasure. But after a while my mind was
especially attracted to the verses in the Philippian letter: "In
nothing be anxious; but in everything by prayer and suppli-
cation with thanksgiving let your requests be made known
unto God. . . . And my God shall supply every need of yours
according to his riches in glory in Christ Jesus."

"So I resolved that I would not go to him any more for
money, and I never did. Sometimes the temptation to do so
was very great, but I did not yield to it; and I got along just
as well, met every obligation just as promptly, and had the
consolation of knowing that I was trusting in God and not in
man."[12]

Harding followed this principle all of his life and was never in
want. Later in life, he started two Bible Colleges, one in Nashville
and one in Bowling Green, Kentucky, without ever asking anyone to contribute. He "believed the Lord would move people

voluntarily to support the school as long as it was pleasing to Him."[13]

This theme of trusting God for support is also found in many Methodist stories.[14] One interesting Methodist story, also found among Mormon missionaries,[15] is of a small sum of money that somehow is multiplied and becomes virtually inexhaustible.[16]

Saved from dangerous men

From the mid-nineteenth through the early twentieth centuries, religious feelings were high in the South. Religious differences were taken seriously, and religious discussions sometimes ended violently. Church of Christ preachers in this period generally spoke harshly of the religious errors of other churches, causing much hostility. For these reasons, many early preachers faced violence from those opposed to their message. One preacher who was threatened extensively was Marshall Keeble, a black Church of Christ preacher, who faced both religious and racial opposition.

[6]

Marshall Keeble's life has been threatened on several occasions including bodily injury. His courage was never reckless but controlled by his wisdom. No matter what the indignities were that he suffered at the hands of Negro or white, he remained calm and courteous. He baptized a Negro woman once in Duck River in Tennessee. Her husband said he would kill Keeble and waited on the bank with a shotgun. Keeble went right on into the water and baptized her and the husband later.

In a West Tennessee town, a white man threatened Keeble: "You preach like this anymore, you'll leave town or we'll kill you."

Keeble answered: "I kissed my wife before I left Nashville, Tennessee. My Lord died for me, I'd just as soon die for him in Lexington, Tennessee, as anywhere else." That concluded the whole matter.

Nor were the Negroes always friendly. While in a meeting in the early part of 1933, in Sarasota, Florida, the sectarians put up a hard fight against Keeble. They threatened to burn his tent, including other veiled threats of one kind or another. Fifty-two were baptized during the meeting.[17]

These three incidents were typical of Keeble's life. He and other preachers consider such opposition a result of Satan's opposition to the gospel, not a result of their own particular caustic preaching style.

This religious opposition was not limited to black preachers, or to Church of Christ preachers. Anecdotes of violent opposition to Methodist and especially Mormon preachers are told. In these stories, just as in the Keeble story, the preachers showed great courage in the face of the danger of mob violence, trusting God to deliver them from those who opposed the "true message."[18]

Special religious guidance

Since Church of Christ preachers did not believe in modern miracles, they relied on the preaching of the gospel to save souls, not on the miraculous intervention of God. One incident that goes against the tide of opinion is the encounter of James A. Harding with a young woman who wished to be baptized, but could not bring herself to leave the church of her upbringing. Harding gives her a New Testament, and they continue their conversation:

[7]

"Mark this verse, Brother Harding. Mark this verse," she cried. The verse read, "Let no man deceive you with vain words; for because of these things cometh the wrath of God upon the sons of disobedience." Harding wondered if she meant him.

"Miss———, have I ever asked you to do a single thing that I have not read to you plainly from the word of God?" he asked.

"No," she replied, "you have not."

"Then my words have not been in vain," Harding said, "for they have been the words of God. It is God who exhorts us to forsake not to assemble ourselves together, who tells us that the disciples came together to break bread upon the first day of the week, who commands us to mark those who cause division contrary to the doctrine which we have learned. These are not vain words but are indeed words of truth and soberness."

As she continued to flip through the pages of the New

Testament, her face again lighted up, and she cried, "Mark this, too, Brother Harding." The verse read, "For this cause we thank God also without ceasing, because, when ye received it not as the word of men, but as it is in truth the word of God, which effectually worketh also in you that believe."

By this time she was deeply affected. She felt she must break away from her mother's church, but it was no light thing to turn from associations of a lifetime, associations made dear by the memory of a mother's tenderness and love.

"The path of duty is the way of happiness," Harding encouraged her, "though it may not seem so in the beginning. True, Jesus tells us to take up the cross daily and follow him; but he also says, 'My yoke is easy and my burden light.' If we follow him lovingly and trustingly, he will delight in us, and it will please him to surprise us with his kindnesses; he will even go beyond our brightest hopes in granting us the desires of our hearts. He loves us and he allows no pain, no sorrow, no disappointment to come to us except it be for our good. He ever watches over us, directs our steps, and causes all things to work together for our good, when we love him as we should."

As they talked she was still turning the leaves of the New Testament, and for the third time she suddenly turned to him, this time with her eyes full of tears.

"Here's another verse; mark this one too," she said. The verse read, "And ye now have sorrow; but I will see you again, your heart shall rejoice, and your joy no man taketh from you."

"It seems that God is guiding you in the very verses you need," Harding said.

"Yes," she replied; "so it seems to me."[19]

Neither Harding nor his biographer call this a miracle (though his biographer does use the word "accident" in quotations), reflecting the church's stand against miracles. Even in this story, God's providential guidance is not direct divine illumination, but direction to Scripture, the heart of Church of Christ preaching.

Correction of moral faults

In addition to the external dangers facing preachers, many also struggled internally with their own moral faults and lack of dedication to God. To them, God was not just a loving God, but one who also disciplined his children. Sometimes this correction from God took an unusual form. One time, James A. Harding had spent a good deal of money on a supply of cigars to last him the winter. The very next day, a little girl knocked on his door:

[8]

"My mother sent me to ask if you would give me money to buy some shoes," she said, as she held up one small bare foot.

Looking down at her pitiful clothes and her bare feet, and keenly aware of the approaching winter, Harding's heart went out to her, and he reached in his pocket and drew out his pocketbook. But it was empty, not one red cent.

"I am sorry," he said. "I wish I could help but I haven't a thing I can give you right now." Ashamed, he watched her turn and go slowly away. As he closed the door, Carrie said, "Mr. Harding, if you had not bought all those cigars yesterday, you would have had the money for that child's shoes."

Perhaps Harding's conscience had already troubled him, for instantly his furious temper flashed. Without a word he grabbed his hat and rushed out the door. All day long he walked the streets and countryside in a torrent of passion. Finally the gigantic struggle within changed from anger to penitence, and it was a sorrowful and repentant young husband who returned to embrace his wife in the evening.

For months the cigars remained untouched in the trunk, a perpetual reminder that he was never to smoke again. After the habit was gone and forgotten they were finally destroyed.[20]

The fault here was not smoking (that was an accepted practice) but squandering money that God had providentially given Harding to support his family and help the poor.

So the theme of God's providence is an important one in Church of Christ folklore. However, it is not as widespread as it is in other traditions, Methodist and Mormon, for example. Instead, it centers upon certain individuals, T. B. Larimore and James A. Harding in particular, who believed strongly in providence and interpreted their experiences accordingly. This limited use of the theme partially results from the church's stand against modern miracles.

HUMOROUS ANECDOTES

Preaching

Saving souls was serious business to a Church of Christ minister, and souls were saved by preaching the Word. Preaching then, along with baptism, was the most important religious activity in the Church. Ironically, since preaching was taken so seriously, when something humorous occurred in a sermon, the amusement of the audience was intensified. For this reason, many humorous preaching anecdotes exist in the biographies.[21]

Misquotes and misunderstandings

Like all public speakers, preachers sometimes became tongue–tied, frequently resulting in hilarious error. At other times, it was the audience's misunderstanding of a properly used word or phrase that prompted the humor. Some preachers displayed their lack of education by ignorantly misquoting a verse, while others tried to cover their ignorance by using a confusing vocabulary. Both types were humorously caught in their errors quite frequently.

One type of misquote was prompted by an attempt to find a suitable Scripture for a sermon on gossip:

[9]

Errors of pronunciation sometimes twisted very plain texts so as to make them fit all sorts of sermons. A case in point was that of an old preacher who selected the familiar passage from the writings of Peter against those who "shall bring in damnable *heresies*," as a text against *gossiping*. It was a mistake in the pronunciation of the word "*heresies*" that suggested the appropriateness of the text as a foundation for the remarks the faithful old preacher wished to make against "*damnable hearsay*." Regardless of the real meaning of the text, the sermon was a timely rebuke against certain old women of the neighborhood whose busy tongues were continually stirring up strife in the community by repeating with appropriate ad-

ditions, subtractions and variations, everything they heard
about other people.[22]

This very same mistake, "hearsay" for "heresy," was made
once by Anson Green, a Methodist circuit-rider, in his preaching.[23]
Sometimes the text was quoted correctly, but the audience
misunderstood, as in this story of N. B. Hardeman:

[10]

At one of the frequent debates of his earlier years, Hardeman had several of his loyal friends sitting around the edge
of the pulpit—for lack of seats in the audience. Among them
was John McDonald, a fine and crusty Irishman whom NBH
had baptized at Enville in one of his earliest meetings. Another
supporter present was Mr. Bill Bray of Henderson. In reference to the building of the Temple, NBH referred to "Hiram,
son of Abiff." He saw a sudden rise of interest among his
friends; when later he came across the same expression,
"Hiram, son of Abiff," Mr. McDonald and Mr. Bray turned
around with startled looks—only then did the speaker realize
what they had *thought* they heard.[24]

Although the context here is a speech in a debate and not a
sermon, the occasion was still a solemn one. No doubt the discrepancy between "church language" and the type of language
the audience "thought they heard" provoked the humor.

A preacher might want his audience to misunderstand him in
order to impress them with the depth of his knowledge. Audiences in this time period were not as educated as today and
so fell prey to a preacher who could wield an impressive vocabulary. James A. Harding heard one of these "impressive"
preachers and tried to straighten out another man who had
heard him:

[11]

Harding heard him lecture on the *Internationual Sunday
School Lessons*. As he walked home with a plain, sensible,
straightforward man, the other remarked:
"Is not Brother——a grand teacher? Was not that fine

tonight? There is only one trouble about it with me, and that is that I am such a numbskull that I cannot understand half that he says. He is too deep for me. I tried hard to catch the drift of his arguments tonight, but I could not do it to save my life."

"Do you want to know what he said?" Harding asked.

"Yes, indeed. I would like very much to know," he replied.

"Well," Harding said, "he expressed the belief that the *International Sunday School Lessons* are providentially designed to turn the minds of the people from the creeds and confessions of faith to the pure word of God."

"Was that all that he said?" the man exclaimed.

"Yes, that was all he said," Harding assured him.

"Well, well," the man said in disappointment. "It is strange I could not get that; I thought he was making a deep argument about something."

"Brother———was practicing the art of circumlocution," Harding said, "and he got what he was working for; that is, a reputation for profundity; people esteemed him profound, when he was only muddy. Such men remind me of the circus people who go bedecked with brass jewelry, tinsel, and faded finery. They are very nice to look upon at a distance, but they will not bear close scrutiny."[25]

This story could almost be classified as a serious anecdote, a warning against pompous preachers, but the situation is so ludicrous it is humorous.

"Stolen" sermons

Sermons, like most speeches, are not often copyrighted. Preachers felt no moral compunction in "borrowing" sermon ideas, outlines, and sometimes entire sermons verbatim from other preachers. The situation became strained, though humorous, when the sermon's original preacher was in the audience; as in this story of Cornelius Abbott, a young preacher, and H. Leo Boles:

[12]

Sometime afterwards the young man attended a meeting where Boles was preaching and memorized one of his sermons. A few weeks later Abbott was preaching one Sunday

at the Green Street Church of Christ when he spied Boles in
the audience and he exclaimed in dismay: "Brother Boles, I
did not see you in the audience, and if I had I would not be
here delivering your sermon." Whereupon Boles arose slowly
from his seat and said, "That's all right; the fellow I got it
from said you could preach it too."[26]

N. B. Hardeman was probably the man whose sermons were
"borrowed" most often. Many young men memorized his "Tabernacle Sermons," first preached in Nashville and later published. On at least one occasion, Hardeman heard one of his
own sermons preached by someone else:

[13]

In 1956, at Hazen, Arkansas, an incident took place about
which his family has teased him: Hardeman and "Miss An-
nie" had stopped there for Sunday morning worship. The
young preacher in charge met him before service, inquired
his name and whether he was a member of the church.
Brother Hardeman answered both questions. Then the young
man called on him to pray—which the visitor did—then
mounted the pulpit and proceeded to preach a Tabernacle
sermon almost verbatim—never realizing that his visitor was
N. B. Hardeman, author of the Tabernacle Volumes.[27]

Both of these stories are humorous, but their humor is based
on a serious issue. Although stealing sermons was a common
and accepted practice, there is an underlying sense of the unethical nature of the practice that provides the humor in this situation. These young men got caught doing what most preachers
did surreptitiously.[28]

Cleverness

Stories of cleverness comprise one major subgroup of humorous anecdotes. This section will examine clever actions of
preachers while the next section will look at clever retorts or
repartee. Early preachers had to rely on their own resources,
and many times showed great creativity in overcoming difficult
situations and the opposition of those of another religious per-
suasion.

Cleverness in advertising a sermon

Traveling preachers on the American frontier faced the challenge of gathering crowds to hear their preaching. Many times the preacher came into town with no advance warning; no other members of his church lived there, and so he was an absolute stranger. In such circumstances, it required cleverness to draw an audience. Walter Scott, a frontier Church of Christ preacher, used children to gather his audience:

[14]

Riding into a village near the close of the day, he addressed himself to the school children who were returning home from school, in such a way that he soon had quite a circle of them gathered round him. He then said to them: "Children, hold up your left hands." They all did so, anticipating some sport. "Now," said he, "beginning with your thumb repeat what I say to you: Faith, repentance, baptism, remission of sins, gift of the Holy Spirit—that takes up all your fingers. Now, again: Faith, repentance, baptism, remission of sins, gift of the Holy Spirit. Now, again, faster, altogether: Faith, repentance, baptism, remission of sins, gift of the Holy Spirit"—and thus he continued until they all could repeat it in concert, like a column of the multiplication table. They were all intensely amused, thinking that he was a harmless, crazy man. He then said: "Children, now run home—don't forget what is on your fingers, and tell your parents that a man will preach the gospel tonight at the schoolhouse, as you have it on the five fingers of your hands." Away went the children in great glee, repeating as they went, "Faith, repentance, baptism, remission of sins, gift of the Holy Spirit"—and soon the story was rehearsed in nearly every house of the village and neighborhood; and long before the hour of meeting the house was thronged, and, of course, not a few of the children were there, all expecting to have great sport with the crazy man.[29]

This spur-of-the-moment gimmick for drawing a crowd became quite significant in the later history of Churches of Christ. Even today, most preachers in the group end their sermons with a five-step "plan of salvation" differing only slightly from Scott's. Today the plan is usually: hearing, faith, repentance, confession,

and baptism compared to Scott's faith, repentance, baptism, remission of sins, and gift of the Holy Spirit. In his preaching,
Scott originally had six steps in what he called the "Ancient
Gospel," but he dropped the last one, the resurrection, to make
it all fit on one hand.[30] This is one instance in which a spon-
taneously clever act became a fixed tradition in the church.

Clever handling of other preachers

There was a competitive spirit among preachers on the frontier, both inside the church and between preachers of different
churches. Preachers tried to "one-up" each other over almost
anything, as shown by this encounter between Raccoon John
Smith and a Methodist minister:

[15]

A storm of rain coming up, the travelers hurried forward
to a little village just ahead of them. They took shelter in a
store, or small shop, where several farmers had gathered in
out of the rain. The preachers were unknown to the company,
but the shopkeeper, seeing that they were cold and wet, set
out a decanter of wine upon the counter, and pressed them
to take a glass.

"You are the oldest, Brother Smith," said the Methodist,
"help yourself first."

Smith went forward, and filling the small wineglass, drank
it off.

"Why, Brother Smith!" said the Methodist, who had
watched his opportunity, "you have been boasting for an hour
past that you observe the Book more strictly than other people. I am surprised now to see that your practice does not
accord with your profession, for you have just violated the
plain injunction, that in all things, whether we eat or drink,
we should give thanks!"

"I admit, my brother," said Smith, "the correctness of your
teaching; but I think that among strangers, and on such an
occasion as this, we may enjoy the good things of the Lord
without making a display of our piety before men. I hope,
though, that you will be as careful to observe all the com-
mandments. Drink; you will find the wine good."

His companion, pouring out a glassful, set it down on the
counter, and reverently closed his eyes; but Smith, seizing

the glass unobserved, emptied it at a mouthful, and quietly replaced it on the counter. The Methodist took up the glass to drink; but, finding it empty, turned, amid the laughter of the crowd, and said:

"That was some of your mischief, Brother Smith, I know."

"Yes," said Smith, "and you have now let these good people see how a Methodist just halfway obeys the Book. We are told to watch as well as to pray, my brother. You prayed well enough, but you neglected to watch, as the Scriptures command, and have lost both your wine and your argument by your disobedience."[31]

Thus, a typical jest over wine (Motif J1310) is cleverly turned into a point of religious discussion (Type 1823, "Biblical repartee").

This clever handling of preachers sometimes turned inward and became a contest among preachers of the same Church. If a preacher could make others of his Church look foolish, especially those of great reputation, he would increase his own standing in the eyes of some. Jack McElroy, a student of S. H. Hall who called him "the cyclone from among my boys,"[32] used his skill as an amateur magician to get the best of several prominent preachers:

[16]

Here I must tell a little humorous story about his magic. He was invited by Brother Boles and Brother Freed to give an exhibition for the students at David Lipscomb College while he was in school there. Besides the students, there were others there to enjoy it. At the close of his program he stated, "I have one more little exhibition to give, if the faculty will cooperate and come to the stage." Most of them did. A string was stretched from one side of the stage to the other, and he had them walk up and put their forefingers and thumbs around the string, somewhat like a ring. Without indicating that anything unusual was to happen, there stood Brothers H. Leo Boles, Sam P. Pitman, A. G. Freed and others, with forefingers and thumbs encircling the string. Jack addressed the audience, expressing appreciation for their presence and rapt attention. Then stated that he sometimes went fishing, but was closing the program with the biggest string of "*suck-*

ers" he had ever caught, and the audience was dismissed.
While it brought quite an applause from the audience, we
must say that the fish caught did not so much enjoy it.[33]

This bit of cleverness no doubt had mixed rewards: McElroy
received renown from his fellow students, but lost influence with
those who were powerful in the Church and could most help
or hinder his preaching career.

Cleverness in ignorance

Churches of Christ do not require a seminary degree for ordination; indeed, no formal ordination exists in the movement.
Early preachers in the movement were usually uneducated, most
without a college education and many who could barely read.
When facing competition from more educated ministers from
other Churches, especially in debate, Church of Christ preachers
would often times play to the audience, who was also uneducated. In this way, Raccoon John Smith once got the best of a
Presbyterian minister who spoke Biblical Greek:

[17]

During the debate, Mr. Whitney at one time forgot the
agreement that no appeal should be made to the Greek or
Hebrew Scriptures. Closely pressed by one of his opponent's
arguments, he introduced, by way of reply, a citation from
the Greek. Smith's ear instantly caught the strange sounds,
and he was about to rise to a point of order; but, looking over
the large audience, he saw that not a man in the house, save
his learned opponent himself, understood one word of the
matter in hand. He suffered him, therefore, to proceed, without interruption to the close. He then arose, and, after reply-
ing to every thing relevant to the question, he said:
"It was my fortune, as you all know, my friends, to be raised
on a frontier, where I had no opportunity to acquire a colle-
giate education. I am unable to say, therefore, whether the
gentleman has spoken good Greek, or even Greek at all. But,
lest some of you may suppose that there is argument in an
unknown tongue, I will attempt to answer the gentleman's
Greek also. When my father first settled in Kentucky, many
Cherokee Indians used to come about on friendly hunting

excursions. I was a lad then, but was always fond of hanging about their camp and observing their ways, and I learned, at last, a little of their language."

Suddenly turning to his reverend opponent and taking the attitude of an Indian brave in the act of letting fly an arrow at his foe, he exclaimed, with a strong Cherokee accent: "Segilluh unuhsohee unaka howee taw!"

With a stamp of his foot, he gave a startling emphasis to the last word; the bow-string twanged, the arrow sped, and his opponent started, as if a Cherokee warrior was upon him.[34]

Many years later Marshall Keeble used the same approach to win the audience when he was challenged by a Methodist:

[18]

Keeble conducted another of his sensational meetings this year in August just two blocks from Lane College (Methodist) in Jackson, Tennessee. Bishop Isaac Lane attended several nights. One Lane professor accused Keeble of preaching false doctrine and later wished he hadn't. He wanted to know if Keeble knew the Greek on Acts 2:38. Keeble said—"The way I talk English you see I can't speak it very well." Keeble said he had the Greek New Testament "shelled" by the finest Greek scholars in the world into English. He called for a show of hands in the audience for all who could read Greek. Not a hand went up. Keeble then sternly reprimanded the Lane scholar for bringing up the subject in the first place. Keeble won again when he extended the invitation and seven came forward. Any preacher who challenged Keeble for a debate before one of his vast audiences wished he hadn't later. Keeble said some preacher from Lane University would jump him, and "he had to shoot one every night."[35]

These stories illustrate the prejudice that many Church of Christ preachers hold against education. The gospel was simple enough to be understood by common people. Knowing "too much" about the Bible, including Hebrew and Greek, tended to lead one away from those simple truths.

Repartee

Debates were common in American religion until the mid-twentieth century. Protestants debated Catholics, Baptists faced Presbyterians, Methodists faced Baptists, and Church of Christ preachers debated them all. It is no surprise then that the largest group of Church of Christ preacher anecdotes centers on cleverness in argument or repartee. After all, the "winner" of the debate was not the most erudite preacher, but the one who could skewer his opponent and win the audience.[36]

Repartee against religious error in general

Church of Christ preachers sometimes faced religious opposition in settings other than debate. These include interpersonal encounters and church settings. Here, too, the preacher many times verbally got the best of his opponent:

[19]

Boles, of course, included a biography of "Raccoon" John Smith with another story from the famous "Raccoon" repertory. John Smith had preached in Sparta, Tennessee, and a number of judges and lawyers were present in the audience. Afterwards he was asked if he were not embarrassed in the presence of so many learned gentlemen. He quickly retorted: "Not in the least, for I have learned that judges and lawyers, so far as the Bible is concerned, are the most ignorant class of people in the world, except Doctors of Divinity."[37]

This story, set in an interpersonal encounter, echoes the theme of the stories of cleverness and ignorance discussed above.

Another Raccoon John Smith story shows the personal hatred that a preacher's teaching could engender:

[20]

Having baptized several members of a certain family in his own neighborhood, he shortly afterward met the father, who had always been his personal friend.

"Good morning, my brother," said Smith to him kindly.

But the old man fixed a scornful look upon him and said:

"Don't call me brother, sir! I would rather claim kin with the devil himself!"

"Go, then," said Smith, "and honor thy father!"[38]

This technique of turning a derogatory term, "devil," back on an opponent was typical of preacher repartee.

On another occasion, Raccoon John was discussing the subject of creeds in front of a Church of Christ audience. The target of Smith's words this time was John T. Johnson, a preacher in the audience who was not as opposed to "human creeds" as Smith thought he should be:

[21]

And he turned his pleasant face toward Johnson, who sat before him nodding his ready promises with a thoughtless confidence that said as plainly as words, "We are all sober-minded Christians here, Brother Smith; so proceed with your illustration." The speaker in his deliberate manner, continued:

A Christian was once discussing the question of creeds with a Calvinistic Baptist, who boldly maintained that his Confession of Faith was a better bond of union among Christians than the Bible alone. So well satisfied was the anti-creed brother, however, that both Scripture and common sense sustained him in the argument, that he proposed, in the end, to submit the question to a Frenchman who had listened attentively to the discussion, and who, from the negative character of his own religion, could not have any prejudice in the case. The matter was accordingly referred to him, and he consented to judge between them. Making each disputant take into his hand the creed that he had defended, he asked of the man with the New Testament who it was that made his creed.

"Jesus Christ," was the answer.

"It was adopted in the city of Philadelphia, in the year 1742," replied the Baptist.

"Very well, then, gentlemen," continued the Frenchman: "that is enough. If you follow your creed, Mr. Christian, when you die, it will take you to Jesus Christ. Follow yours, Mr. Baptist, and, when you die, you will go to *Philadelphie!*"

The amiable Johnson, taken by surprise, struggled very hard to keep his promise and his gravity; but when he saw his brother's droll look of admonition, bending down upon him from the pulpit, he laughed outright![39]

Raccoon John Smith was obviously known for this interpersonal repartee with strangers, friends, and even his fellow preachers.

Repartee against specific religious groups

Most religious conflict occurred either during "gospel meetings" when non–Church of Christ preachers interrupted a sermon (a common practice) or during formal religious debates. In these cases, specific denominations were attacked by name, sometimes quite literally by name:

[22]

Keeble had a way of answering his "shouting religious neighbors" so as to quiet them. The preacher of the Primitive Baptist Church would say that mine is the oldest church—it was here "before the clouds were flying." Keeble would say, "That's too soon. When Christ came to set up his church the clouds were already flying. You are too early." Keeble would have to wait until the audience finished laughing.[40]

After playing on the word "Primitive," Keeble turned on another church:

[23]

Another "Keeble classic" happened in a California meeting. A young white man got up and challenged Keeble.

"You have spoken about every other church, now what about mine?"

Keeble said—"I don't know what church you are a member of."

The young man responded—"The Latter Day Saints."

Keeble shot back—"You're too late!"

The next night he was up a little closer, "and here he comes to be baptized," Keeble said.

The young man told Keeble—"I don't stay in anything that is too late." Keeble often related the incident—"Lot of you sitting out there are too late."[41]

Keeble did not hold formal debates, but in several of his tent meetings he did have these impromptu discussions. His usual method on these occasions is illustrated by these stories: he used short, pithy sayings to put his opponent down and win the audience.

In more formal debates, Church of Christ preachers had to utilize more elaborate arguments, but there was still room for the snappy comeback. Sometimes, these discussions digressed into personal name–calling, as in this debate between J. D. Tant and a Methodist preacher named Smith:

[24]

After the debate several Methodist women brought a big bouquet of roses and put them in Smith's arms (to which Tant commented: "That's right, Sisters; we always decorate the dead with flowers"), and pinned a huge blue ribbon on him. Upon seeing the blue ribbon, Tant got to his feet and made a little speech:

"Ladies and Gentlemen, when I was a young man we used to always have a State Fair every fall. Farmers would bring in their hogs, their mules, their cows and chickens to compete for the blue ribbon. Now in these competitions a jack or a stud or a bull would always be judged in good part by the quality of his colt or his calf. Since I have made no stand along that line in this community, I consider myself not in competition with this good Methodist preacher. But apparently he is well known in Bloomington, and the Methodist sisters feel that he deserves the blue ribbon."

There was an awesome silence—for there had been three illegitimate babies born to ladies in the community that year. And, whether rightly or wrongly, the Methodist pastor was reported to have had more than a nodding aquaintance with at least two of the unhappy mothers.[42]

Such a charge was certainly beyond proper decorum, though such charges against ministers are common in preacher repartee.[43] On another occasion Tant got in serious trouble with his brethren by using the word "bull" in a sermon. Such a term was considered too vulgar for women's ears; "Mr. Cow" was preferred.[44]

Many of Tant's debates reached this level of acrimony, as shown by this example of a discussion he had with J. K. P. Williams, a Primitive Baptist:

[25]

"Tant has acknowledged," he replied, "that I am going to be in heaven. You heard him say that when he and I meet in heaven we will ask the Apostle Paul about some of his writings. Now, I am a Baptist. I was born a Baptist, raised a Baptist, and I'll die a Baptist. Therefore it is my Baptist doctrine that will take me to heaven. If Baptist doctrine will take a man to heaven (and Tant admits I'll be there), then I see no point in continuing the discussion."

Without a moment's hesitation Tant responded, "Why, yes, I am confident J. K. P. Williams will be walking the street of heaven after the final judgment. And I am not alone in that conviction. I believe most of this audience are fairly certain he will be there. For four days now we have been listening to his miserable efforts to make some kind of sensible argument. He has been unable to do so, but has spouted the most nonsense and foolish gibberish I have ever heard from the lips of any idiot in all my life. I feel very certain that when J. K. P. Williams stands at the judgment bar of God, and the books are opened, revealing every deed of his life, and the Lord takes a look at the arguments he has made in this debate, he is going to admit Williams to heaven!"

"He is going to poke him in through the fool hole!!"[45]

To modern ears, such strong language in a religious context seems extremely rude, but to early preachers the importance of salvation called for the truth to be defended in any possible way. In dealing with false teachers, no language was too strong. As one Mormon preacher put it, "I do pray for my enemies: I pray that they may all go to hell."[46]

Repartee on baptism

The belief that set most Churches of Christ apart from other churches was its insistence on the necessity of adult baptism for salvation. Church of Christ preachers even debated Baptists, who believed in adult baptism, over whether it was absolutely necessary to be baptized to be saved. Presbyterians, Methodists, and others who did not practice adult immersion as the exclusive mode of baptism met with more of the ire of the Church of Christ preachers.[47]

Most of the debates and informal discussions on baptism cen-
tered on biblical precedents on baptism, especially Jesus' baptism in the Jordan river. Some Presbyterians and Methodists
insisted that the Jordan was too shallow for Jesus to have been
immersed. Church of Christ preachers had several snappy re-
sponses to that argument:

[26]

One amusing incident marked the discussion, a story that
was to follow Tant the rest of his days. Smith had argued that
Jesus was sprinkled by John the Baptist, and of necessity had
to be, since the Jordan was only a trickle of water at the place
of the baptizing, and in the summer time ceased to flow altogether. It was so small, in fact, he said, that "a man could
dam it up with his foot, and stop the flow of water entirely,
even in the rainy season!"

To this Tant replied: "Brethren and friends, I have travelled
from one end of this nation to another, and have seen many
marvellous sights in it. I have always had a desire to travel
around the world and behold the glories and grandeurs of
ancient cities and far places. I have a longing to travel to the
country where my Lord lived and died, to stand in old Jerusalem and view the city o'er. I have wanted to visit ancient
Egypt, and see the great pyramids and the mighty Nile River.
But there is now one thing I'd rather see than all these other
mighty wonders combined. There is one sight which I believe
would be more awesome, more marvellous, more wonderful
than all the seven wonders of the world. Brethren, I want just
one time in my life to catch a glimpse of that foot that could
dam the Jordan River!"[48]

This argument from Tant to the Methodist Smith is repeated
in a classroom setting by N. B. Hardeman:

[27]

"Some sectarians say, 'Oh, the Jordan River doesn't amount
to anything—a little stream you could dam with your foot.'
Well, *you* may spend fifteen hundred dollars to see the Jordan,
but as for me, I'd rather see that *foot*! The Jordan is the most
important river on the globe, because of its history."[49]

Hardeman and Tant knew each other, and it seems likely, in light of the statement of Tant's biographer that this incident "was to follow Tant the rest of his days," that Tant originated the argument and Hardeman borrowed it. The settings of the stories, Tant's in the rough and tumble of debate and Hardeman's in the more controlled environment of the classroom, also point to Tant as the author of the "foot" illustration. Of course, it is possible Tant borrowed the argument from another preacher. Whatever its origin, this "big foot" argument was a common reply to the shallow Jordan theory.

Another "Jordan" incident occurred in a Presbyterian church:

[28]

A descendant of Stone gave me a traditional story of Thomas Miller Allen, who was ordained by Stone and was long associated with him. Allen was preaching in a Presbyterian church. It was a warm day. He preached fervently and long. He had a withered hand which he frequently struck with his good hand at periods of emphasis. He perspired. Thirsty and obsessed with his message he drank deeply from the baptismal font. Recovering instantly for a timely thrust of wit, he said to his pastoral friend on the rostrum: "I'm sorry. I beg your pardon. I have drunk your Jordan dry."[50]

Here the argument, stemming from an action no doubt considered rude and sacrilegious by the audience, is that the font was not deep enough to be the Jordan, the opposite of the argument of Methodist Smith against Tant.

Another "depth of water" argument occurred in a debate between Jonas Hartzel and Rev. Waldo, a Congregational minister. In speaking of the baptism of the Ethiopian eunuch, Waldo argued the water he was baptized in was no bigger than a crawfish hole; Hartzel responded by burlesquing Waldo's argument:

[29]

With great adroitness, the advocate of immersion responded: "If the supposition of the gentleman be correct, it will make good sense to insert the term he has chosen in the place of *water* in the text." He then proceeded, with all the gravity possible, to read as follows: "And as they went on their way, they came to a certain *crawfish hole*, and the eunuch said, See here is a *crawfish hole*, what doth hinder me to be baptized?" At this there was a slight titter in the audience, and the preacher proceeded with the reading, but when he came to read "and he commanded the chariot to stand still, and they went down into the *crawfish hole*, both Philip and the eunuch," the titter became a subdued laugh; but the inexorable preacher continued, "and he baptized him; and when they were come up out of the *crawfish hole*"—this proved too much, and the audience burst into loud and long-continued laughter; and the preacher, when silence was in a measure restored, turning to his now discomfited opponent, very gravely observed: "Were we not discussing a serious and important matter, I should feel inclined to say that my friend here was crawfishing." This reference to the peculiar style of this animal's advancing backwards was too much; the audience again exploded, and the advocate of the crawfish hole theory had nothing more to offer.[51]

Preachers from many denominations accused the Campbellites (as they called them) of believing that the act of immersion itself caused one to be saved. Though this was not the position of most Church of Christ ministers, some went so far in their defense of baptism it seemed they gave the act an automatic saving power. Witness this saying by Marshall Keeble:

[30]

His arguments were never complex or subtle. They were plain and he meant for them to be understood. Baptism was often a subject for controversy. And he would say in few words so much. "If you get saved before you hit baptism— you're too fast. God never dry cleaned a man dry since his Son died on Calvary. You put God in the dry cleaning business when you have him saved before baptism." Keeble would have to wait until people would get through laughing.[52]

This charge of "baptismal regeneration" against Church of Christ preachers was put into poetry by John T. Nichols, a Methodist minister debating James A. Harding:

[31]

Every time you tackle Harding, he said, he makes "a bee-line for the water, and cries:

'Every mother, son and daughter,
  Here's the gospel in the water;
O, ye blinded generation,
  Won't you have this cheap salvation?' "[53]

Harding responded with a poem of his own on the Methodist mourner's bench where repentant sinners waited for salvation:

'Ho, every mother, son and wench,
  Come, get religion at the mourner's bench;
Yes, white man, Indian, Negro, squaw,
  Come, find pardon by rolling in the straw.'

The incongruity of such a jingle from a man of natural courtesy and dignity convulsed the audience, and there was no more "poetry" in the debate.[54]

Just as "baptismal regeneration" was a whipping boy for Methodists, so waiting for a divine sign of salvation on an "anxious seat" or "mourner's bench" was a favorite target of Church of Christ preachers. Raccoon John Smith once succinctly pointed out their difference:

[32]

At another time, after he had shown the absurdities of the mourners'-bench theory of getting religion, he was asked: "What is the difference between your baptism and our mourners' bench?" He replied: "One is from heaven, the other is from the sawmill."[55]

Discussion on baptism sometimes approached physical violence, as in this case of Raccoon John Smith forcing a Methodist minister to be baptized:

[33]

Seizing the preacher by the arm, he pulled him gently but firmly along toward the water. Resistance would have been in vain; for the *Dipper*, as the people now began to call him, was a man of powerful muscle. "What are you going to do, Mr. Smith," said the man uncertain what the strange procedure meant.

"What am I going to do!" said Smith, affecting surprise at the question; "I am going to baptize you, sir!"

"But I do not wish to be baptized," said the man, trying to smile at what he deemed to be rather an untimely jest, if, indeed, it was a jest at all.

"Do you not believe?" said Smith.

"Certainly I do," said the preacher.

"Then come along, sir," said the Dipper, pulling him still nearer to the water; "believers must be baptized!"

"But," said the man, now uneasy at the thought that possibly it might not be a joke at all, "I'm not willing to go. It certainly would do me no good to be baptized against my will."

Smith now raised his voice so that the multitude could hear, for the song had ceased, and every ear was open to catch his words. "Did you not," said he, "but yesterday, baptize a helpless babe against its will, though it shrunk from your touch, and kicked against your baptism? Did you get its consent first, sir? Come along with me, for you must be baptized!" and with one movement of his powerful arm, he pulled the unwilling subject to the water's edge. The preacher loudly and earnestly protested, and the Dipper released his hold.[56]

Smith's actions were really a clever *reductio ad absurdum*[57] of the Methodist position: if an infant must be baptized against its will, so must an adult.

Predictably, in the biographies of Church of Christ preachers, they always get the best of their opponents in debate. In the memoirs of non-Church of Christ preachers, of course, the situation is reversed, the "Campbellites" are completely thrashed.[58] The one exception to this pattern in the Church of Christ biographies is related by N. B. Hardeman:

[34]

Claud Cayce, a Baptist, once said to, and of, me: "Hardeman will strain out a gnat and swallow A. Campbell."[59]

This brief glimpse of an opponent's skill at repartee implies that the Church of Christ preachers got as good as they gave in religious debates.

Repartee in other situations

The quick wit of the preacher, developed in religious controversy, sometimes displayed itself in other settings. Once Raccoon John Smith turned a practical joke back on three boys:

[35]

Many stories are told concerning "Raccoon" John Smith's wit and repartee. He was accustomed to rise early and take a long walk through the woods. This time was spent in solitary prayer and meditation. One morning three boys, wishing to play a practical joke on the old preacher, hid themselves at various points along the path that Elder Smith's walk would take him. The first boy meeting him said very politely, "Good morning, Father Abraham." John Smith replied kindly, "Good morning, son." A few moments later the second boy interrupted John Smith's solitude by stepping out from the tree behind which he had been hiding and said, "Good morning, Father Isaac." "Raccoon" John Smith looked at him sharply, but he answered gently, "Good morning, son" and continued on his walk. After he had taken only a few paces, the third boy appeared in the pathway and cried in a loud voice, "Good morning, Father Jacob." That was more than John Smith could take and he answered tartly, "I am neither Abraham, Isaac, nor Jacob, but I am Saul, seeking his father's asses, and lo, I have found three of them already this morning!"[60]

Another incident that showed Church of Christ preachers would not take criticism kindly, not even from their sisters in the church, involved a religious meeting held by J. D. Tant:

[36]

The summer was a hot one, and when Tant came back to Joe Johnston Church for a meeting in June, the whole city was sweltering. Once again, and nearly every day, he removed his coat when he started to preach. This was entirely too informal and "country" to suit one of the good sisters of

Joe Johnston church; so after three or four days, she told Tant she felt it was somewhat beneath the dignity of a gospel preacher to remove his coat in the pulpit and preach in his shirt sleeves.

Tant very carefully looked at the woman, beginning at her feet and letting his eyes slowly and deliberately travel from sheer-hosed legs, to sleeveless, extremely low-cut dress, made of the frothiest kind of material, then he intoned with a slow nasal twang:

"Why, sister, I could pull off my pants right now and still have on more than you are wearing!"[61]

So, while the serious anecdotes show the preachers as courageous men, full of faith in God, the humorous anecdotes display another side to their personalities. Preachers sometimes made embarrassing faux pas in their preaching, cleverly got the best of others (both their "brothers" in the church and preachers of other churches), and skewered all opponents with their sharp wit.

III.

ORAL ANECDOTES

Most people, especially religious ones, have heard stories about preachers. Parson stories were common in the Middle Ages as shown in the writings of Boccacio, Chaucer, and others. Even in the highly literate American culture of the twentieth century, oral preacher stories still circulate.

For several reasons—the origin of the church in a colorful time in American history, the exclusive nature of this religious group, and other reasons to be explained in chapter 6—oral preacher stories are particularly numerous among members of the Churches of Christ. The anecdotes presented in this chapter were collected in the southeastern United States in 1985–1986. All of the informants were members of the Churches of Christ.

The themes of these stories are similar to those of the written anecdotes with a few significant differences. Only two serious oral anecdotes were collected, compared to several serious written ones. Among the humorous oral anecdotes, the Church of Christ preacher is more often the butt of the joke; also, there are more stories of physical humor in the oral collection. These differences between oral and written will be discussed more fully in chapter 5.

SERIOUS ANECDOTES

Alexander Campbell's Ghost

Ghost stories are a staple of folk narratives,[1] but it is unusual to find a Church of Christ preacher ghost story. Perry Gresham, the former president of Bethany College (a college founded by

Alexander Campbell where Gresham spent the greater part of his life), has lived for years just a few feet from Campbell's grave. Gresham tells of his encounter with Campbell:

[37]

It was a very snowy night. The snow was falling in great flakes that covered the hills around Bethany. One could hardly see through the falling snow outside the window there at old Pendleton Heights. But I discerned, as the snow let up a little, a lantern, as if it were someone riding on horseback across the country. I couldn't believe my eyes because there was no road there; I knew there was no road there. Just as if it were a lantern on the, on the edge of a saddle of one riding horseback, this light bobbed up and down across the landscape.

And I made certain the next morning that I went out to see what kind of tracks there were there. For it had stopped snowing shortly after that, and I knew I would find the tracks. And there was not a track in the snow.

That's how I came to know about Alexander Campbell.[2]

Later Gresham told of disagreeing with some scholar on Campbell's thought. The scholar commented that Gresham should know Campbell since he lived at his college. Gresham commented, "I didn't tell him I'd seen his ghost."[3] This story shows the continued respect shown to the founders of the Church of Christ movement.

Burning the Piano

Religious controversies could become quite heated as shown in the previous chapter. Some of the most acrimonious clashes occurred within the Churches of Christ over instrumental music in worship. This issue eventually split the movement, but when the instrument was first introduced into some churches, there were violent results. Charlie Jones tells the reaction of J. H. Johns, a preacher at Smedley, Indiana, in the 1890s:

[38]

So one week they moved a piano in. He said that he, uh, and six other fellas went up there then and saw that piano in

there and they took that piano outside and they busted it up
and set it on fire. He said, he, uh, took, uh, the idols of Baal
and, uh, ah, burned them, uh, made an altar of wood and
burned them. And he said that was an actual truth.[4]

Although the informant thought this was an amusing story,
it is a serious example of how religious feeling could lead to a
violent act, even among those who were "brethren."

HUMOROUS ANECDOTES

Preaching and Other Speeches

Lengthy sermons

As with the written anecdotes, preaching furnished the setting
for many oral anecdotes. One subject on which preachers were
open to good-natured criticism was the length of their sermons.
Sermons were generally longer in the frontier period; in later
years, they were expected to be a more reasonable length. Perhaps that is why the three examples here all date from the twentieth century.

Adult church members may have been too polite to complain
of long sermons but sometimes children were not so reticent:

[39]

Brother B. C. Goodpasture was preaching in a meeting in
Nashville, Tennessee. His granddaughter, little Kathy King,
went with him one night. He preached longer than usual.
And the next day, he asked Kathy, "Are you goin with me
tonight?" She said, "Paw-Paw, you preached so long last
night, you about quit me from goin to church."[5]

Audience members sometimes used wit to try to shame the
preacher into shortening his sermons:

[40]

Reminds me of anothuh preacher that, uh, preached a long
sermon and while he was still preaching, a man started walkin
out. And the preacher said, "Brother, whair you're goin?" He

said, "To get a haircut." "Well why didn't, uh, you git one
before you came to church?" And he said, "I didn't need one
then."[6]

Particular preachers had reputations as long-winded speakers.
Deserved or not, these reputations followed the preachers even
in speaking situations where there was no formal preaching:

[41]

Brother Guy N. Woods was conductin the open form
[forum], which he did for many years, at one of the lecture-
ships at Freed–Hardeman College. Someone asked a question. Brother Woods said, uh, "Brother Gus Nichols is here,
let's let him anzer that question." The fella said he really didn't
wanna know that much about it.[7]

Misquotes, misunderstandings, and inappropriate language
Though this type of anecdote was found in the biographies it is
more frequent in oral lore. The oral stories also are generally
more embarrassing to the preacher than the written ones. The
first two stories below make the written anecdotes tame by comparison.

One of the most successful revivalists in recent Church of
Christ history (success being measured by the number of con-
verts) was W. A. Bradfield, but even he could have trouble with
his words when preaching:

[42]

Brother W. A. Bradfield was known for his ability to, as
they say in the salesman language, close. In other words,
some of us preach our sermons, and make our appeals and
invitations, and, and, hope you'll come and that's about it.
But Brother Bradfield was a closer; he would, he would, you
know, as he'd draw near to the end of that sermon he would
really be tightening the message into a very, very tight pack-
age about the need for salvation and the dangers of hell, and
really painting the glories of heaven and the imperative nature
of your responding and responding now.

Well on this night, he closed the lesson and at, uh, after a
verse or so he stopped the singing and made an additional
appeal. I don't know if this was the first, second, or third

appeal (he was prone to do this several times), but at one point he was appealing and thinking of all the people who would be blessed if the sinner repented, and, and he said, "Oh, why don't you come? You daddies, for your children's sake, why don't you come? Oh, why don't you come, you husbands, for your wives's sake? Why don't you come? Oh, for heaven's sake, why don't you come? Oh, why in the hell don't you come?"[8]

To understand the enormity of Bradfield's error, one should know that profanity is still strongly condemned by Churches of Christ, in some places even euphemisms like "gosh," "darn," and "heck," are preached against. Bradfield's mistake was completely unintentional (though Freud might disagree) since he was not convinced he had actually said the offending word until he heard it played back to him on tape.

A more severe mistake was made by a young preacher in the Midwest. The informant refused to use the man's real name, so he called him Jim:

[43]

Jim was a little, little preacherish in his style, I mean artificial in his style at times, and that's one of the things I wanted him to get over. And so he got into Toastmasters and made a few speeches. And so he decided on a certain occasion he would speak to the men's group there in town, "secular men's group" is the way he announced it, I believe. He said to the church on this particular Sunday, he said, "I'm going to be speaking to these businessmen," and he said, "I want to, want to warn them of the errors of the clergy class in Protestant America." (I'm not quoting you understand, but just giving the general gist of what he said.)

And he said, "I thought this morning for my sermon I'd simply do an expanded version of what I'm going to do when I speak Tuesday night." And so he began his little presentation with "Don't call men Reverend, only God is Reverend—'Holy and Reverend is his name.'" And he then began to wax eloquent, and he became very irate at these pompous people who dress in robes and the very finest of clerical garb and who parade around the community as someone special with special language, and special style, and special clothing. He said, "They remind me of the Pharisees of old who enjoyed parading before the people in their broad prophylactics." He said, "They put on their broad prophylactics and strut before the people."[9]

Again the preacher did not catch his error, substituting pro-phylactic for phylactery, until privately confronted by almost every brother in the small church. The mistake may have been a subconscious attempt to intensify the charges against "de-nominational" preachers: not only are they pompous, but they are secretly sexually promiscuous.

Another story deals with these themes of pomposity and ap-parent sexual immorality, although in this story the Church of Christ preacher is the guilty one:

[44]

Pfeiffer told a story, not on himself, but on a different preacher who used a very sophisticated vocabulary. And when two widows of the congregation came forward one Sun-day (he had been talking with them during the past week, trying to counsel them), they had decided to make confession of some things. And so after the, uh, uh, song was over, he announced their names and said to the congregation, which was not a sophisticated congregation, said, uh, uh, "Brethren, I have had intercourse with these women during the past week," (meaning he had talked with them). And everybody's jaws hit the floor. A poor choice of words to say the least.[10]

A similar blunder was made by Willard Collins in a chapel announcement at David Lipscomb College in Nashville:

[45]

Brother Collins and, uh, I can't remember the sister's name, but one of the ladies on campus who'd be the equivalent of Dean of Women (I don't think they had anybody with that title at this particular point), but they had been talking over the problem they'd been having with some of the couples who were not behaving themselves in a very becoming kind of way. And so they talked it over and decided that something was to be done about it. And so, Brother Collins decided to announce that fact to the student body one day. And so he got up and did a little bit of preamble about the importance of Christian behavior and, and, he realized some things had been going on that were not appropriate, and he said, "I simply want the student body to know that Sister Margaret Leonard and I are going to stop smooching on campus."[11]

Margaret Leonard was a pseudonym invented by the informant. Collins is a renowned revivalist among Churches of Christ, but he is famous at Lipscomb for his inadvertent humor in chapel.

As mentioned above, Church of Christ preachers were sometimes short of formal education. One preacher's lack of scientific education got him in trouble during a sermon illustration:

[46]

In Chicago back several years ago, we had, uh, what I call a cornfed, hillbilly preacher type. Very little formal education, but, uh, thought quite highly of himself. He was quite an exuberant, thundering preacher at times. And he was, he was explaining baptism. And so he went to the board and he put it up on the board. He said, "There are some things that are difficult to be understood and there are some things that are simple to be understood." And he said, "I want you to take a look at this: repentance plus baptism equals salvation, now that's Acts 2:38. Now look at it again. Repentance plus baptism equals remission of sins." He said, "Now is that plain, or is that plain? That's as plain as H-twenty equals water!"[12]

This story illustrates a theme found in many of the anecdotes, both oral and written: although Church of Christ preachers were generally less educated than preachers from other churches, they display an arrogance when it comes to preaching and Bible interpretation.

Many mistakes were understandable substitutions of one biblical character for another. This was especially humorous when done by a polished, well-respected preacher like N. B. Hardeman:

[47]

> Brother Hardeman was preaching under a tent. Brother L. L.
> Brigance came in during the sermon. When services were
> dismissed, Brother Hardeman said, "Brother Brigance, I
> didn't know you were here." He said, "Yes, I came in while
> you had Moses building the ark."[13]

This may not have been an error on Hardeman's part, but an
attempt at humor by Brigance. If Hardeman indeed had Moses
(not Noah) building the ark, he must not have realized his mistake until told by Brigance.

Some preachers would not tolerate humor in church. Since
preaching and salvation affected eternity, there was no room for
levity in the pulpit or in the audience. Other preachers were
known for their wit. John T. Lewis, the serious type, and a
preacher named Emmons (the not-so-serious type) displayed
these opposing reactions to an error in a sermon:

[48]

> Brother J. H. Boles was preaching the sermon, they say,
> that night. And he was really driving home his points. And
> he got to a certain place and he says, "There they stand."
> And he was going to say, "Like lighthouses on veritable rocks
> of Gibraltar." But he didn't say that. He said, "There they
> stand like outhouses." Uh, then he corrected himself, "Like
> lighthouses," but it was too late. Everybody was laughing,
> but Brother John T. Lewis didn't. They say he twitched, he
> turned, he adjusted his seating, but not one time did he crack
> a smile. Said Brother Emmons had a harder time. Said, he
> got down between the seats and just shook on his knees,
> because it just, just tickled the fire out of him.[14]

This is one time the preacher realized his mistake and tried to
correct it.

The next three anecdotes are examples of intentional plays on
words or inappropriate wording. That is, they seem intentional,
although the first one could be an unintended malapropism:

[49]

Brother W. Curtis Porter in debate used to say, "I deny the allegation and I charge the alligator."[15]

Porter was given to plays on words:

[50]

This same Brother Porter was in a debate in Birmingham, Alabama, with a fella named Tinsley, who said, "I am brutally honest." Brother Porter said, "I wonder what he thinks I am? Honestly brutal?"[16]

As mentioned above, Churches of Christ are quite strict on profanity and euphemisms. However, preachers did get so worked up at times that they forgot the distinction between "plain language" and "church language":

[51]

Brother Hardeman told about another country preacher, and he said in his sermon, "I want to talk to yuh about the thief on the cross. And I want to say three things about it: I don't know if he was baptized; I don't know if he was saved, number two; and number three, who wants to be saved like a dadburn thief?" Brother Hardeman said he put it that way.[17]

The thief on the cross was the example of salvation without baptism that most non-Church of Christ preachers used against the Churches of Christ. This explains the preacher's vehemence against the thief. His language is mild by modern standards, but its offensive nature is shown by the informant's insistence that he really "put it that way."

Physical incidents in sermons

It was not always what was said in sermons that was humorous, sometimes it was what happened. Preachers were interrupted many times by various things. One of the most common intruders in country churches was the dog.[18] There are two versions of an anecdote in which the dog disrupted the

service and was removed in an unusual way. The first involves
a sermon of James P. Miller in a country congregation:

[52]

Anyhow, Miller was preaching away one night and a big
dog, sort of an ole hound dog, walked in out in the back of
the church building (and he said it happened); he walked right
up the center, very slowly, and sat down in dog-like fashion
between the front two rows. And he said he cocked his head
and just looked at him while he was preaching. No one paid
the dog any attention, but he said "it was eating the life out
of me." He cocked his head the other way, you know, and
finally Miller, he said, he nodded to one of the brethren there
and pointed to the dog and just went on with his preaching.

The brother nodded. He went over to the center aisle and
he picked that dog up by the nap of the neck and by the tail.
He said, he looked over at one side to the window over there,
and looked over at the other side at the window over there.
And from that position he threw that dog out the window.[19]

The second version is longer. Jay Andrews was the preacher:

[53]

And just about time for services to start, the door opened,
he looked down and this tall, distinguished looking man
stepped in, he had an Abe Lincoln beard. He took off his coat
and hung it on the peg; he took off his stovepipe hat and
hung it on the hook. And without a change of expression
walked down front, sat down, pulled out his watch. And
when it was time for services to begin, he turned to this fella
and nodded to him, and the guy got up and led some songs.
At a certain point, he nodded to this other fella, and the guy
got up and led a prayer. He said, after that he looked at
Andrews and nodded to him, and he said he "figured it was
my turn."

So he got up to the pulpit and was preaching. And in the
middle of the sermon, this, uh, real, uh, wrinkled, scrawny
hound dog came into church, walked right down front and
laid down in the middle of the floor. And everybody was
looking at him. And, uh, Brother Andrews said he stopped
preaching and looked at the guy with the beard sittin' in the
front row, and nodded at the guy. So the guy got up off the

pew, and grabbed that dog by the loose skin of his neck and
back and heaved him out the window and sat down.[20]

It is hard to say which version is earlier. The second one explains how the dog-thrower understood the nod: nodding was
common in that church. Both versions are told secondhand; the
preacher to whom it happened told the informants personally.
The first informant even felt it necessary to buttress the veracity
of his story with "and he said it happened." It is possible that
two similar incidents occurred, although the extent of the similarities—country church, hound dog, the nod, the heave out the
window—makes this unlikely. One story could derive from the
other, though the settings of the stories are contemporary, or
both could stem from an earlier, uncollected story.

Church furniture was made by hand from the early history of
the movement until the mid-twentieth century. Pulpits many
times were built to fit the local preacher. This could have humorous effects when there was a visiting preacher.

[54]

Brother Foy E. Wallace, Jr., preached his first, uh, sermon
at Stephenville, Texas. Brother Wallace's stature was very
close to mine. I might be a little taller. The regular preacher, Brother Rube Porter, was six-feet plus. Brother Wallace,
uh, couldn't see over the stand. And so, he looked around,
uh, the corner and said, "If you don't see me anymore, remember that 'faith comes by hearing,' Romans 10 and 17."[21]

This skillful play on the word "hearing" shows Wallace was a
masterful wit even at an early age (it was his first sermon).

Preachers sometimes embarrassed themselves by their own
actions in the pulpit, as did this anonymous preacher who in
trying to cover one embarrassment made things worse:

[55]

The preacher was preaching and somehow noticed that his
fly was unzipped. And so he was real embarrassed. (I guess
he was one of those who walks back and forth a lot when he
preaches.) So he decided the easiest way out of this would
be to call on somebody to lead prayer. And he knelt down

behind the podium and during the prayer he hastily zipped up his fly. And when the prayer was over, he started to straighten up, and he had zipped his tie up in his zipper; it was a silk tie, it was all hung up in his zipper and he couldn't get it undone. I don't know how he managed to get out of that situation, but if he had a pocket knife he could just cut it off.[22]

Baptisms

Ignorance of baptism technique

Churches of Christ have a traditional method for immersing baptismal candidates: the subject is lowered backward into the water from a standing position (while the subject holds his or her nose) and then brought back to a standing position by the minister. There is no evidence as to when this tradition began, but there are no known references to another method. For a new minister, this process requires some practice, since a great deal of leverage is sometimes required to raise the candidate from the water. Ignorance of the technique caused Lou Pfeiffer great trouble at his first baptism:

[56]

One of the stories he told was about, ah, the first time he ever baptized anyone. That was the one about the Texas cattle rancher, uh, he preached to and the guy wanted to be baptized in the cattle pond of his ranch. So he went out to the guy's cattle pond and it was so shallow, that they had to wade out to the middle of it before the water was deep enough to baptize him. Nobody told him how to baptize anybody before. And nobody told him that you stand one step behind the person before you lean back to immerse him, so he stood squarely even with this guy, who was a two-hundred and something pound hefty rancher. So he tipped over the guy and leaned him back under the water and started to pull him back up. He bent over so far, he couldn't lift the man, so he tried to step out with his right foot and get under him, and he was up over his ankles in mud, and he couldn't move his feet. So here the guy was under water, blowing bubbles; I mean, he couldn't get the guy back up. And he said he held him under about half a minute, while he was puffing, wheezing trying to get him, finally he got him back up. I guess the guy got a double good baptism.[23]

Falling in the baptistry

On the frontier, baptism took place outside in rivers, lakes, or ponds. As the movement grew and became more urban, churches began to build baptistries inside the church building, so that today practically all Churches of Christ have a baptistry in the building. Traditionally, the baptistry is located at the front center of the church building, behind the pulpit. There are usually two dressing rooms, one on each side of the baptistry (one for men, one for women), where the candidates can change into baptismal clothes (usually white robe–like affairs).

The presence of a large tub of water in a church can be surprising to those of other faiths not familiar with the practice:[24]

[57]

But one day, a fella, the doorbell rang and Norman [Gibson] went to the door and here stood a fella soaking wet. And he had a sheepish look on his face, and he said, "Uh, Brother Gibson, uh, uh, no wonder you got, uh, uh, uh, a short in the, in, in, the electricity on the church building, the whole basement's flooded."

The problem was, there was no basement. But the lights were off and this electrician came into the building, and looking around and trying to search for the problem, and probably hunting for the fuse box, he saw a door, opened the door, immediately stepped into the baptistry and fell flat. He thought, he thought those stairs he could see were stairs going into the basement and in the dark just didn't realize there was water. So, when he stuck one foot into the water, he, of course, immediately panicked, took another step, and into the baptistry.[25]

Falling into the baptistry could occur not from ignorance but from a mere slip. In the following story, the slip had further consequences:

[58]

There was this little country church where the auditorium and the dressing room were separated only by a sheet draped over a wire or a string. And those who wanted to be baptized would go back behind there, get dressed for baptism, and come out from behind the sheet and be baptized. And the bap, baptistry would just sit in the floor.

And I guess a hell–fire and brimstone preacher that day, an especially tough sermon, they had a bunch of people to request baptism. There were so many people being baptized, there weren't enough baptismal garments, so some of the people being baptized would go back behind the sheet, peel off their wet clothes, someone else would put them on, then they would be baptized. And you know how there's always a whole flock of ladies to go back and help them change clothes, whatever they do, I don't know, but, uh. The preacher was standing in the water with one of the people baptizing.

One of the ladies who went back as an assistant wanted to watch the baptism, so she was standing up on her tiptoes, peeping over the sheet behind the preacher (which is kind of curious in itself). She was a very heavy woman, a couple of hundred pounds, and when the preacher went down under the water with the person, she leaned forward to see the whole thing, and the wire or string broke, she put too much weight on it. And she fell, with the sheet, into the baptistry, on top of the preacher and the person being baptized, nearly drowned them before they got her off. But of course as soon as she fell, the sheet had exposed three or four people in the back who didn't have a stitch on. They were running all over the place trying to hide themselves.[26]

A second version of the story, including the untimely exposure of the candidates, but omitting the fall in the baptistry, has Jim Cope doing the baptizing:

[59]

And there were one, or two, or three who responded to the invitation, some girls. And they didn't even have dressing rooms, so what they had was some curtains that could be pulled from the wall around the construction they had put there, they went from one wall over to the other; and they could get over behind there, and, and, prepare.

And, uh, according to this, they were getting ready for that, uh, baptizing. They'd been there a little while, and one of the brothers, sort of put his hand on the edge of the wire, and just sort of said something to one of the sisters, "Uh, is everything ready?" He wasn't really peeping. But what happened was, he put too much pressure on that wire and the whole thing fell down. And it was just, nobody laughed, 'cause it was embarrassing. 'Cause they were in varying states of readiness at the time, two or three or four of them were back there.

And so they took care of it, I understand, as best they could, I never got the details of that.

But, they, uh, went on with the service, with everybody, no doubt, doing his or her best to keep very well under control. At any rate, they, uh, decided afterward it would be best to have a quick dismissal. So they called on the brother that they knew was always under control, a John T. Lewis type, and they said, would they ask him to lead closing prayer. And he started, "Our Dear Heavenly Father, ho, ho, ho, ho, ho, ho." And continued to laugh and broke up the entire service.[27]

Obviously this is a second version of the same story. Both have the flimsy partition (sheet or curtain) that falls revealing unclothed women (without "a stitch on" or "in varying stages of readiness"). However, there are significant differences. In the first version a large woman falls from behind the sheet partition into the baptistry, while in the second a "brother" accidentally ("He wasn't really peeking") pulls the curtain down. The first version adds the interesting, but extraneous, detail of the shared baptismal garments. The second version tells more of the audience's reaction. In both stories, the role of the preacher is minor. He does the baptizing, but is a passive victim of circumstances.

"Swimming" in the baptistry

A recent addition to baptistry style in Church of Christ buildings is the inclusion of a clear glass or Plexiglas panel in the front of the baptistry. This allows the audience to see the candidate actually under the water during baptism. One man was ignorant of or had forgotten this feature in his church:

[60]

There were several people who responded to the invitation song and wanted to be baptized and so they had to all go back and change. And, uh, uh, they had a woman's dressing room on one side with a door leading into it and a men's room on the other side. And the preacher was down in there just taking them from both sides. And so this, uh, they, uh, had one of those, uh, glass front baptistries where you could see through the water, you could see the people's feet down there too.

This guy came down from the left hand side and he was baptized, and, uh, there was another man coming in behind him, so he went on up the stairs to the right hand side with his back to the door that led to the women's dressing room, he couldn't get out. So, instead of waiting until the guy behind him got baptized and then walking back across and exiting with him, he thought he would just go under water and go down behind the preacher. So he took a deep breath and submerged and was kind of swimming across the baptistry under water. When he got half-way, he looked back past the preacher's legs and and the people were sitting out there looking at him.[28]

Baptism in running water

Though all Church of Christ members took the Bible literally on baptism, only a few went to the extreme of insisting on baptism in running water, as Jesus was baptized in the Jordan. In the early years, this was no problem since most baptisms were performed in creeks and rivers. With the advent of baptistries in the church, the practice of running water baptism became an inconvenience. Gus Nichols on one occasion solved the problem quite easily:

[61]

A lady came farward [forward] in response to a sermon Brother Gus Nichols preached and told him that she wanted to be baptized in running water. Brother Nichols told her, uh, it wouldn't be a problem, that they would go into the baptistry, he would turn the water on, while the water was running, he would baptize her.[29]

It is implied that this procedure satisfied the woman's conscience.

Repartee

In public religious discussions

There are many oral stories of repartee in debate, as well as written ones. In both, the Church of Christ speaker always gets the best of his foes, but the oral anecdotes tend more toward personal degradation of the opponent than the written ones. J. D. Tant, for example, was known for his cutting remarks:

[62]

Brother J. D. Tant was in another debate, he had over 300, and this debate was held in Louisville, Kentucky. Brother Tant got disgusted with his opponent and told him in one of his speeches, that he had met a lot of men in public debate and some wanted to lead all the way and some wanted to follow, but he said, "You are the first one I've ever met that wouldn't lead nor follow." And he said, "I'll tell you what I believe. We could put your brain in a mustard seed and it would have as much room to play around as a tadpole in the Atlantic ocean."[30]

The technique of ridiculing an opponent's ignorance was common in religious discussions among all denominations on the frontier,[31] but few were as personally vehement as Tant.

One of the most popular terms used by preachers to refer to their opponents is "ass," perhaps because of its use in the Authorized version of the Bible—Balaam's ass and the ass Jesus rode into Jerusalem.[32] This word was a particular favorite of Joe S. Warlick:

[63]

Brother Warlick debated a Baptist preacher in this section of Kentucky, several years ago, and the Baptist preacher called him a "long–horned ox from Texas." Brother Warlick told,

uh, his brethren that they had sinned, because the Bible said
not to yoke the ox and the ass up together. Of course that
took care of that.[33]

The reference here is to Deuteronomy 23:10, "Thou shalt not
plow with an ox and an ass together."

Warlick's clever turning of an opponent's taunt is shown in
this confrontation during a sermon:

[64]

Brother Joe S. Warlick had a question box during a series
of meetings. Someone asked, "What's the difference between
a jackass and a Campbellite preacher?" Brother Warlick
thought he knew who wrote the question and so he said, "If
whoever wrote this question will come up here and stand by
me, well, I'll show you the difference."[34]

In personal conversations

Repartee was such a part of the preacher's public life that some
kept an adversarial outlook at all times. This caused them at
times to answer innocent questions in a caustic manner:

[65]

A lady on a train found out Brother Srygley was a preacher.
She asked him, "What kind of preacher are you?" And he
told her he was a good one. She wanted to know what branch
of the church that he belonged to. He said he belonged to his
wife.[35]

Here F. D. Srygley goes to great lengths to avoid the answer "I
am a Church of Christ preacher." He may have been afraid that
such a term was too "denominational," it would place the church
alongside other denominations ("Baptist preacher," "Methodist
preacher," etc.) while he believed it was not a denomination.
This also explains the strange second answer—"he belonged to
his wife"—since the church is not a denomination one can join
or "belong to" in Church of Christ teaching. One must be baptized into Christ and then Christ adds one to the church.

The exclusive attitude of Church of Christ preachers, that they alone had the truth, is shown by the Srygley story and by this story of another innocent question:

[66]

A barber asked Brother John L. Fye of Arkansas, "Brother Fye, if you didn't belong to the Church of Christ, what would you be?" And he said, "Lost."[36]

This combative spirit even spilled over into preacher's dealings with other Church of Christ preachers. The language in these situations was slightly less strong than in fighting the denominations, but even the "ass" epithet was used in an indirect way:

[67]

Brother G. K. Wallace said he was riding a train out West to hold a meeting. In Kansas, they ran into a snowdrift and stopped the train. Brother Wallace, uh, knew the preacher in the town and he called him and he came and got him. He said, "Brother Wallace, just get on my back and I'll take you to your appointment." Brother Wallace said, "No, no." The brother said, "Why?" Brother Wallace said, "When they saw me coming, they would think I was Balaam."[37]

One assumes this was said with a smile, or the preacher there had a great deal of patience; he did take Wallace home.

Another Wallace, Foy E., repays a preacher's rudeness to a sister in the church by ridiculing him:

[68]

Brother A. G. Freed and Brother Foy E. Wallace, Jr., went to a place for dinner. The sister asked Brother Freed if he'd like a cup of coffee. He said, no, he was a Christian. Brother Wallace said, "Sister, you may pour me a cup, I'm a Christian too, but I didn't let it make a fool out of me."[38]

The feelings of Church of Christ preachers toward educated preachers, especially Doctors of Divinity, is shown by this reply of Foy E. Wallace to the question of a fellow Church of Christ preacher:

[69]

Another preacher said to Brother Wallace, "Brother Wallace, a man called me a Doctor. I felt like a fool. Do I look a Doctor?" "No," said Brother Wallace, "you look more like you said you felt."[39]

It is not clear why Wallace characterized this preacher as a fool, perhaps because of the extent of his concern over being called a Doctor of Divinity. These two Wallace stories indicate he habitually ridiculed others as fools.

The final two stories of this section are examples not of ridicule, but of cleverness in conversation with other Church of Christ preachers. The first is set in N. B. Hardeman's Bible class at Freed–Hardeman College:

[70]

A young man, Solomon, Brother Solomon, a preacher of the gospel, whom I know, was in one of Brother Hardeman's, uh, classes and a question, uh, came up that was kind of difficult. Brother Hardeman said, uh, "Well, uh, let's ask, uh, Solomon, he'll know the answer." And Solomon said, "Beholdah, a greater than Solomon is here."[40]

These two preachers try to outwit one another by their use of Scripture. Hardeman's reference is to the proverbial wisdom of Solomon. Brother Solomon outwits his teacher by quoting the words of Jesus (Matt.12:42). Hardeman was genuinely amused at Solomon's retort.[41]

The pride in ignorance of many Church of Christ preachers is seen in this story of the grammar of F. B. Srygley:

[71]

One of the McQuiddys was looking over an article that Brother Srygley wrote for the *Gospel Advocate* [a religious periodical] and he said, "Brother Srygley, how do you spell 'occurred'?" And he spelled it with one "c." Brother McQuiddy said, uh, "That's not the way Webster spells it." Brother Srygley said, "You didn't ask me, 'How does Webster spell it?', you asked how do I spell it, and that's the way I spell it."[42]

Though deficient in formal education, Srygley had plenty of the quick-witted cleverness which was more respected than college degrees in the Churches of Christ.

Oral anecdotes about Church of Christ preachers are then almost all humorous. Although a few of them ridicule the "denominational" preachers, most tell of the foibles of Church of Christ preachers. These men make fools of themselves by inappropriate, sometimes scandalous, remarks in sermons. They face embarrassing interruptions in sermons and baptisms. They even make fools of other Church of Christ preachers.

IV.

ORAL AND WRITTEN ANECDOTES

Some anecdotes are written in biographies and histories. Others are passed on orally. This chapter deals with preacher anecdotes occurring in both written and oral forms. In some cases it is clear that the written and oral forms are practically identical. In others there is significant variation so that there are two or more versions of the anecdote; some written and oral stories are so different they may not, in fact, be related.

The oral stories below must be related to the written ones in one of three ways, from the informant's point of view.

1. The oral anecdotes are completely independent tellings of a story. The informant is unaware of the written version.

2. The oral story is remembered from the written version, but the informant does not recall that the source of the story was a biography. He tells it as if he heard it orally.

3. The informant does recall reading a similar story but tells his story with significant variation. In this case, the oral story may be an unconscious changing of the written story or a genuine parallel oral version the informant heard.

All of the stories found in oral and written forms are humorous. The themes are similar to those found in the solely written or solely oral stories.

REPEATED SERMONS

Preachers not only made fools of themselves by preaching sermons that other people wrote, but they also sometimes confused and amused their audience by preaching on the same subject for successive Sundays. In this written version, N. B. Hardeman tells of Raccoon John Smith:

[72]

In connection with the last quotation, Hardeman told a story of Raccoon John Smith, who preached on Repentance for several successive Sundays. When his crowd remonstrated, he said: "All right, when you *do* it, I'll quit preaching on that and take up something else."[1]

Smith's repetition of the same topic is intentional. His audience thus reacts with confusion, even anger that church propriety has been violated; preachers are expected to have a different sermon each Sunday. Smith's implication that they had not repented, reflects his frustration in reaction to theirs.

In the first of two oral versions of the "repeated sermon," it is unclear whether the repetition is intentional or not:

[73]

Brother T. B. Larimore, after he got along in years, was preachin' in a series of meetings and he preached, uh, two nights on the same thang, the conversion of the Eunuch. And as his wife, uh, came out the door, and she always called him Brother Larimore, and, uh, she said, "Brother Larimore, you preached that last night." And he said, "It's a good one, idn't it?"[2]

Larimore's response to his wife implies that he intended to, repeat the sermon; however, other parts of the story point in the opposite direction. Larimore is "along in years," so his memory might have faded causing him to forget the previous night's sermon. His wife's action in informing him of the repetition shows that she thought he had forgotten. With either interpretation, the story is humorous. If the repetition is intentional, Larimore's reply to his wife is a humorous retort, much like Smith's. If unintentional, the humor is in his forgetfulness and his lame attempt to cover it.

In a second oral version, the repetition is made not by the same preacher, but by successive preachers. In this story, four teachers at Freed–Hardeman College, N. B. Hardeman, L. L. Brigance, C. P. Roland, and W. Claude Hall, each preached one Sunday a month at a country church. It was Hall's Sunday:

[74]

And, uh, according to the story, why Brother, uh, Hall got up and started preaching one, uh, uh, Sunday on a subject, seems like it was repentance. And, he, he, uh, from the very beginning of it he saw people smile. And as they went along, they, it was just obvious everybody was so tickled. Uh, it, he had no idea what was wrong, but he knew something was wrong because the audience never had been this way before. Uh, they just obviously were amused about something that was a private joke to them.

After it was over, he inquired about it and, uh, they said, "Why, Brother Hall, you are the fourth person this month to speak on the subject of repentance; you all preached the same sermon."

They had never checked with each other, and it was just one of those things that, uh, happen. And probably it was an outline that Brother L. L. Brigance used because he used to provide sermon outlines, or at least help Brother Hardeman with his sermons.[3]

The humor here lies in the impropriety of the repeated sermon and the lack of coordination between the four preachers.

Are these stories related? There are similarities; in each a sermon is repeated, the preacher is confronted by the audience, and the preacher gives an explanation for the repetition (although in the second oral version it is the informant, not the preacher, who gives the explanation).

There are also significant differences. Comparing the first two stories, the preachers are different (Smith and Larimore), the sermon topics are different, though related ("repentance" and "conversion of the Eunuch"), the preacher is confronted by different individuals ("his crowd" and "Mrs. Larimore"), and the explanation for the repetition is different (one preaches until they repent, the other repeats a good sermon). In spite of these differences, these could be two versions of the same story; either the oral or the written could be the prior one, or they could be two variations on an earlier, unrecorded story.

The third story is different from the first two in that there are four (actually three) preachers who repeat the sermon topic. The topic is identical to that in the written story: repentance. The explanation for the repetition is different since there are four preachers: they independently use the same outline. Could this third story come from the other two? It is possible since the sermon topic is the same. The third story could be a reworking of one or both of the first two stories (or an unrecorded original), replacing the less believable motif of a single preacher repeating a sermon with a more logical explanation of four preachers who unknowingly use the same outline.

It is most likely that each story is an independent telling of an incident common in preaching. Most preachers preached the same sermon on different occasions during their preaching careers, especially if it was a good one,[4] so it is not inconceivable that they could purposefully or inadvertently preach the same sermon, or at least on the same topic, on successive Sundays.

REPARTEE

Against Religious Foes

As seen in the written and oral anecdotes in the previous chapters, Church of Christ preachers were constantly trying to get the best of "denominational" preachers, both in public debates and in more informal discussions. Alongside this partisan spirit there was also an impulse on the frontier for unity among different churches. Some preachers supported these unity efforts while others tried to disrupt them. J. D. Tant managed to disrupt a unity meeting while participating in it. The written version is from N. B. Hardeman:

[75]

Here he again made reference to J. D. Tant. The latter, at insistence of some of his friends, agreed not to mention baptism in a "union meeting." But he got around it by such remarks as "Repent and do that which I have promised not to mention, etc."[5]

The oral version is fuller:

[76]

Years ago, Brother J. D. Tant learned that the denominations in the town whur he lived were planning a union meeting. He went to the leaders and told them that he lived in that town and that he was a preacher of the gospel and he wanted to be one of the preachers in the meeting. They told him, uh, that they had made an agreement not to mention baptism in that meeting. Well, he said, that wouldn't bother him in the least. And so they let him preach.

He went through the New Testament, presented all of the passages on baptism, and referred to baptism as "that which I'm not allowed to mention."[6]

This story shows how clever Church of Christ preachers could be in conflict with other churches; here the preacher is a wolf in sheep's clothing, preaching under false pretenses.

In this case, it is likely that the oral version of the story grows out of the written version. The informant told this story and then immediately told another story found on the next page of Hardeman's biography.[7] The brief written account is expanded in the oral version to a more detailed narrative.

Another J. D. Tant story tells how far Church of Christ preachers could go in their personal attacks against debate opponents. The written version is set in a debate between Tant and a Mormon Elder named Wyatt:

[77]

"Elder Tant has shown himself even less of a gentleman than Warlick," he complained in one speech. "He has called me every kind of belittling and ridiculous thing a man could think of. I can't call to mind any kind of animal he has failed to compare me with unless it be a tumble-bug. I guess now that I've mentioned it he will be calling me a tumble-bug in his next speech."

"Not at all," responded Tant when he got the floor. "Why, before God, friends, I thought everybody recognized what is happening in this debate—J. D. Tant is the tumble-bug, and Elder Wyatt is the stuff the tumble-bug is rolling down the road!!"[8]

The first of two oral versions is similar to the written one:

[78]

Brother J. D. Tant was in a debate. His opponent said, "Brother Tant has called me everything but a tumblebug. I guess he'll call me that next." Brother Tant said, "No, I'm not going to call you a tumblebug. I'm the tumblebug, you're that stuff the tumblebug rolls down the road."[9]

This version could certainly have come from the written one.

A second oral version is longer and more complex. The informant was not sure who the Church of Christ preacher was, but knew it was "an old timer," possibly "Joe S. Warlick or J. N. [sic] Tant":

[79]

But, in the course of the debate, our brother, whoever he was, was really bringing the pressure to bear on the person, the Baptist preacher, making it pretty rough on him, and, uh, probably accusing him of being dishonorable, uh, not quite, uh, as uh, as uh, level headed as he could be, bright. And so, uh, the Baptist preacher was really feeling the pressure, and he, he began to make an appeal to the audience. Uh, he said, "I, I have just been treated shamefully in this debate." He, he says, "I have just been called everything." He says, "I, I've been called everything but a tumblebug." And, and, and, he was just almost to the point of tears.

And our good brother when he got up for his rebuttal, said, "I, I would call, uh," (he called his name, probably called him brother, I'm not sure), but he said, "I wouldn't call him a tumblebug." He said, "I would want to be more accurate than that. I, I'd rather call him that little ball that the tumblebug pushes along in front of him."[10]

This is obviously the same story, but with significant differences. The preacher is Baptist and the story is more sympathetic to him. This version could be a faint memory of the written story or may have been heard by the informant in an oral setting.

Another Tant story focuses on his manner of dress. Tant was a farmer as well as a preacher and frequently dressed in overalls. In a debate with a Methodist named Pigue, Tant wore his farming clothes:

[80]

Pigue commented with some disgust on the "uncouth and sloven" appearance of his opponent, and opined that the dignity and importance of the occasion demanded a more respectable presence than Tant offered.

"I grew up on a farm," Tant responded with his nasal twang even more pronounced than usual, "and my old pappy always told us boys to dress for the kind of work we had to do. I come down here to do a hogkillin' job on a fat, overgrown over-stuffed 'pigue,' and I dressed for the occasion. Let's get on with the job!"[11]

Tant, of course, is making a play on the Methodist's name (Pigue is pronounced "pig").

An oral version of the story has the debate between different preachers:

[81]

Brother Joe S. Warlick went to engage Ben, uh, Bogard, Missionary Baptist preacher of Little Rock, Arkansas, in debate. Brother Warlick was wearing a suit that had been dyed black. It had been a light colored suit, but a bottle of ink had turned over on it in his suitcase, so he had it dyed black. And on the trip, he perspired and the dyed coat faded on his white shirt.

And he had to make the first speech in the debate, and so he didn't have time to change clothes. And in his speech he introduced Galatians 3:26 and 27, where Paul said, "For as many of you as have been baptized into Christ have put on Christ." Brother Warlick, uh, pulled his coat off to illustrate and demonstrate. And he said, "Before I can put my coat on I have to get into it. And before you can put Christ on, according to Galatians 3:27, why you have to get into him, and you're baptized into him."

Mr. Bogard, uh, thought he'd just, uh, laugh it off. And he said, "I tell yuh what, if my shirt had been as dirty as Elder Warlick's, I would have kept, uh, on my coat." Brother Warlick said in reply, "I'll have you know, Mr. Bogard, these aren't the best clothes that I have. I have clean clothes in my suitcase. But my father taught me when I was a boy, not to wear the best that I had when I went to clean a hog."[12]

Are these two versions of the same story? Their differences are many: different preachers, different reasons for the inappropriate clothing, and a difference in the "pig" comment (it is not a play on words in the second story). One cannot be sure, but the similar circumstances and endings in the stories makes it likely that they are somehow related.

Another set of stories, oral and written, tells how Church of Christ preachers deal with interruptions during sermons. In the written story, Raccoon John Smith is preaching against Spiritualism when a woman medium in the audience interrupts him and goes into a trance:

[82]

"Excuse me," said the medium, who was now sitting with her head thrown back, her bonnet fallen off, and her eyes still closed; "excuse me," she said, "I am not responsible for what I say; I have no control over myself."

"Well," said he, "you are in a bad fix if you have no control over yourself, and you had better go home."

She immediately arose to her feet, and stepped forward; extending her hand to him, which, however, he refused to take, she said:

"Well, I will go. Farewell, my brother; I hope to meet you in another world."

"It depends, madam, on which world you are going to," said he, "whether I wish to meet *you* or not."

At this, she seemed to get angry, and started abruptly down the aisle. Just as she passed out at the door, he closed the scene by saying:

"I raised the devil, and have now cast him out!"[13]

Although the woman interrupted Smith's sermon, she is cordial and wishes to part in friendship. Smith's rude reply to her stems from his belief that Spiritualism really was from Satan. His "casting out the devil" comment is to be taken literally.

Gus Nichols is the preacher in the oral version. His sermon is interrupted by two drunks:[14]

[83]

Brother Gus Nichols was holding a meeting somewhere, and two inebriated fellows walked in off the street and sat down. A few minutes went by and one of 'em hopped up and said, "We want to see a miracle." And, uh, Gus said, uh, "Just be quiet, sit down and listen, and don't cause any trouble." A few minutes went by and he jumped up again. "We want to see a miracle." "Be quiet, you're interrupting the service, just sit down." The second guy jumped up the third time. He said, "We want to see a miracle." About that time, a big ole deacon walked down the aisle, picked them up by the shirt collar and started to escort 'em out and said, "We don't perform miracles here, but we do cast out demons."[15]

This story is quite different from the written one. There are different preachers; the interruption is motivated by doctrinal differences in the written story, by drunkenness in the oral; the interrupter leaves on her own power in the Smith story, the drunks are thrown out. Even the "cast out" demons (or "the devil") line is used differently: in the Smith story, it is literal—the medium is a tool of Satan; the deacon in the Nichols story makes a play on words—no miracles, but casting out "demons" (both supernatural acts). Though these anecdotes may be related, it is more likely they are separate stories that share the "cast out demons" theme.

Against Other Church of Christ Preachers

Preacher repartee did extend to other preachers of the same church. However, when verbally fencing with "brothers," Church of Christ preachers generally used the counterthrust instead of the offensive barrage used against other churches. The snappy comeback was admired by these preachers, especially when it got them out of a jam, like being caught smoking:

[84]

Once, when Brother T. Q. Martin was caught smoking, "I see you're burning incense to the devil," Brother Jimmy Smith said to him. "Yes," replied Brother Martin, "but I didn't expect him to catch me at it."[16]

The oral version is almost identical:

[85]

Once Brother T. Q. Martin, who was a preacher of great renown, was, uh, caught smokin'. Brother Jimmy Smith said, "I see you're burning incense to the devil, Brother Martin." He said, "Yes but I never thought he would, uh, catch me at it."[17]

The similarities between these versions, and the informant's telling of another story found in the Hardeman biography just before he told this one, make it almost certain that this oral story is a memory of the written one. This story, and the Smith and Nichols stories before it, show that calling someone a demon or devil was common in the church.

Catching a preacher in a moral fault was a frequent occasion for repartee. For Martin, it was being caught smoking; for James A. Harding, it was his famous temper:

[86]

From his Irish grandmother Harding may have inherited his flashing, furious temper, which made his mother sometimes fear to let him play with other children. But in his childhood he learned the necessity of self–control. John Garner was the playmate whom he loved best. One day another child in a fit of anger threw a stone and knocked out John's eye. Jimmy was deeply grieved. For the first time he resolved to master his own temper. In this he was amazingly successful. All his life he had to hold it strictly in check. Once when his face flushed with anger and he was with difficulty fighting to keep silence, a friend scolded him.

"Jimmy, you ought to control your anger."

"Don't scold me," Harding flashed. "For the past fifteen minutes I have been controlling more anger than you have had to control in a lifetime!"[18]

The setting for this story is ambiguous: "once" may mean during childhood (the context of the paragraph), or much later in life (since he had to control his anger "all his life").

In the oral version, the setting is more specific, and the friend is David Lipscomb, known as a calm, controlled preacher:

[87]

And they were journeying to some location buggy style. And, uh, uh, they were riding down the road and the, uh, the horse began to balk (it was a mule actually), the mule began to balk. And Harding had the reins and was getting very, very frustrated, very frustrated with the whole situation.

At this point, there are two versions of the story. OK. I've heard it in two sources, and I can't remember the other source.

One source was that in the buggy Harding was real frustrated and lashing and spewing and spitting, uh, uh, with the horses, and yanking and just as mad as he could be.

Uh, and the other is, he got out of the buggy, picked up a big rock, and threw it right into the side of the horse. And that's uh, Jimmy Allen's source of throwing the rock into the side of the horse.

And at that point Brother Lipscomb turns to him and says, "Now, Brother Harding, you know that you must work to control that temper. That you're not solving anything with that. God challenges us to control our temper."

And Harding turns to Lipscomb and says, "Brother Lipscomb, I control more temper in one minute than you control in your entire life."[19]

Which is prior, the written version or the oral ones? The written one gives little detail to the story and is probably set in Harding's boyhood (the address, "Jimmy," points in this direction). The oral story is specific in detail: the buggy ride, the stubborn horse or mule, the expression of anger (here the two oral versions diverge: one has only an oral expression of anger, the other is more violent), Lipscomb's scolding, and Harding's reply. If the written version is the prior one, then the oral versions supply gaps in the story, a characteristic of oral lore. It is also possible Harding's biographer had a vague recollection of the oral version, but he reset it in Harding's childhood. Indeed, the imprecise setting in the written version reflects this partial memory of the story. Since he discusses Harding's temper in his chapter on childhood, he places the anecdote in that setting.

So, although it is impossible to know for certain, it seems that both the written story and the oral story (with its variations) have a basis in oral lore.

Inappropriate Answers

Another type of humorous anecdote found in written and oral forms is the humorous answer to a question. In this written example, the story is told by "Miss Joe," the wife of N. B. Hardeman:

[88]

An incident that amused "Miss Joe" considerably is this: the Third Tabernacle Meeting, in 1928, for obvious reasons was the first one to be aided by radio. The noonday services were broadcast daily from Central Church in Nashville. A dear friend of "Miss Joe's," Mrs. Ed McCann, was listening in Henderson to the broadcast one day. She called her colored maid into the room and said, "Sophie, see if you know who this is." The maid listened intently, and then said, with assurance, "Oh, sure, yes ma'am! That's Reverend Keeble."[20]

Keeble was a famous black preacher in Churches of Christ. The humor here then is not simply mistaking one preacher for another, but mistaking a white preacher for a black one. The "considerable amusement" this anecdote engendered clearly shows the racial attitudes of most Church of Christ members in the 1920s.

There is great similarity to the written version in this oral one:

[89]

Brother Hardeman was speaking on the radio, WLAC in Nashville, Tennessee. Sister Hardeman, at home, called the colored maid and said, "Tell me, who's speaking on the radio?" And she said, "The Reverend Marshall Keeble."[21]

This version simplifies the story to directly involve Mrs. Hardeman and her maid, instead of her friend, Mrs. McCann, and her maid. The confusion between Hardeman and Keeble is a much greater mistake, and more humorous, when made by Hardeman's own maid. The oral story probably comes from the written one since this informant is familiar with Hardeman's biography.

Another type of inappropriate answer is given in response to a question asked in a sermon or a Bible class. The following story is Type 1833 and Motif X435, "The boy applies the sermon." In stories of this type, someone in the audience, usually a boy, misunderstands the question and shouts out an answer.[22] Here David Lipscomb is teaching a college Bible class:

[90]

Once, Brother Lipscomb asked Brother Alexander Yohannan "What became of Adonijah?" Brother Yohannan soberly replied, "He died!"[23]

This non sequitur seems like nonsense, unless Yohannan was trying to be funny, which evidently ("soberly replied") he was not. However, in most stories of this type, the hearer confuses the historical person in the question, Adonijah, with someone he knows. The biographer explains after this story that Yohannan was a Persian student; this makes it more likely that he actually knew someone named Adonijah or that the language barrier caused him to misunderstand the question.

The oral version must be a memory of the written version, since the informant knew the written source and quotes it verbatim.[24]

These examples show that there are degrees of variation between the written and oral versions of preacher anecdotes. In some cases, the stories are identical, implying the oral informant knew the written version. Some oral versions vary slightly from the written ones. Other stories have significant differences in oral and written versions. Sometimes the variation is so great that oral and written stories may be separate anecdotes sharing only certain motifs, instead of versions of the same anecdote. The implications of these similarities and differences will be discussed in the next chapter.

V.

THE STYLE OF ORAL AND WRITTEN ANECDOTES

As suggested in chapter 1, the written anecdotes presented in chapters two and four are not living folklore, but what might be called folklore once removed. Anecdotes are folklore in their living, oral performance, but when a performance is reduced to print it is fixed, stripped of its traditional context, and becomes no longer folklore per se, but "folklore in literature."[1]

Thus, what one has in these written anecdotes is not folklore, but the literary use of folklore. What happens to folklore when placed in a literary work (in this case biographies) is the subject of this chapter. In other words, how does writing restructure the form and language of the anecdotes?[2]

It is helpful to remember at this point the three levels of analysis of folklore given by Alan Dundes: text, texture, and context.[3] Comparison of the written and oral texts of the anecdotes ("text" meaning a version or single telling) was made in the previous chapter. This chapter concerns itself mainly with the texture of the anecdotes, that is, their linguistic features: rhyme, stress, pitch, juncture, tone, etc. The context of the anecdotes, the relations of narrator and audience, will also be examined in this chapter. Texture and context together constitute the style of the anecdotes.

Two difficulties arise immediately. One is the inability to completely convey in print the linguistic features and the kinetic aspects of a folklore performance. These oral anecdotes must be seen and heard to be fully appreciated. How can one adequately express on paper the physical setting, the verbal and nonverbal nuances, and the audience's reaction? Folklorists have responded to this problem in various ways. Some have constructed elaborate symbol systems to express voice change and physical movements in the performers.[4] Such esoteric symbols are hard to master and actually distract the uninitiated from the power of the folklore text. Other folklorists simply print folklore texts with little, if any, attempt to express their texture and context.

The approach here will be to let the texts stand by themselves without any additional symbols, but to describe narratively some significant aspects of their language and performance contexts. While individual texts will be referred to, the primary emphasis will be on the linguistic and contextual aspects of the oral texts as a group. This group analysis is made necessary in part by the brevity of most of the anecdotes.

The second difficulty is in using the folklore categories texture and context to compare written with oral texts. The linguistic features of writing are characterized differently from oral linguistic features. Context in writing means something different from context in oral performances. Writing style is not oral style. How then can they be compared? There are some stylistic features that are parallel in oral and written media. Sandra K. D. Stahl discusses seven paired stylistic features she discovered.[5] Dropping one of these features that had little application to anecdotes, and adding a new one, she compares the style of the oral anecdotes as a group to the style of the written anecdotes as a group in the following seven ways:

1. The physical structuring of the presentation.
2. Use of a common frame of reference.
3. Directives given to the audience.
4. Word choice.
5. Length of the presentation.
6. The relation of context to language.
7. The variability or fixity of the text.

THE PHYSICAL STRUCTURING OF THE PRESENTATION

In the oral anecdotes, the storyteller structures the presentation in the course of his interaction with his audience. The audience informs the teller by laughter, facial expressions, and displays of attentiveness whether they understand the anecdote. The teller responds to these cues by giving needed explanations of the material.

Examples of this teller-audience interaction are fewer in discussions of anecdotes than in other types of oral folklore, folktales for example. This relative scarcity is due to the brevity of the anecdotes, the limited audience of anecdotal performances (usually only one individual), and the social setting of the performances (tellers of anecdotes rarely view their storytelling as a performance, but as interpersonal communication). In spite of these limiting factors, there are some instances in the oral anecdotes of the informant giving explanatory material in response to nonverbal cues from the collector.

In three of the anecdotes, the teller feels compelled to reinforce the truth of the anecdote. The form of this assurance is almost identical in the three stories. Charlie Jones says, "And he said that was an actual truth."[6] O. B. Perkins says, "Brother Hardeman said he put it that way."[7] H. A. Fincher parenthetically says, "and he said it happened."[8] These assurances may result from an unintentional expression of incredulity on the part of the collector. The placing of the assuring sentence at the very end of the stories by Jones and Perkins makes this more likely. Those informants, and perhaps Fincher as well, have structured their stories in response to a need for assurance on the part of the audience that the story really happened that way.

Another type of responsive structuring is the explanation of an unfamiliar term or situation. Dale Smith explains the term "close" (a sales term, not a religious term) in great detail in the Bradfield story.[9] In his story of the preacher with the unzipped fly, Mike Glenn digresses to explain that the preacher was one who walked back and forth when he preached.[10] Without that information, the story makes no sense; if the preacher stayed behind the pulpit, there would be no embarrassment. H. A. Fincher explains that the deacon who pulled down the dressing room partition "wasn't really peeping"[11] to make it clear that the incident was accidental and not intentional. These explanations probably are in response to expressions of misunderstanding on the part of the audience.

If oral stories are structured by interaction between storyteller and audience, what parallel feature of writing structures the written anecdotes? Paragraphing serves this structuring function. In comparing the paragraphing of the various written anecdotes, one interesting feature emerged: the number of paragraphs used in the anecdotes is generally determined by the number of speakers in the story.

Of forty-five written anecdotes, twenty-five are told in one paragraph. In eighteen of those twenty-five stories, there is no direct dialogue; either no one is quoted directly or only one speaker is quoted directly.[12] In the other seven stories, dialogue occurs in the one paragraph.[13] Note that six of these seven stories are from the N. B. Hardeman biography or from biographies by J. E. Choate. The placing of dialogue in only one paragraph may thus be a stylistic device of these authors.

Two or more paragraphs are used in telling twenty of the forty-five written anecdotes. In seventeen cases, the paragraphing is determined by the dialogue in the story.[14] In three cases, more than one paragraph is used even though there is no dialogue.[15]

So in the vast majority of the written stories, where there is dialogue, more than one paragraph is used; and if there is no dialogue, only one paragraph is used. What is the cause of this particular patterning of structure? The oral source of the written stories. In writing stories the authors have heard orally, they use paragraphing to distinguish the speakers, just as an accomplished oral storyteller might use different voices in telling the story. In this case then, the written structuring of the story is dependent on an earlier oral structure—the use of dialogue.

USE OF A COMMON
FRAME OF REFERENCE

In the oral anecdotes the common frame of reference is shown by certain omissions and casual allusions. Certain terms unfamiliar to the general public are used without explanation in the stories. For example, there are many references to biblical passages in the stories, some of which are obscure to the general public, but well known as "proof texts" to members of the Churches of Christ. These include Old Testament references prohibiting plowing with an ox and an ass[16] commanding the destruction of the idols of Baal,[17] and telling the stories of Balaam,[18] Solomon,[19] and Adonijah.[20] New Testament references include the casting out of demons[21] and two baptism proof texts—the thief on the cross[22] and the conversion of the Eunuch.[23] These references are made in passing and are not extensively quoted. The oral anecdotes are therefore told in a context of individuals who have great familiarity with the Bible.

Other terms are used freely that would have a special meaning only to Church of Christ members. One such term is "brother." In some religious groups, "brother" is a title for the clergy or members of a religious order. In the Church of Christ, it is used to refer to preachers, but also to any male member of the church (the term for a female member is "sister"). Thirty-seven of the forty-five oral anecdotes call the preacher, "brother." Two make reference to "the brethren" (referring to the entire church),[24] one to "one of the brothers"[25] and two to a "sister."[26] An exception to calling only members of the Church of Christ "brother" is found in a J. D. Tant story, and even there, the informant states Tant "probably called him [the Baptist preacher] brother."[27] If Tant did call him "brother," he is violating usual Church of Christ practice, since calling one "brother" implies an agreement with his teaching and a recognition of his Christianity. From the other Tant stories, it is clear he did not consider Baptists as true Christians.

Another unusual exception to the use of "brother" is the reference to "the Reverend Keeble."[28] "Reverend" was a forbidden title for Church of Christ preachers, and many sermons were preached against using the term.[29] Why is it used in this case? The preacher referred to is a black preacher and the comment is made by a black woman. It may be that in black Churches of Christ the term "reverend" is not as objectionable as it is in white Churches of Christ and so is used alongside the usual "brother" designation.

A third type of casual reference is the use of the name of a preacher without additional personal information. It is assumed by the performer that the audience knows these preachers, since most of them are famous in Churches of Christ. The only personal information given about the preachers is their location, and this information is provided in only fifteen of the forty-six oral anecdotes.[30] Similar casual references are made to two

Church of Christ colleges, Freed-Hardeman and David Lipscomb, and to a Church of Christ periodical, the *Gospel Advocate*.[31]
These stories thus assume that the hearer is familiar with Church
of Christ papers, schools, and preachers.

Familiarity with Church of Christ worship is also assumed.
The anecdotes on baptism[32] would make little sense to someone
unfamiliar with the Church's method of adult baptism, yet no
effort is made to explain the procedure. Another Church of
Christ custom is to close the worship with prayer; without this
closing prayer the service feels incomplete. To a Church of Christ
audience, the two anecdotes that seek to avoid an embarrassing
situation by quickly calling on someone to lead prayer[33] make
perfect sense. To an outsider unfamiliar with the "closing
prayer" tradition, these anecdotes are unclear.

To summarize, the oral anecdotes display a common frame of
reference by what they do not say. A knowledge of Church of
Christ preachers schools, papers, and customs is assumed.

In written anecdotes this common frame of reference is usually
shown by the use of popular allusions, brief references to people,
places, and events known by the general public. These particular
written preacher anecdotes, however, contain no popular allusions, but instead make the same kind of casual allusions that
the oral anecdotes make.

For instance, the written anecdotes make frequent references
to the Bible, usually without mentioning the location of the Scripture.[34] Familiarity with these particular Bible passages is assumed, just as in the oral anecdotes.

The title "brother" is used in the written anecdotes, though
not as frequently as in the oral ones (eleven of the forty-five
written anecdotes use "brother").[35] Preachers are also referred
to as "Mr.," "Elder,"[36] once as "Reverend,"[37] and many times
by name without a title. "Sister" occurs twice, once referring to
Methodist women.[38]

Since the written anecdotes occur in biographies, the anecdotes themselves tell little of the setting of the stories, but the
larger context supplies this information. No anecdotes mention
Church periodicals, and only one concerns a Church college.[39]

To understand the written anecdotes on baptism[40] the reader
does not need to know the Church of Christ method of baptism,

but must know the Church's doctrinal stand that baptism is essential for salvation.

So both oral and written anecdotes show their common frame of reference in similar ways. Instead of using popular allusions that reflect a general audience, the written anecdotes make the same casual allusions the oral anecdotes make, allusions easily understood only by Church of Christ members. However, these casual allusions occur less frequently in the written anecdotes, indicating that although the biographies are written for a Church of Christ audience, there is some concern in them for the non-Church reader. This concern is not shared by the oral tellers, since they know their listeners are Church of Christ members privy to the terminology and customs of the church.

DIRECTIVES GIVEN TO
THE AUDIENCE

Every oral performance has elements that go beyond the mere words of the story: acoustic, visual, and kinetic cues to the audience. These oral directives are expressed in gestures, noises, facial expression, bodily motion, pitch, volume, pantomime, and pauses. Three difficulties occur in discussing the directives in oral anecdotes. One is the problem, discussed earlier, of expressing non-verbal aspects of a performance in print. The other two arise from the nature of anecdotes: they are usually brief and they are told informally. The informant is usually not consciously concerned with creating a "good" performance.

Few directives were given visually in the oral performances. Most gestures were simply movements of the hand to emphasize certain points. For example, H. A. Fincher in telling of two "lighthouses" mentioned in a sermon, pointed upward with the index fingers of both hands.[41] This was the most elaborate gesture encountered in the oral performances. Little bodily motion was used, usually just a shifting of weight backwards or forwards, and there was no pantomime. The facial expression of the informants was animated, but not unusually so.

Verbally, no special noises were used and little dynamics. Dale Smith, the most dramatic of the tellers, did vary the pitch of his

voice to distinguish different characters in a story.[42] By far, the
device used most often to direct the audience is the pause. Most
of the oral anecdotes end with a "kicker," a line that makes the
point, in most cases the joke of the story. Usually there is a long
pause before this line to let the audience know the "kicker" is
coming.[43]

The audience-directing feature in the written anecdotes is
punctuation, both conventional punctuation and manipulation
of type-face (italics, etc.). The punctuation of the stories is standard (although there are more errors in punctuation than one
would expect in a published work) except for various marks to
emphasize certain words or sentences. Exclamation points, for
example, occur quite frequently; two stories even include sentences with double exclamation points.[44] Italics are used in several stories and bold type, coupled with double exclamation
points, is used once.[45]

Why do the written stories use such devices to emphasize so
many words? Because these stories attempt to express oral anecdotes in print. What the oral storyteller expresses by pitch and
volume of voice and by visual expressions, the biographers express by italics, bold type, and exclamation points. In this instance, then, the oral features of the anecdotes directly affect
their stylistic representation in print.

WORD CHOICE

Oral presentations of anecdotes are marked by a great number
of repetitions, especially of formulas, as well as by the use of
slang, clichés, and the overuse of connective conjunctions, especially "and." Much has been written on the subject of formulaic repetition in oral narratives. Formulas function as a tool
for oral composition, enabling a performer to easily fit new material into a story form.[46] In the oral anecdotes, formulas occur
at the beginning, in the verbs, and at the end of the stories.

The majority of the oral stories open with the name of the
preacher who is the main character in the story. "Brother" followed by the preacher's name opens twenty-three of the forty-
six anecdotes. The name without "brother" begins three of the
stories, and two begin with "the preacher," since the name is

unknown. This opening formula allows the storyteller to immediately introduce the main character of the story.

The verb phrase "he said" is repeated several times in eighteen of the anecdotes. This repeated verb, a type of formula found in many stories,[47] allows the performer to structure his story around dialogue.

As discussed earlier, several of the anecdotes end with a summary phrase, a "kicker," that makes the point of the story or joke. Placing the punchline at the end is characteristic of jokes, but even some of the serious anecdotes use a formulaic closing phrase.

Besides formulaic language, oral anecdotes also use more informal terms, e.g., slang, than written anecdotes. Slang terms in the oral anecdotes include "quit me"[48] (for "stop me"), "fella,"[49] "dadburn,"[50] "anyhow"[51] (for "anyway") and "idn't it."[52]

An excessive number of connective conjunctions mark these anecdotes. Nineteen of the stories use "and" repeatedly, two use "and so," and two use "so."

Another characteristic of oral stories is the frequent use of verbal fillers, words that have no meaning but are used to fill dead space in the performance. "Uh" is the most popular, used in twenty-six of the forty-six oral anecdotes, while "ah" is used repeatedly in two of the stories.

Written narratives, on the other hand, use variety and innovation in word choice and phrasing. The formulas used in the oral narratives occur less frequently or not at all in the written ones. The name of the preacher is used at the beginning of the story in only nine of the forty-five written anecdotes. When it is used at the beginning, it usually is not preceded by "brother" (although "brother" is used later in the text of some of the stories). Direct quotes are introduced by a variety of phrases, compared to the repeated use of "he said" in the oral stories. Closing formulas, "kickers" or "punchlines," occur less frequently in the written stories.

The other characteristic word choices of the oral stories are also missing in the written ones. Little slang is used. Phrases are joined by a variety of grammatical methods, not simply by connective conjunctions. No verbal fillers are used.

In this case then, there is a great difference in the way the two media, oral and written, handle the choice of words. Oral stories make use of formula, repetition, and an informal style that includes words with no lexical significance. Written stories have a much greater variety of word choice and avoid the use of slang and words with no significance. No doubt the writers of the biographies have taken their oral sources for their anecdotes and "cleaned them up." That is, they have restructured them, removing repetitive words and phrases and adding a variety of introductory phrases, connectives, and conclusions.

LENGTH OF THE ANECDOTES

Related to word choice is the length of the anecdotes. With the repetition characteristic of oral anecdotes, one would expect them to be longer than the written anecdotes. However, the opposite is true. The written anecdotes of chapter 2 are, on the average, sixty-eight percent longer than the oral anecdotes of chapter 3.[53] However, in chapter 4, where similar oral and written anecdotes are compared, the oral ones are on the average thirty-four percent longer.[54] This pattern continues in the six pairs of stories in chapter 4 in which the oral and written versions are practically identical;[55] there the oral stories are twenty-five percent longer.[56]

How can this conflicting evidence be explained? The greater length of the written anecdotes may be due to the inclusion of more contextual information in the anecdotes. In other words, since these anecdotes are part of a section in a biography, it is hard to tell exactly where the anecdotes begin and end. By contrast, the formulaic openings and endings of the oral anecdotes make it easier to determine their length.

Another explanation for the increased lengths of the written stories is their roots in oral lore. The biographers may have expanded the stories they heard, adding more contextual features and detail. The performance setting of the oral anecdotes in an interpersonal, conversational mode may also have led to their brevity.

What about chapter 4, where the oral anecdotes are longer? Here the characteristic repetition of oral stories may account for their increased length. The expansion would work in both media: both writers and tellers of anecdotes tend to add details to their source stories.

THE RELATION OF CONTEXT TO LANGUAGE

Another stylistic characteristic related to word choice is the relation of context to language. In oral stories, context means interaction between storyteller and audience. The language of the oral stories is chosen with the sensibilities of the audience in mind. In written narratives, words are chosen appropriate to the anticipated sensibility of the reading audience. The difference between oral and written contexts and language choices is readily apparent in the handling of offensive language and themes in the two media.

Stronger language, for example, is used in the oral stories. "Hell"[57] and "dadburn"[58] (a euphemism) are used. Opponents are called "devils,"[59] "fools,"[60] or "asses."[61] Even sexual terms such as "prophylactic"[62] and "intercourse"[63] serve as the major focus in certain stories. By contrast, the written stories use "devil"[64] more often, but "ass"[65] and "fool"[66] less. No profanity is used, and the only reference to sexual immorality is made by use of an analogy.[67]

This difference in use of offensive language is paralleled in the different themes of the oral and written stories. In none of the biographies are there stories of Church of Christ preacher immorality; the anecdote closest to this theme is the story of Raccoon John Smith drinking wine.[68] On the other hand, there are several oral stories of preachers who were sexually immoral or drug-dependent. They do not appear here because the informants would not allow them to be printed for fear of ruining the reputation or offending the families of the subjects of the anecdotes. This reticence on the part of the informants shows the difference between the handling of offensive material in oral and written media. Since the oral stories are told in an informal setting, themes and language which might be offensive to the general public can be used, if not offensive to the listeners of that particular oral performance. On the other hand, since the written stories are intended for a larger audience, whose composition is beyond the control of the biographer, the writer is more reluctant to print material that may be offensive. Context thus affects the themes and language of anecdotes in both media.

VARIABILITY OR
FIXITY OF THE TEXT

One characteristic of folklore is that it exists in different versions.[69] Even in brief oral anecdotes, one finds variation among different performances. Compare, for example, the two versions of the "dog out the window" story. The first is told by H. A. Fincher:

[52]

Anyhow, Miller was preaching away one night and a big dog, sort of an ole hound dog, walked in out in the back of the church building (and he said it happened); he walked right up the center, very slowly, and sat down in dog-like fashion between the front two rows. And he said he cocked his head and just looked at him while he was preaching. No one paid the dog any attention, but he said "it was eating the life out of me." He cocked his head the other way, you know, and finally Miller, he said, he nodded to one of the brethren there and pointed to the dog and just went on with his preaching.

The brother nodded. He went over to the center aisle and he picked that dog up by the nap of the neck and by the tail. He said, he looked over at one side to the window over there, and looked over at the other side at the window over there. And from that position he threw that dog out the window.

Another version is told by Mike Glenn:

[53]

And just about time for services to start, the door opened, he looked down and this tall, distinguished looking man stepped in, he had an Abe Lincoln beard. He took off his coat and hung it on the hook. And without a change of expression walked down front, sat down, pulled out his watch. And when it was time for services to begin, he turned to this fella and nodded to him, and the guy got up and led some songs.

At a certain point, he nodded to this other fella, and the guy got up and led a prayer. He said, after that he looked at Andrews and nodded to him, and he said he "figured it was my turn."

So he got up to the pulpit and was preaching. And in the middle of the sermon, this, uh, real, uh, wrinkled, scrawny hound dog came into church, walked right down front and laid down in the middle of the floor. And everybody was looking at him. And, uh, Brother Andrews said he stopped preaching and looked at the guy with the beard sittin' in the front row, and nodded at the guy. So the guy got up off the pew, and grabbed that dog by the loose skin of his neck and back and heaved him out the window and sat down.

Chapter 3 concluded that these were two versions of the same anecdote. Note the differences in the stories. In the first, James P. Miller is the preacher; in the second, Jay Andrews. The second version gives a setting to the story: a strange bearded man controls the order of worship by nodding. Even in the descriptions of the ejection of the dog, there are variations between the stories. Other oral anecdotes, discussed in chapters three and four, display variation between versions.[70]

Not only is there variation between oral anecdotes told by different performers, but even when the same anecdote is told by the same performer on different occasions, variation occurs. Here is the same anecdote told by O. B. Perkins ten months apart:

[68]

Brother A. G. Freed and Brother Foy E. Wallace, Jr., went to a place for dinner. The sister asked Brother Freed if he'd like a cup of coffee. He said no, he was a Christian. Brother Wallace said, "Sister, you may pour me a cup. I'm a Christian too, but I didn't let it make a fool out of me."[71]

Now, the later performance:

Brother Foy E. Wallace Jr. and Brother A. G. Freed went to dinner together. The lady said, "Brother Freed, have a cup of coffee." And he said, "No, I'm a Christian." Brother Wallace saw she was embarrassed, and he said, uh, "Pour me a cup. I'm a Christian too, but I didn't let it make a fool out of me."[72]

Note that there is a reversal of names in the beginning, and the ending of the two versions is identical. In the body of the story, the second version has more direct quotations, and the "sister" of version one is now a "lady." In the second version, Wallace's remark is prompted by the embarrassment of the lady.

In another instance of repeated anecdotes by Perkins, the differences are fewer:

[69]

Another preacher said to Brother Wallace, "Brother Wallace, a man called me a Doctor. I felt like a fool. Do I look like a Doctor?" "No," said Brother Wallace, "you look more like you said you felt."[73]

Compare this with:

A preacher said to Brother Foy E. Wallace, Jr., "A fella called me Doctor the other day. I felt like a fool. Do I look like a Doctor?" Brother Wallace said, "No, you look like you said you felt."[74]

Though the differences are minor, this example too shows that even an informant like Perkins, with a phenomenal memory and a large stock of preacher anecdotes, will vary his stories from telling to telling.

Written anecdotes on the other hand are fixed, since they are written but once and remain the same no matter how many times they are printed.[75]

Writing, then, restructures the oral anecdotes in several ways. Little change is made in the length of the anecdotes from speaking to writing. Both spoken and written anecdotes are told in the setting of a common frame of references, but this frame is narrower in the oral anecdotes. The opposite is true in regard to the relation of context to the language of the anecdotes: oral anecdotes are broader in their use of offensive terms than are written anecdotes. In these three instances, the differences in style between oral and written stories are differences in degree, not kind. That is, they use very similar structures in different ways.

In the four other areas of comparison, there is greater diversity. Oral stories are structured by verbal or kinetic signs. Written stories are structured quite differently, that is, by paragraphs. Directives are given to the audience in oral stories by verbal or kinetic signs also. Written stories rely on punctuation, sometimes special stress marks like bold type or italics, to give direction. On word choice, oral and written stories exhibit opposite patterns. Oral stories use repetition, slang, and non-lexical terms ("uh," "ah"), but writers use variety in wording, as opposed to repetition, and choose words with precise meaning. Finally, oral stories are by nature variable. Written and printed stories are fixed.

Written stories thus not only display a different style from oral stories, but these stylistic changes produce differences in the meaning of the stories. Oral stories are personable, direct, and informal. Written stories are more circumspect, formal, and precise in language. Writing restructures the thoughts of the anecdotes.

VI.

THE FUNCTIONS
OF THE ANECDOTES

This chapter will interpret the anecdotes in terms of function. Function is not to be confused with authorial intent, but instead deals with the meaning of the story in the entire context of teller and audience. Function is then "an abstraction made on the basis of a number of contexts."[1] Context refers to the material surrounding the stories in the written biographies and to narrator–audience interaction and the community's shared beliefs in the oral stories. With the oral stories, an attempt has been made to elicit interpretations of the functions of the stories from the storytellers themselves. This attempt, however, was not always fruitful, since storytellers are many times unreflective about the stories they tell. As O. B. Perkins put it, "I've been telling stories all my life, it's just a part of me. I don't have any purpose in mind."[2]

The preacher stories in this collection display three broad functions. Some serve as exempla, either positively as models of what a preacher should be, or negatively as a warning against moral and religious faults. Many have a humorous function. As humor, they entertain, laugh at others, and tell truths not easily told in a more serious tone. Thirdly, some stories serve to create or reinforce an identity; they mark the tellers and listeners as part of a special group. Many of the stories simultaneously perform more than one of these three functions.

PREACHER ANECDOTES AS EXEMPLA

One historic function of anecdotes has been to serve as a moral example or warning.[3] Since preachers are expected to be moral models to the community, it is not surprising to find several stories that have this function. Preachers are presented as positive examples in two ways. More than most Christians, they are called on to trust God's care in keeping them from accident, sickness, and poverty.[4] Preachers also are expected to be clever in publicizing their preaching and in overcoming religious opposition.[5] In trusting both God and their own cleverness, they were personal examples of Jesus' command to be "wise as serpents and harmless as doves" (Matt.10:16).

The emphasis on preachers as examples grew out of the practice in southern churches of training for the ministry through an apprenticeship.[6] Since formal education was not encouraged by many churches (some, like the Church of Christ, even discouraged it), young preachers usually learned their craft by imitating older preachers. This placed pressure on the older ministers to be models of good preaching and good morals.

Since a higher morality was expected of preachers, when they were unethical they stood out as warnings against evil behavior. Only one preacher, James A. Harding, is accused of moral faults in these stories, since they are presented by people who wish to portray the Church of Christ preachers in the best light. In one case Harding is wasteful with his money[7] and in another he loses his temper.[8] He repents of his wastefulness, but defends his loss of temper.

More often, Church of Christ preachers are accused not of moral faults, but of bad preaching. Twisting Scriptures to fit sermon topics[9] and excess verbiage in sermons[10] are specifically condemned. The embarrassment felt when those who "stole" sermons were caught, implies that this too was a taboo practice.[11] Poor theology is condemned in the "swallow A. Campbell" statement made against N. B. Hardeman.[12]

Preachers thus serve as positive models morally, but as negative examples in their preaching. It is interesting to note that all of these exempla are found in biographies or in oral versions of stories found in the biographies. This implies the biographers are more concerned with presenting their subjects as examples of Christianity than the oral storytellers are (although one oral storyteller told me that preachers today are not as good as the "old-time preachers").[13]

PREACHER ANECDOTES AS HUMOR

Most of the preacher anecdotes are humorous, yet this humor has a serious function. Unfortunately only recently has humor been discussed from a serious philosophical viewpoint. This scarcity of scholarly treatment of humor stems from four characteristics of humor. First, humor is a living entity. Any attempt to analyze or systematize a joke tends to diminish its humor. Dissecting a joke kills it. Secondly, the subject of humor is complex. There are so many humorous situations, they seem beyond classification. Similarly the omnipresence of humor makes it difficult to study. Since humor pervades our lives, it is difficult to establish an objective stance for studying it (like the proverbial fish who cannot write scholarly papers about water). Finally, humor seems too frivolous for serious study; "a serious study of humor" is itself an ironic phrase.[14]

However, in spite of these obstacles, humor deserves, and has recently received more scholarly treatment simply because it is such an important part of human existence. But when it comes to religious humor, as in these preacher anecdotes, there are additional objections. Some find a biblical basis for rejecting the importance of humor, claiming there is nothing funny about the Bible. This view ignores both the ubiquity of humor in human society and the humorous sections of the Bible. A second objection to the study of religious humor comes from the nature of Christianity itself. Since, theologically speaking, Christianity is an historical religion set in the real world, then the comic view of the world as illusion is impossible. This objection falls when one remembers the transcendent nature of Christianity. Although Christianity teaches the world is real, it also says it is not ultimate. Belief in a transcendent reality actually gives Christians a stance for comic detachment.[15] Thirdly, the seriousness of social problems—war, racism, hunger—leads some to reject the place of humor in religion. Such a view confuses humor with apathy. The opposite of seriousness in this case is not humor, but tragedy or resignation.[16] One can laugh at problems and still work for their solution.

In spite of these objections, there has been a consensus lately among scholars of religion that humor is important as a religious subject. This consensus informs this discussion on the functions of humorous preacher stories.

Before discussing how these humorous stories function, first one must ask "What makes a story humorous?" or, in other words, "How does humor work?"

Scholars agree that humor results from incongruity and discrepancy. Something is funny because it catches one off guard; it derails the normal train of thought, and it represents something indirectly and absurdly.[17] The perception of this incongruity has a physiological aspect, as when a child laughs at a suddenly withdrawn face in the peek-a-boo game.[18] Verbally, incongruity occurs when more than one line of thought belongs simultaneously to one sign.[19] This clash of unrelated matrices (in its simplest form, a pun) produces humor.

In these preacher anecdotes humor is usually produced by a clash between the serious themes of religion and the mundaneness of human life. This discrepancy between man and universe is itself a sign of transcendence. Thus, humor itself functions religiously as an indication of the sacred in human existence.

Besides this general "religious" function of humor, specific humorous anecdotes function in various ways. Some are therapeutic play. Others serve as socially acceptable forms of aggression. Like the exempla discussed above, some warn against pride and intolerance, revealing unpleasant truths. Finally, by bringing conflicting thoughts together, some anecdotes serve to reconcile opposing thoughts.

The Therapeutic Function of Humor

Jokes produce laughter. Laughter produces pleasure. Jokes then are a form of play. As such they carry little obvious meaning, but simply liberate the individual. Such jokes share in the innocence and joy of childhood. They usually involve plays on words, puns, and other forms of silly humor.[20]

Among the preacher anecdotes, many display this playful attitude toward words. Curtis Porter plays with "alligation" and "alligator,"[21] "brutally honest" and "honestly brutal;"[22] Foy E. Wallace works over the word "hearing;"[23] Gus Nichols uses "running water;"[24] N. B. Hardeman plays with the name "Solomon;"[25] and F. B. Srygley twists the "how do you spell?" question.[26] In each of these cases one can see the clash of thought that produces humor, as well as a playful attitude toward life and words.

Another type of joke that produces this playful humor is the situational joke, based on an embarrassing slip. This may be a literal slip into the baptistry,[27] a social faux pas such as drinking the baptistry water[28] or throwing a dog out a window,[29] or a verbal slip such as confusing N. B. Hardeman with "the Reverend Keeble."[30] In each of these cases the laughter produced seems to be mostly innocent, like laughing at a pratfall.

However, as one grows older the innocent laughter of childhood is constrained by the inhibitions of adulthood. With adults, then, these jokes may not be merely innocent, but rather an attempt to free oneself from inhibition and recapture some of the innocence of childhood. These jokes are therapeutic because they release the tension and anxiety produced by inhibition.[31] In Freud's words, "The pleasure in jokes has seemed to us to arise from an economy in expenditure upon inhibition."[32] In other words, the repressed tendency toward play is released and the energy previously required to suppress this tendency expresses itself in laughter.

This release from repression is most clearly seen in the preacher anecdotes involving sex. Since Christianity, especially the Church of Christ variety, has a strict moral code, any apparent, but inadvertent violation of that code can result in laughter. Thus stories involving preachers in profanity,[33] scatology,[34] sexual situations,[35] or even stories involving nudity,[36] are particularly funny. Laughing at such stories meets "the need to relax occasionally from the repressiveness of a moral system without denying or abandoning that system."[37] As one storyteller put it, these stories provide a "break from the seriousness of salvation."[38]

It is interesting to note that the vast majority of these therapeutic stories, and all of the sexually oriented stories, are oral. It seems that the informal and personal setting of the oral stories makes it easier to overcome the inhibition to tell and laugh at these stories. The medium in this case affects the function of the stories. Oral stories, more often than written ones, serve a therapeutic function of overcoming inhibition, repression, and anxiety.

The Aggressive Function of Humor

Jokes are not only told to amuse, they may be told to wound. Such jokes release inhibition, just like those mentioned earlier, but in this case the inhibition of hostility. These jokes are doubly funny since they allow both the pleasure found in all jokes and the pleasure found in releasing hostility.[39]

Almost half of the preacher anecdotes are aggressive jokes. Most of these occur in the contexts of debates or other situations in which the Church of Christ preacher is attacked. In these cases the Church of Christ preachers are players in a type of game where repartee and one-upmanship are ways of skewering an opponent.[40] They are therefore aggressive, but in a socially approved situation.

Of more interest are the stories in which the Church of Christ preacher is the instigator or the recipient of an unprovoked attack.[41] In most cases these attacks are merely verbal, though in two of the stories there is some physical violence.[42] These stories are humorous only to those who share the hostile impulses of the teller. No therapy is found in these stories; instead they point to an obsession on the part of the characters and perhaps on the part of the teller, if he shares the same hostile outlook.

The preponderance of stories with this hostile function, found equally among written and oral storytellers, has several important implications. The setting of most of the stories in debate situations implies that they are part of a cultural milieu somewhat foreign to the tolerant attitude of twentieth century America. Let us not judge these preachers too harshly. If their words and actions seem too violent for modern tastes, remember that such vehemence was expected in nineteenth century religious discussions. To their mind, entering the kingdom of heaven was too important a goal for preachers to worry about the tone of their preaching.

On the other hand, the unprovoked verbal attacks launched

by these preachers against those innocent of hostility show a mean-spiritedness that sometimes characterized the Church of Christ. The intensity of their belief in the truth of their message led certain preachers to see opposition when there was none. Conviction led to intolerance. The exclusive nature of Church of Christ teaching led some preachers to a petty cruelty toward those who did not "accept the truth." Indeed, this hostile spirit carried over to their dealings with other Church of Christ preachers. This unprovoked hostility apparently was widespread, since these stories involve eleven different Church of Christ preachers mentioned by name and three mentioned anonymously.

Such humorous stories deal with attempts to hurt those whose doctrine differed with the Church of Christ preachers. This was an accepted practice. Unfortunately, these preachers also turned their wit against others innocent of doctrinal disagreement. These stories are told to release aggressive impulses suppressed by societal standards. Words meant to harm can be safely told if wrapped in humor.

The Prophetic/Revelatory Function of Humor

Scholars agree that one important function of humor is to reveal truths.[43] In this function there are two movements: a negative move that tears down the incomplete knowledge of the proud and a positive move that reveals something of the true state of humans in the universe.

In the preacher stories the negative movement predominates. These stories portray the Church of Christ preachers as intellectually arrogant, narrow-minded, and insensitive. However, in many of the stories this portrayal serves as a critique of these negative attitudes. Intellectual pride is ridiculed in the anecdotes in which the Church of Christ preachers mishandle the Scriptures,[44] misunderstand science,[45] display their contempt for Doctors of Divinity,[46] and "swallow A. Campbell."[47] These stories serve the prophetic function of tearing down the false god of pride. By doing this they also make way for a new, more balanced self-understanding for these preachers, and for those coming after them.

Preachers were also proud of their speaking ability. Stories lampooning long sermons[48] or repeated sermons[49] served to warn against that pride and call the preachers back to their role as humble servants of God.

As shown above, some preachers in their pride and haughtiness struck out maliciously at whomever happened to be near. The story of A. G. Freed contemptuously dismissing a woman's offer of coffee, and his subsequent humbling by Foy E. Wallace, shows how humor could be used to show a preacher what kind of person he had become.[50]

These stories exposed pride of intellect, skill, and morals and by doing so they revealed the preacher as he really was. These anecdotes function today as warnings against arrogance and as reminders of human finitude. Even the preacher who speaks from God is still human, limited, and sinful.

Some humorous anecdotes are thus humorous exempla, similar in function to the serious exempla discussed above. However, while most of the serious exempla are found in biographies, the humorous ones are almost all oral. Since the biographies are hagiographic, it is not surprising they do not include stories in which their hero is the butt of a well deserved joke.

The Reconciling Function of Humor

Søren Kierkegaard bases his theological thought on the infinite qualitative distance between the finite and infinite and the supreme paradox of Christianity that in Christ the infinite and finite come together and are reconciled. Since humor is also based on a paradoxical collision of conflicting thoughts, it plays an important role in Kierkegaard's theology.

The comic in two forms, irony and humor, forms the boundaries among Kierkegaard's stages of existence. Irony forms the boundary between the aesthetic stage, where one lives for pleasure and is uncommitted to any higher cause, and the ethical stage, where one commits oneself to keeping the universal moral law. "Irony arises from the constant placing of the particularities of the finite together with the infinite ethical requirement, thus permitting the contradiction to come into being."[51] Recognition of this ironic contradiction does not itself move one into the ethical sphere, but it does permit one to make the leap into the ethical.

Humor realizes an even greater contradiction, that is, the one between the infinite and the finite. Humor is thus the boundary between the ethical and the religious stages of existence. Humor, however, does not make one religious, but only prepares one to take the leap of faith.

All humor, including humorous preacher anecdotes, realizes the contradiction between the infinite and the finite and seeks to transcend the contradiction. However, according to Kierkegaard, humor is the painless way out of the contradiction; it does not take the contradiction as ultimately serious. Faith seriously accepts and even affirms the contradiction, transcending it in absurdity.[52]

Humor thus not only arises from contradiction, but it seeks to reconcile this contradiction. This reconciliation between the infinite and the finite is especially seen in the preacher anecdotes, since they contain religious humor. Slips of the tongue, falling in water, or throwing a dog out a window might be humorous in any situation, but the humor is intensified when it occurs in church, a place of ultimate seriousness where the transcendent is to be seen. Stories of such events remind humans of their finitude in the very act of reaching toward the infinite. This reminder does not provoke despair, but laughter. "By laughing at the imprisonment of the human spirit, humor implies that this imprisonment is not final but will be overcome."[53]

This function of humor might even be called sacramental. Like the sacraments, humor mediates the grace of God. It brings the infinite into a finite situation. It strengthens and encourages faith.[54]

In saying this, one must not ignore Kierkegaard's warning that humor is not faith. Humor does reconcile the infinite and the finite, but in a painless way. It, unlike faith, does not change the basic situation of human beings, their finite existence with longings for the infinite, but it does change their attitude toward that situation.[55] Humor provides a comic outlook on life that affirms the value of being human in the midst of the tragedies of life.

Such an outlook is not itself faith, in Kierkegaard's view, but it is a precursor to faith.[56] Indeed, persons of faith will be viewed by most as comics; comedy will be their incognito. Humor and religious faith are closely intertwined.

So, the humorous preacher stories have four functions. Some

act as play therapy, releasing one from anxiety and inhibition. Most of these therapeutic stories are oral since the oral speech situation is less inhibitory than a formal writing situation. The majority of the stories have an aggressive function, releasing pleasure by harming an opponent. These stories are found equally in both oral and written media. Some humorous stories are used to puncture pride and tell harsh truths. Most of these stories are oral; the biographers tend to avoid criticism of their subjects. Finally, religious humor is life–affirming. The anecdotes—both written and oral—that are not hostile and negative share in this reconciling function.

PREACHER ANECDOTES AS MARKS OF IDENTITY

Some anecdotes function as exempla, some as humor. Others are used to develop and reinforce a group identity. As discussed in chapter 1, folk groups are not necessarily racial, ethnic, or regional. Each human is a part of several folk groups simultaneously. One switches codes, depending on the group in which one is participating at the time. This idea of a part-time folk raises the question of how folk groups can be recognized. "Jokes about groups do provide an index of the existence of such groups."[57] One function of the preacher anecdotes, then, is to establish the Church of Christ as a folk group and provide its members with a group identity.

Although these stories do mark the Church of Christ as a separate folk group, that does not mean these stories are unique to the Church of Christ. Indeed the parallel stories noted in earlier chapters from several denominations active on the American frontier, Methodists and Mormons in particular, demonstrate that the Church of Christ stories are part of a wider cultural milieu.

This group identity is reinforced in the stories by the use of esoteric terms, known only to those who are members of or very familiar with the Church of Christ. These terms concerning Church of Christ preachers, schools, customs, Scriptural proof-texts, and controversies were discussed in full in chapter 5. By participating in telling and listening to these stories, church members strengthen their ties to these church traditions.

More of these "insider" terms are used in the oral stories than in the biographies. Again, this shows how media can affect both style and function. The biographies are intended primarily for a Church of Christ audience, but their public nature makes it necessary to explain certain terms for the occasional non-Church of Christ reader. In the oral storytelling situation, both storyteller and audience are almost always Church of Christ members, so there is no need to explain these terms. Indeed, the unspoken assumption that both teller and audience understand these terms bands them together as fellow-members of the group.

CONCLUSION

The preacher anecdotes in this study support the view that a change from oral to written media affects the meaning of discourse. It is likely that all of the anecdotes here were originally passed on orally; none claims to be creative written fiction. Some of them have been used in written biographies, with a resulting shift in the style of presentation and the functions of the stories.

Stylistically, oral and written anecdotes differ in the way they are structured, in the way they give instructions to the audience, in their choice of words and in their degree of variation. Functionally, oral anecdotes serve to reduce anxiety, express hostility, humorously reveal truth, reconcile opposites, and develop and reinforce identity. Written anecdotes share the functions of hostility, reconciliation, and to a lesser extent, identity development, but also function as serious exempla. So although there is some similarity in the style and functions of oral and written stories, their differences are significant enough to support the view that a change in media is a change in the message. A story, in the sense of oral anecdote, is not the same as a story, in the sense of an anecdote used in a biography.

I. INTRODUCTION

1. Walter J. Ong, *Orality and Literacy* (New York: Methuen, 1982), pp. 156–73.

2. Ibid., p. 156.

3. Jan Harold Brunvand, *The Study of American Folklore*, 2d ed. (New York: W. W. Norton & Co., 1978), p. 1.

4. Richard M. Dorson, *Folklore and Fakelore* (Cambridge: Harvard University Press, 1976).

5. Brunvand, pp. 2–4.

6. Brunvand, p. 114; William Hugh Jansen, "Legend: Oral Tradition in the Modern Experience," in *Folklore Today*, ed. Linda Dégh, Henry Glassie, and Felix J. Oinas (Bloomington: Indiana University Press, 1976), p. 265; Stith Thompson, *The Folktale* (Los Angeles: University of California Press, 1946), p. 188.

7. For the similarities and differences between folktales and one particular group of anecdotes, see E. 'Nolue Emenanjo, "The Anecdote as an Oral Genre: The Case in Igbo," *Folklore* 95 (1984):172–73.

8. Ibid., pp. 173–74.

9. Linda Dégh, "Folk Narrative," in *Folklore and Folklife: An Introduction*, ed. Richard M. Dorson (Chicago: University of Chicago Press, 1972), pp. 69–71.

10. Emenanjo, p. 174.

11. Richard M. Dorson, *Buying the Wind* (Chicago: University of Chicago Press, 1964), p. 351.

12. Ibid.

13. Most of the material in this section is from Dorson, *Folklore and Fakelore*, pp. 127–43.

14. Ibid., p. 141.

15. Ibid., p. 140.

16. Ibid., p. 139.

17. For an overview of the history of the Churches of Christ see Sydney E. Ahlstrom, *A Religious History of the American People*, vol. 1 (Garden City, N. J.: Doubleday, 1975), pp. 524–548.

18. Francis Lee Utley, "Folk Literature: An Operational Definition," *Journal of American Folklore* 74 (July 1961):200.

19. Richard M. Dorson, "The Identification of Folklore in American Literature," *Journal of American Folklore* 70 (1957):5–8.

20. Charles C. Ware, *Barton Warren Stone* (St. Louis: Bethany Press, 1932), p. 326.

21. H. Leo Boles, *Biographical Sketches of Gospel Preachers* (Nashville: Gospel Advocate Co., 1932), pp. 40–41; Leo Lipscomb Boles and J. E.

Choate, *I'll Stand on the Rock: A Biography of H. Leo Boles* (Nashville: Gospel Advocate Co., 1965), p. 7; J. E. Choate, *Roll Jordan Roll: A Biography of Marshall Keeble* (Nashville: Gospel Advocate Co., 1968), p. 105; S. H. Hall, *Sixty Years in the Pulpit or Compound Interest in Religion* (Ann Arbor, Michigan: John Allen Hudson, 1955), p. 182; James Marvin Powell and Mary Nelle Hardeman Powers, *N. B. H., A Biography of Nicholas Brodie Hardeman* (Nashville: Gospel Advocate Co., 1964), p. 280; F. D. Srygley, *Seventy Years in Dixie: Recollections and Sayings of T. W. Caskey and Others* (Nashville: Gospel Advocate Co., 1954), p. 30; Fanning Yater Tant, *J. D. Tant—Texas Preacher* (Erlanger, Kentucky: Faith and Facts Press, 1958), pp. 77, 129, 459; and John Augustus Williams, *Life of Elder John Smith* (Nashville: Gospel Advocate Co., 1956), p. 402.

22. See James H. Penrod, "Teachers and Preachers in The Old Southwestern Yarns," *Tennessee Folklore Society Bulletin* 18 (December 1952):91–96.

23. Alan Dundes, *Essays in Folkloristics* (New Delhi, India: Folklore Institute, 1978), pp. 22–27.

24. See Claude Lévi–Strauss, *The Raw and the Cooked* (Chicago: University of Chicago Press 1969), as well as the other three volumes in his *Introduction to a Science of Mythology* (*From Honey to Ashes; The Origin of Table Manners; The Naked Man*).

25. Vladimir Propp, *Morphology of the Folktale*, 2d ed., trans. Laurence Scott (Austin: University of Texas Press, 1968), pp. 21–24.

26. Propp himself points out the difference in structure between anecdotes and other folklore genres: Vladimir Propp, *Theory and History of Folklore*, trans. Ariadna Y. Martin and Richard P. Martin (Minneapolis: University of Minnesota Press, 1984), p. 41.

27. See chap. 5 for additional reasons for not using this approach.

28. Dundes, *Essays in Folkloristics*, pp. 40–45.

II. WRITTEN ANECDOTES

1. These are the two major types according to *Funk and Wagnalls Standard Dictionary of Folklore, Mythology, and Legend*, 1972 ed., s.v. "Anecdotes" by B. A. Botkin.

2. Annti Aarne, *The Types of the Folktale*, trans. and enlarged by Stith Thompson. 2d revision. (Helsinki: Academia Scientiarum Fennica, 1964).

3. Stith Thompson, *Motif–Index of Folk Literature*, Indiana University Studies 22 (Bloomington, Indiana University Press, 1934); see also Ernest W. Baughman, *Type and Motif Index of the Folktales of England and North America*, Indiana University Folklore Series 20 (The Hague: Mouton & Co., 1966).

4. Motif V540, "Intervention of Providence saves person's life."

5. Mrs. T. B. Larimore, *Life, Letters, and Sermons of T. B. Larimore* (Nashville, Tenn.: Gospel Advocate Company, 1955), pp. 21–22.

6. Donald E. Byrne, Jr., *No Foot of Land* (Metuchen, N. J.: Scarecrow Press, 1975), pp. 141–42.

7. F. D. Syrgley, *Smiles and Tears, or Larimore and His Boys*, 5th ed. (Nashville, Tenn.: Gospel Advocate Co., 1955), p. 239. A similar Mormon story tells of a man pulled to safety by one of the Nephites (ghostly Mormon apostles who appear to do good deeds); see Hector Lee, *The Three Nephites* (Albuquerque: University of New Mexico Press, 1949), pp. 151–52.

8. Syrgley, p. 239.

9. Barton W. Stone, *The Biography of Barton Warren Stone* (Cincinnati: J. A. and U. P. James, 1847), p. 43.

10. Charles Crossfield Ware, *Barton Warren Stone: Pathfinder of Christian Union* (St. Louis: Bethany Press, 1932), p. 125.

11. For a similar Methodist example, see Byrne, p, 136. In the Mormon tradition, some preachers were not only healed, but had the power to heal others; see Stanley B. Kimball, *Heber C. Kimball: Mormon Patriarch and Pioneer* (Chicago: University of Illinois Press, 1981), p. 38. The three Nephites of Mormon tradition also heal others, Lee, pp. 140–44. All of these anecdotes fit motif F950, "Miraculous cures."

12. Lloyd Cline Sears, *The Eyes of Jehovah: The Life and Faith of James Alexander Harding* (Nashville: Gospel Advocate Co., 1970), pp. 36–37.

13. Ibid., p. 218.

14. Byrne, pp. 136–41.

15. Kimball pp. 67–68; for Nephite parallels, see Lee, pp. 135–40.

16. Motif D1652.18, "Inexhaustible article."

17. J. E. Choate, *Roll Jordan Roll, A Biography of Marshall Keeble* (Nashville: Gospel Advocate Co., 1968), p. 107.

18. Byrne, pp. 134–35; Kimball, pp. 31–32, tells of a spectacular deliverance from a mob by a sudden hailstorm.

19. Sears, pp. 226–27.

20. Ibid., pp. 18–19.

21. Type 1833, "Anecdotes of Sermons."

22. F. D. Srygley, *Seventy Years in Dixie: Recollections and Sayings of T. W. Caskey and Others* (Nashville, Tenn.: Gospel Advocate Co., 1954), p. 193.

23. Byrne, p. 257; he lists other errors of the same type. This twisting of Scriptures was also known in the black Baptist tradition, see Douglas Glenn Adams, "Humor in the American Pulpit from George Whitefield Through Henry Ward Beecher" (Th.D. dissertation, Graduate Theological Union, Berkeley, California, 1974), p. 28; and J. Mason Brewer, *The Word on the Brazos: Negro Preacher Tales from the Brazos Bottoms of Texas* (Austin: University of Texas Press, 1953), p. 24.

24. James Marvin Powell and Mary Nelle Hardeman Powers, *N. B. H., A Biography of Nicholas Brodie Hardeman* (Nashville, Tenn.: Gospel Advocate Co., 1964), pp. 354–55.

25. Sears, pp. 60–61.

26. Leo Lipscomb Boles and J. E. Choate, *I'll Stand on the Rock: A*

Biography of H. Leo Boles (Nashville, Tenn.: Gospel Advocate Co., 1965), p. 208.

27. Powell and Powers, p. 355.

28. This was a common, but stigmatized, practice among Methodists as well, see Byrne, pp. 246–48.

29. William Baxter, *Life of Elder Walter Scott* (Nashville, Tenn.: Gospel Advocate Co., n.d.), pp. 184–85.

30. Raccoon John Smith followed the six-step form of the Gospel due to Scott's influence in his periodical "The Evangelist." See John Augustus Williams, *Life of Elder John Smith* (Nashville, Tenn.: Gospel Advocate Co., 1956), p. 168.

31. Ibid., pp. 411–12.

32. S. H. Hall, *Sixty Years in the Pulpit or Compound Interest in Religion* (Ann Arbor, Michigan: John Allen Hudson, 1955), p. 182.

33. Ibid.

34. Williams, p. 433; the Methodist preacher Peter Cartwright in a similar situation answered Greek with Dutch; see Adams, p. 191.

35. Choate, p. 59.

36. Motif J1262, "Repartee based on doctrinal discussions."

37. Boles and Choate, p. 168. The Methodist Peter Cartwright, when asked about Doctors of Divinity, responded "Divinity is not sick and don't need doctoring." Adams, p. 1. Sam Jones, another Methodist preacher, once said, "Half of the literary preachers in this town are A. B.'s, Ph.D.'s, LL.D's, and A. S. S.'s.,''' Adams, p. 169. Opposition to an educated clergy thus was not limited to Church of Christ preachers.

38. Williams, p. 180. Adams mentions a Baptist preacher who makes a similar retort; Adams, p. 10.

39. Ibid., p. 402.

40. Choate, pp. 103–104.

41. Ibid., p. 105.

42. Fanning Yater Tant, *J. D. Tant—Texas Preacher* (Erlinger, Kentucky: Faith and Facts Press, 1958), pp. 197–98.

43. Motif J1270, "Repartee concerning the parentage of children."

44. Tant, pp. 54–55. "Bull" is still considered vulgar in some parts of the Ozarks; see Vance Randolph and George P. Wilson, *Down in the Holler: A Gallery of Ozark Folk Speech* (Norman: University of Oklahoma Press, 1953), pp. 95–96.

45. Tant, pp. 185–86.

46. Kimball, p. 279.

47. Motif V81, "Religious services—baptism."

48. Tant, pp. 196–97.

49. Powell and Powers, p. 282.

50. Ware, p. 326.

51. Baxter, pp. 381–82. This method of substituting an opponent's definition in a text in order to make it seem absurd was also used by the Methodist William Milburn against an "infidel," and by the Congregationalist Timothy Dwight against a Unitarian; see Adams, pp. 89, and 105–106.

52. Choate, p. 103.

53. Sears, p. 116; Byrne, p. 271, ascribes the first two lines of this poem to another Methodist, Rev. Samuel Clawson. This may be a standard Methodist answer to the Church of Christ position on baptism.

54. Sears, p. 116.

55. H. Leo Boles, *Biographical Sketches of Gospel Preachers* (Nashville, Tenn.: Gospel Advocate Co., 1932), p. 41; Williams, p. 413.

56. Ibid., pp. 189–90.

57. Motif J1290, *"Reductio ad absurdum* of question."

58. Byrne, pp. 271–72.

59. Powell and Powers, p. 280; the traditional form of the rebuke, "strain at a gnat and swallow a camel" was used earlier against the "Campbellites" by John Burgess, a Methodist, see Byrne, p. 271.

60. Boles and Choate, p. 7; Motif J1352, "Person calls another an ass."

61. Tant, p. 410.

III. ORAL ANECDOTES

1. Motifs E220-E599, "Ghosts and other revenants."

2. Perry Gresham, interview, Abilene, Texas, July 1985; motif E581.2, "Dead person rides a horse." The theme of "no footprints in the snow" is also found in several Nephite stories, see Hector Lee, *The Three Nephites* (Albuquerque: University of New Mexico Press, 1949), pp. 60 and 137.

3. Gresham, interview.

4. Charlie Jones, interview, Barnesville, Georgia, April 1986. There were also Methodist and Congregationalist ministers who objected to instrumental music in worship, but their opposition was not as extreme; see Douglas Glenn Adams, "Humor in the American Pulpit from George Whitefield through Henry Ward Beecher" (Ph.D. dissertation, Graduate Theological Union, Berkeley, California, 1974), pp. 9 and 249.

5. O. B. Perkins, interview, Munfordville, Kentucky, March 1986.

6. Ibid.

7. Ibid.

8. Dale Smith, interview, Dallas, Texas, August 1985.

9. Ibid.

10. Mike Glenn, interview, Norcross, Georgia, April 1986.

11. Smith, interview.

12. Ibid.

13. O. B. Perkins, interview, Munfordville, Kentucky, May 1985.

14. H. A. Fincher, interview, Norcross, Georgia, April 1986.

15. Perkins, interview, March 1986.

16. Ibid.

17. Ibid.

18. Donald E. Byrne, Jr., *No Foot of Land* (Metuchen, N. J.: Scarecrow Press, 1975), pp. 229–30, gives examples of dogs interrupting Methodist

meetings; see also Julia Hull Winner, "Some Religious Humor from the Past," *New York Folklore Quarterly* 21 (March 1965):58.

19. Fincher, interview.

20. Glenn, interview.

21. Perkins, interview, March 1986.

22. Glenn, interview.

23. Ibid.

24. The author's wife once heard a young woman who was not a member of the Church of Christ exclaim when she saw a church's baptistry, "My, you have a Jacuzzi in your church."

25. Smith, interview. Motif 1823, "Misunderstanding of church custom causes inappropriate action."

26. Glenn interview.

27. Fincher interview.

28. Glenn interview.

29. Perkins, interview, March 1986.

30. Ibid.

31. Byrne, pp. 267–72. Motif 1263.1, "Repartee based on clerical ignorance."

32. Methodists seemed especially fond of the term, Ibid., pp. 222–23. Motif J1352, "Person calls another an ass."

33. Perkins, interview, May 1985.

34. Ibid.

35. Ibid.

36. Ibid.

37. Ibid. Compare motif J1261.1.5, where a woman speaks of riding on two men as Jesus rode an ass into Jerusalem. Also there is a similar story of H. K. Stimson, a Baptist chaplain in the Civil War, who refused to ride the back of a Lt. Colonel over a mudhole, calling him a "jackass"; see Adams, p. 150.

38. Perkins, interview, May 1985.

39. Ibid.

40. Perkins, interview, March 1986. Type 1847, "Biblical repartee."

41. Ibid.

42. Perkins, interview, May 1985. A similar story is told of Heber Kimball, the Mormon preacher. When his grammar was questioned, Kimball boasted, "I can make grammar faster than you can swallow it; and my grammar is as good as anybody's, if theirs is not better than mine," Stanley B. Kimball, *Heber C. Kimball: Mormon Patriarch and Pioneer* (Chicago: University of Illinois Press, 1981), p. 275.

IV. ORAL AND WRITTEN ANECDOTES

1. James Marvin Powell and Mary Nelle Hardeman Powers, *N. B. H., A Biography of Nicholas Brodie Hardeman* (Nashville: Gospel Advocate Co., 1964), p. 280. An almost identical story is told of Dwight Moody, see Douglas Glenn Adams, "Humor in the American Pulpit from

George Whitefield through Henry Ward Beecher" (Ph.D. dissertation, Graduate Theological Union, Berkeley, California, 1974), p. 35.

2. O. B. Perkins, interview, Munfordville, Kentucky, March 1986.

3. H. A. Fincher, interview, Norcross, Georgia, April 1986.

4. N. B. Hardeman, for example, reportedly said, "Well, there are those whose sermons really don't need to be repeated; the sermons I preach are worth repeating," Fincher interview.

5. Powell and Powers, p. 279.

6. Perkins interview.

7. See the T. Q. Martin smoking story in chap. 4.

8. Fanning Yater Tant, *J. D. Tant—Texas Preacher* (Erlanger, Kentucky: Faith and Facts Press, 1958), p. 305. Edward Taylor, a Methodist, compared a Unitarian to "a beetle bug rolling over the sand his ball of dirt," Adams, p. 203.

9. Perkins, interview.

10. Fincher interview.

11. Tant, pp. 313–14.

12. Perkins interview.

13. John Augustus Williams, *Life of Elder John Smith* (Nashville: Gospel Advocate Co., 1956), pp. 467–68.

14. A common interruption also in Methodist circles, Donald E. Byrne, Jr., *No Foot of Land* (Metuchen, N. J.: Scarecrow Press, 1975), p. 234, and among Congregationalists,, Adams, p. 77.

15. Don Brown, interview, Dallas, Texas, August 1985.

16. Powell and Powers, p. 280.

17. Perkins, interview.

18. Lloyd Cline Sears, *The Eyes of Jehovah: The Life and Faith of James Alexander Harding* (Nashville: Gospel Advocate Co., 1970), p. 8.

19. David Fincher, interview, Norcross, Georgia, July 1986.

20. Powell and Powers, p. 352.

21. O. B. Perkins, interview, Munfordville, Kentucky, May 1985.

22. For examples see Stith Thompson, *The Folktale* (Berkeley: University of California Press, 1946), p. 213.

23. Powell and Powers, p. 270.

24. Perkins, interview, May 1985.

V. THE STYLE OF ORAL
AND WRITTEN ANECDOTES

1. John Mies Foley, *Oral Formulaic Theory and Research* (New York: Garland Publishing, 1985), p. 34.

2. For an extended discussion of how writing in general restructures consciousness, see Walter J. Ong, *Orality and Literacy: The Technologizing of the Word* (New York: Methuen, 1982), pp. 78–116.

3. Alan Dundes, *Essays in Folkloristics* (New Delhi, India Folklore Institute, 1978), pp. 25–27.

4. For example see the folktale in Elizabeth C. Fine, *The Folklore Text:*

From Performance to Print (Bloomington: Indiana University Press, 1984), pp. 180–95.

5. Sandra K. D. Stahl, "Style in Oral and Written Narrative," *Southern Folklore Quarterly* 43 (1979):42–49.

6. Anecdote 38.

7. Anecdote 51.

8. Anecdote 52.

9. Anecdote 42.

10. Anecdote 55.

11. Anecdote 59.

12. Anecdotes 1, 2, 3, 4, 9, 10, 13, 14, 16, 18, 19, 27, 28, 29, 30, 34, 72, 75.

13. Anecdotes 12, 22, 32, 35, 84, 88, 90.

14. Anecdotes 5, 6, 7, 8, 11, 15, 20, 21, 28, 25, 26, 31, 33, 77, 80, 82, 86.

15. Anecdotes 17, 24, and 36.

16. Anecdote 63.

17. Anecdote 38.

18. Anecdote 67.

19. Anecdote 70.

20. Anecdote 91.

21. Anecdote 83.

22. Anecdote 51.

23. Anecdote 73.

24. Anecdotes 44 and 63.

25. Anecdote 59.

26. Anecdotes 68 and 89.

27. Anecdote 79.

28. Anecdote 89.

29. Anecdote 43.

30. Anecdotes 37, 39, 41, 45, 50, 54, 62, 63, 66, 67, 70, 74, 81, 89, and 91.

31. Anecdotes 41, 70, 74, 45, and 91.

32. Anecdotes 56–61.

33. Anecdotes 55 and 59.

34. Anecdotes 7, 9, 10, 15, 29, 35, 81, 82, and 90.

35. Anecdotes 7, 11, 12, 13, 15, 16, 20, 21, 82, 84, and 90.

36. Anecdote 77.

37. Anecdote 88.

38. Anecdotes 24 and 36.

39. Anecdote 16.

40. Anecdotes 26–33; 75.

41. Anecdote 48.

42. Anecdotes 42, 43, 46, and 57.

43. This pause occurs in twenty-six of the forty-six oral anecdotes.

44. Sixteen of forty-five stories use exclamation points; the double exclamation points are in Anecdotes 25 and 77.

45. Italics: Anecdotes 1, 2, 3, 9, 10, 16, 21, 27, 29, 33, 72, and 82; bold type: Anecdote 25.

46. Albert B. Lord, *The Singer of Tales* (Cambridge: Harvard University Press, 1960), pp. 30–67.

47. Ibid., p. 34.

48. Anecdote 39.

49. Anecdote 50.

50. Anecdote 51.

51. Anecdote 52.

52. Anecdote 73.

53. The written stories in chapter 2 average 20.7 typed lines per anecdote, while the oral stories in chapter 3 average 12.3 lines.

54. The written stories in chapter 4 average 9.6 lines; the oral ones 12.9.

55. Anecdotes 75 and 76; 77, 78, and 79; 84 and 85; 86 and 87; 88 and 89; 90 and 91.

56. The written anecdotes average 8.7 lines; the oral ones 10.9.

57. Anecdote 42.

58. Anecdote 51.

59. Anecdotes 83 and 85.

60. Anecdotes 68 and 69.

61. Anecdotes 63, 64, and 67.

62. Anecdote 43.

63. Anecdote 44.

64. Anecdotes 20, 82, and 84.

65. Anecdote 35.

66. Anecdote 25.

67. Anecdote 24.

68. Anecdote 15.

69. Jan Harold Brunvand, *The Study of American Folklore* 2d ed. (New York: W. W. Norton & Co., 1978), p. 5.

70. Compare anecdotes 58 and 59, and 78 and 79, for example.

71. Perkins, interview, May 1985.

72. Perkins, interview, March 1986.

73. Perkins, interview, May 1985.

74. Perkins, interview, March 1986.

75. For a discussion of this "fixed" characteristic of written stories, see Foley, p. 34.

VI. THE FUNCTIONS OF THE ANCEDOTES

1. Alan Dundes, *Essays in Folkloristics* (New Delhi, India: Folklore Institute, 1978), p 27.

2. O. B. Perkins, interview, Williamson, Georgia, October 1986.

3. Funk & Wagnalls; Gerald L. Davis, *I Got the Word in Me and I Can*

Sing It, You Know: A Study of the Performed African–American Sermon (Philadelphia: University of Pennsylvania Press, 1985), pp. 82–88.

4. See anecdotes 1–7.

5. See anecdotes 14, 17, 18, 75, and 76.

6. Bruce A. Rosenberg, *Can These Bones Live? The Art of the American Folk Preacher*, rev. ed. (Chicago: University of Illinois Press, 1988), pp. 30–32.

7. Anecdote 8.

8. Anecdotes 86 and 87.

9. Anecdote 9.

10. Anecdote 11.

11. Anecdotes 12 and 13.

12. Anecdote 34.

13. O. B. Perkins, interview, October 1986.

14. These four difficulties are discussed by Jackson Lee Ice, "Notes Toward a Theology of Humor," *Religion in Life* 42 (Autumn 1973):389–90; see also Wilbur H. Mullen, "Toward a Theology of Humor," *Christian Scholar's Review* 3 (1973):4; and Eivind Berggrav, "Humor and Seriousness," *Dialog* 22 (Summer 1983):206.

15. Harvey Cox, *The Feast of Fools* (New York: Harper & Row, 1969), p. 184; Mullen, pp. 4 & 5.

16. Cox, p. 185; Mullen, p. 4; Conrad Hyers, "A Funny Faith," *One World* 78 (July/August 1982), p. 10.

17. W. A. Welsh, "Homo Ridens," *Lexington Theological Quarterly* 2 (October 1967):98; Berggrav, p. 207; Sten H. Stenson, *Sense and Nonsense in Religion* (New York: Abingdon Press, 1969), p. 112; Sigmund Freud, *Jokes and Their Relation to the Unconscious*, trans. James Strachey (New York: W. W. Norton & Co., 1960), pp. 88–89.

18. Ice, p. 393.

19. Henri Bergson, *Laughter*, trans. Cloudesley Brereton and Fred Rothwell (London: Macmillan and Co., 1911), p. 96; Arthur Koestler, *The Act of Creation* (New York: Dell Publishing Co., 1967), pp. 32–42; Stenson, p. 107.

20. For a fuller discussion of jokes as play see Mullen, pp. 6 & 7; Roy Branson, "The Theology of Joy," *Encounter* 34 (1973):244; Hyers, *One World*, p. 11; and Robert Detweiler, "The Jesus Jokes: Religious Humor in the Age of Excess," *Cross Currents* 24 (Spring 1974):69.

21. Anecdote 49.

22. Anecdote 50.

23. Anecdote 54.

24. Anecdote 61.

25. Anecdote 70.

26. Anecdote 71.

27. Anecdotes 58 and 59.

28. Anecdote 28.

29. Anecdotes 52 and 53.

30. Anecdotes 88 and 89.

31. Ice, pp. 394–96; Detweiler, pp. 61–62.

32. Freud, p. 236.

33. Anecdotes 10, 42, and 51.

34. Anecdote 48.

35. Anecdotes 43, 44, and 45.

36. Anecdotes 55, 58, and 59.

37. Detweiler, pp. 66–67.

38. H. A. Fincher, interview, 1986.

39. Freud, p. 136.

40. Anecdotes 17, 18, 20, 24, 25, 26, 27, 29, 31, 32, 35, 62, 63, 64, 68, 72, 77, 78, 79, 80, 81, 82, 84, and 85; see also Berggrav, p. 208.

41. Anecdotes 15, 16, 19, 21, 22, 23, 30, 33, 34, 36, 38, 40, 41, 47, 51, 65, 66, 67, 69; for a discussion of this hostile function see Conrad Hyers, *The Comic Vision and the Christian Faith* (New York: Pilgrim Press, 1981), pp. 26–27; idem, "The Comic Vision in a Tragic World," *Christian Century* 100 (April 20, 1983):364; Welch, p. 99; Detweiler, p. 62.

42. Anecdotes 33 and 38.

43. Mullen, p. 7; Ice, pp. 396–97; Hyers, *The Comic Vision and the Christian Faith*, p. 43; idem, "The Comic Vision in a Tragic World," p. 366; idem, "A Funny Faith," p. 10; Cox, p. 180; Berggrav, p. 208; Detweiler, p. 70; Peter L. Berger, *A Rumor of Angels* (Garden City, N. Y.: Doubleday & Co., 1969), p. 71; Kenneth Hamilton, "Laughter and Vision," *Soundings* 55 (Spring 1972):172–74; Bob W. Parrott, *Ontology of Humor* (New York: Philosophical Library, 1982), p. 10.

44. Anecdote 47.

45. Anecdote 46.

46. Anecdote 69.

47. Anecdote 34.

48. Anecdote 39.

49. Anecdotes 73 and 74.

50. Anecdote 68.

51. Søren Kierkegaard, *Concluding Unscientific Postscript*, trans. David F. Swenson and Walter Lowrie (Princeton: Princeton University Press, 1941), p. 448.

52. Ibid., pp. 459–64.

53. Berger, p. 88.

54. Branson, p. 236; Mullen, p. 10.

55. Detweiler, p. 68.

56. Jackson Lee Ice disagrees here with Kierkegaard and calls this life-affirming function of humor a "fiduciary" function; see Ice, p. 398–99.

57. Dundes, *Essays*, p. 9.

BIBLIOGRAPHY

FOLKLORE

Aarne, Antti. *The Types of the Folktale*. Translated and enlarged by Stith Thompson. 2d ed. Helsinki: Academia Scientiarum Fennica, 1964.

Baughman, Ernest W. *Type and Motif Index of the Folktales of England and North America*. Indiana University Folklore Series 20. The Hague: Mouton & Co., 1966.

Brewer J. Mason. *The Word on the Brazos: Negro Preacher Tales from the Brazos Bottoms of Texas*. Austin: University of Texas Press, 1953.

Brunvand, Jan Harold. *The Study of American Folklore*. 2d ed. New York: W. W. Norton & Co., 1978.

Davis, Gerald L. *I Got the Word in Me and I Can Sing It You Know: A Study of the Performed African–American Sermon*. Philadelphia: University of Pennsylvania Press, 1985.

Dégh, Linda. "Folk Narrative." In *Folklore and Folklife: An Introduction*. Edited by Richard M. Dorson. Chicago: University of Chicago Press, 1972.

Dorson, Richard M. *Buying the Wind*. Chicago: University of Chicago Press, 1964.

————. *Folklore and Fakelore*. Cambridge: Harvard University Press, 1976.

————. "The Identification of Folklore in American Literature." *Journal of American Folklore* 70 (1957):1–8.

Dundes, Alan. *Essays in Folkloristics*. New Delhi, India: Folklore Institute, 1978.

Emenanjo, E. 'Nolue. "The Anecdote as an Oral Genre: The Case in Igbo." *Folklore* 95 (1984):171–76.

Fine, Elizabeth C. *The Folklore Text: From Performance to Print*. Bloomington: Indiana University Press, 1984.

Foley, John Mies. *Oral Formulaic Theory and Research*. New York: Garland Publishing, 1985.

Funk and Wagnalls Standard Dictionary of Folklore, Mythology, and Legend. 1972 ed. s.v. "Anecdotes," by B. A. Botkin.

Jansen, William Hugh. "Legend: Oral Tradition in the Modern Experience." In *Folklore Today*. Edited by Linda Dégh, Henry Glassie, and Felix J. Oinas. Bloomington: Indiana University Press, 1976.

Lévi-Strauss, Claude. *The Raw and the Cooked*. Chicago: University of Chicago Press, 1969.

Lord, Albert B. *The Singer of Tales*. Cambridge: Harvard University Press, 1960.

Ong, Walter J. *Orality and Literacy*. New York: Methuen, 1982.

Penrod, James H. "Teachers and Preachers in the Old Southwestern Yarns." *Tennessee Folklore Society Bulletin* 18 (December 1952):91–96.

Propp, Vladimir. *Morphology of the Folktale*. Translated by Laurence Scott. Austin: University of Texas Press, 1968.

———. *Theory and History of Folklore*. Translated by Adriadna Y. Martin and Richard P. Martin. Minneapolis: University of Minnesota Press, 1984.

Randolph, Vance, and Wilson, George P. *Down in the Holler: A Gallery of Ozark Folk Speech*. Norman: University of Oklahoma Press, 1953.

Rosenberg, Bruce A. *Can These Bones Live? The Art of the American Folk Preacher*. Revised Edition. Chicago: University of Illinois Press, 1988.

Stahl, Sandra K. D. "Style in Oral and Written Narratives." *Southern Folklore Quarterly* 43 (1979):39–64.

Thompson, Stith. *The Folktale*. Los Angeles: University of California Press, 1946.

———. *Motif-Index of Folk Literature*. Indiana University Studies 22. Bloomington: Indiana University Press, 1934.

Utley, Francis Lee. "Folk Literature: An Operational Definition." *Journal of American Folklore* 74 (July 1961):193–206.

PREACHER BIOGRAPHIES

Baxter, William. *Life of Elder Walter Scott*. Nashville: Gospel Advocate Co., n.d.

Boles, H. Leo. *Biographical Sketches of Gospel Preachers*. Nashville: Gospel Advocate Co., 1932.

Boles, Leo Lipscomb, and Choate, J. E. *I'll Stand on the Rock: A Biography of H. Leo Boles*. Nashville: Gospel Advocate Co., 1965.

Choate, J. E. *Roll Jordan Roll: A Biography of Marshall Keeble*. Nashville: Gospel Advocate Co., 1968.

Hall, S. H. *Sixty Years in the Pulpit or Compound Interest in Religion*. Ann Arbor, Michigan: John Allen Hudson, 1955.

Larimore, Mrs. T. B. *Life, Letters, and Sermons of T. B. Larimore*. Nashville: Gospel Advocate Co., 1955.

Powell, James Marvin, and Powers, Mary Nelle Hardeman. *N. B. H., A Biography of Nicholas Brodie Hardeman*. Nashville: Gospel Advocate Co., 1964.

Sears, Lloyd Cline. *The Eyes of Jehovah: The Life and Faith of James Alexander Harding*. Nashville: Gospel Advocate Co., 1970.

Srygley, F. D. *Seventy Years in Dixie: Recollections and Sayings of T. W. Caskey and Others*. Nashville: Gospel Advocate Co., 1954.

———. *Smiles and Tears, or Larimore and His Boys*. 5th ed. Nashville: Gospel Advocate Co., 1955.

Stone, Barton W. *The Biography of Barton Warren Stone*. Cincinnati: J. A. and U. P. James, 1847.

Tant, Fanning Yater. *J. D. Tant—Texas Preacher*. Erlanger, Kentucky: Faith and Facts Press, 1958.
Ware, Charles C. *Barton Warren Stone*. St. Louis: Bethany Press, 1932.
Williams, John Augustus. *Life of Elder John Smith*. Nashville: Gospel Advocate Co., 1956.

ORAL ANECDOTES

Brown, Don. Dallas, Texas. Interview, August 1985.
Fincher, David. Norcross, Georgia. Interview, July 1986.
Fincher, H. A. Norcross, Georgia. Interview, April 1986.
Glenn, Mike. Norcross, Georgia. Interview, April 1986.
Gresham, Perry. Abilene, Texas. Interview, July 1985.
Jones, Charlie. Barnesville, Georgia. Interview, April 1986.
Perkins, O. B. Munfordville, Kentucky. Interview, May 1985.
———. Munfordville, Kentucky. Interview, March 1986.
———. Williamson, Georgia. Interview, October 1986.
Smith, Dale. Dallas, Texas. Interview, August 1985.

RELIGIOUS FOLKLORE

Adams, Douglas Glenn. "Humor in the American Pulpit from George Whitefield through Henry Ward Beecher." Ph.D. dissertation, Graduate Theological Union, Berkeley, California, 1974.
Ahlstrom, Sydney E. *A Religious History of the American People*. 2 vols. Garden City, N.J.: Doubleday, 1975.
Byrne, Donald E., Jr. *No Foot of Land*. Metuchen, N.J.: Scarecrow Press, 1975.
Kimball, Stanley B. *Heber C. Kimball: Mormon Patriarch and Pioneer*. Chicago: University of Illinois Press, 1981.
Lee, Hector. *The Three Nephites*. Albuquerque: University of New Mexico Press, 1949.

RELIGION AND HUMOR

Berger, Peter L. *A Rumor of Angels*. Garden City, N.J.: Doubleday, 1969.
Berggrav, Eivind. "Humor and Seriousness." *Dialog* 22 (Summer 1983):206–10.
Bergson, Henri. *Laughter*. Translated by Cloudesley Brereton and Fred Rothwell. London: Macmillan & Co., 1911.
Branson, Roy. "The Theology of Joy." *Encounter* 34 (1973):233–45.
Cox, Harvey. *The Feast of Fools*. New York: Harper & Row, 1969.
Detweiler, Robert. "The Jesus Jokes: Religious Humor in the Age of Excess." *Cross Currents* 24 (Spring 1974):55–74.

Freud, Sigmund. *Jokes and Their Relation to the Unconscious.* Translated by James Strachey. New York: W. W. Norton & Co., 1960.

Hamilton, Kenneth. "Laughter and Vision." *Soundings* 55 (Spring 1972):165–77.

Hyers, Conrad. *The Comic Vision and the Christian Faith.* New York: Pilgrim Press, 1981.

———. "The Comic Vision in a Tragic World." *Christian Century* 100 (April 20, 1983):363–67.

———. "A Funny Faith." *One World* 78 (July/August 1982):10–11.

Ice, Jackson Lee. "Notes Toward a Theology of Humor." *Religion in Life* 42 (Autumn 1973):388–400.

Kierkegaard, Søren. *Concluding Unscientific Postscript.* Translated by David F. Swenson and Walter Lowrie. Princeton: Princeton University Press, 1941.

Koestler, Arthur. *The Act of Creation.* New York: Dell Publishing Co., 1967.

Mullen, Wilbur H. "Toward a Theology of Humor." *Christian Scholar's Review* 3 (1973):3–12.

Parrott, Bob W. *Ontology of Humor.* New York: Philosophical Library, 1982.

Stenson, Sten H. *Sense and Nonsense in Religion.* New York: Abingdon Press, 1969.

Welsh, W. A. "Homo Ridens." *Lexington Theological Quarterly* 2 (October 1967):95–103.

Winner, Julia Hull. "Some Religious Humor from the Past." *New York Folklore Quarterly* 21 (March 1965):56–61.

Overcoming Common Problems Series

Overcoming Common Problems Series

In loving memory of my father Ron

Contents

Foreword to the first edition

Although most headaches and migraines are not life-threatening, the profound effect they can have on your ability to function and carry out your usual daily activities means that they are now recognized by the World Health Organization as one of the leading causes of disability. But it has been a battle to gain this attention – for centuries headaches have been ignored, or worse, they have been seen solely as a psychological problem. Fortunately, recent research confirms that headaches have an organic basis and there are now specific and effective drugs to help prevent and treat the most severe types of headaches, particularly migraine and cluster headache.

However, drugs are only a part of managing headaches; an understanding of what the condition is caused by and how treatments work can make the difference between being in control of migraine and feeling controlled by it. It is not just you who can benefit from this understanding – family, friends and employers are also indirectly affected by migraine.

Alison Frith is well placed to share her expertise in helping you cope with your headaches and migraines. It has been a privilege to work with her over the past 9 years. She has the advantage of writing from the heart, having experienced her own battle with migraine. But she also has the rare ability of being able to look objectively at the problems, learning from the good and the bad experiences of the patients that she sees every day.

I have no doubt that you will find this book an invaluable source of information to help you understand and gain better control of your headaches.

Dr Anne MacGregor
The City of London Migraine Clinic

Foreword to the second edition

Since the first edition was published I have had much pleasure from hearing numerous patients and colleagues expressing how much they enjoyed reading Alison's book and how helpful it has been to them. This comes as no surprise to me. Alison writes from the heart and talks directly to the reader. She understands what the problems are as she has faced some of them herself. She also knows how isolated you can feel during the throes of an attack, wondering if anything can make it better and fearing that it is never going to end.

In this Second Edition, Alison expands on some of the research that has since come to fruition, including the role that our genetic make-up may play. Also new is the increasing data on the use of non-drug management of headache, particularly the use of nerve stimulation. These techniques have the significant advantage over medication of minimal side effects.

While there is unlikely ever to be a cure for headache, those who suffer can take much comfort from reading Alison's sound advice and words of wisdom.

Professor Anne MacGregor
10 Harley Street, London

Acknowledgements for the first edition

Firstly, many thanks to all those who have attended the City of London Migraine Clinic, talked to me about their headaches and offered themselves so willingly to participate in our clinical studies. Your contributions help us to discover new ways of coping and offer hope to others.

Thank you to Dr Anne MacGregor, Clinical Research Director at the City of London Migraine Clinic. Working with you is as joyful as it is challenging. Thank you for being a mentor, for gently encouraging me to achieve new things and for being a special friend.

All my wonderful colleagues at the City of London Migraine Clinic are also greatly appreciated. I have never been happier in my work, and I know that is good for my migraine. Drs Nat Blau and Marcia Wilkinson, who set up the Clinic as a charity almost 30 years ago, created a very special place. I am very proud to work with you to help people cope with their headaches.

I also thank my husband Alan, whose sense of humour always brightens my day. Thank you for keeping me fed and hydrated – I don't always practise what I preach, and you have kept away many a migraine.

Also deserving thanks are my mother Cathy, brother Andrew, sister Catherine and my many friends for unfailing support.

Finally, thank you to Fiona Marshall at Sheldon Press. I am grateful for your encouragement, patience and wise words.

Acknowledgements for the second edition

I have been overwhelmed by the response to this book since its first publication in 2009. I am delighted that in some small way it has helped so many in their battles to cope with headaches and migraine. Thank you to everyone for your positive feedback. People have told me that they found something new to try, have felt more able to cope or simply found the courage to ask for help. Help is out there. There are now numerous headache clinics in the UK and, thanks to amazing work by charities such as the Migraine Trust, Migraine Action, Migraine Association of Ireland and OUCH (Organization for the Understanding of Cluster Headache) UK, migraine and other headaches are now taken more seriously than ever.

Although we have now lost both Dr Nat Blau and Dr Marcia Wilkinson, the consultant neurologists who set up the City of London Migraine Clinic, their legacy lives on. The Clinic in London is now called the National Migraine Centre and continues to help people with headaches. I worked in cutting edge headache research alongside Professor Anne MacGregor, former Medical Director at the City of London Migraine Clinic, for 12 years. I had the most enormous fun and I am so proud to have assisted in work which helped to gain worldwide recognition for menstrual migraine in women. Anne continues to be a dear friend and I'm grateful for her help with this new manuscript. Under her guidance I've brought the information up to date to bring you the latest research on treatments and ways to cope. I've not changed the format, which has worked well. Dr Blau and his wife Jill became friends of mine and I remember 'Dr B.', as I called him, telling me just to imagine that when I'm writing, I'm talking with one of my patients. I've tried to do that and this book will have fulfilled its aim if people reading it feel as though they are speaking with a friend who really understands what they are going through.

Finally, I owe grateful thanks once again to Fiona Marshall at Sheldon Press for her enthusiasm for the new edition of this book and to my husband Alan for never-ending love, support, laughter and food.

Abbreviations

CBT	cognitive behavioural therapy
CGRP	calcitonin gene-related peptide
CHC	combined hormonal contraceptive
CSD	cortical spreading depression
DHE	dihydroergotamine
ECG	electrocardiogram
GP	general practitioner
HOOF	Home Oxygen Order Form
HRT	hormone replacement therapy
5-HT	5-hydroxytryptamine
5-HTP	5-hydroxytryptophan
mcg	micrograms
mg	milligrams
MHRA	Medicines and Healthcare Products Regulatory Agency
MOH	medication overuse headache
MRI	magnetic resonance imaging
NICE	National Institute for Health and Care Excellence
NSAID	non-steroidal anti-inflammatory drug
OUCH	Organization for the Understanding of Cluster Headache
PACAP	pituitary adenylate cyclase-activating polypeptide
PET	positron emission tomography
PFO	patent foramen ovale
PMS	premenstrual syndrome
POP	progestogen-only pill
rTMS	repeated pulse transcranial magnetic stimulation
SSRI	selective serotonin re-uptake inhibitor
sTMS	single pulse transcranial magnetic stimulation
SUNA	short-lasting unilateral neuralgiform headache attacks with cranial autonomic features
SUNCT	short-lasting unilateral neuralgiform headache attacks with conjunctival injection and tearing
TAC	trigeminal autonomic cephalalgia
TENS	transcutaneous electrical nerve stimulation
THR	traditional herbal registration
TMS	transcranial magnetic stimulation
TTH	tension-type headache
VNS	vagus nerve stimulation

Note to the reader

This book is not intended to replace advice from your medical practitioner. The author and publisher have made every effort to ensure accuracy when this book was published, but this is not guaranteed. Information included here may become out of date with new advances in medicine. Do consult your doctor if you are experiencing symptoms with which you feel you need help.

Introduction

A personal experience

Matron escorted me back to the nurses' home just after midnight. Despite her obvious concern and my dazed state, I could tell she was really cross. I was a nurse on night duty in charge of 28 patients and now I would have to be replaced, leaving another ward short staffed. And just because I had a headache.

I was in no fit state to care for my patients that night. On matron's ward round I got everyone muddled up and couldn't get my words out. I excused myself to be violently sick in the sluice room, where the smell of disinfectant seemed noxious and bored into my brain. When I staggered back my hat was lop-sided and my own vomit was splattered down my starched apron and over my shoes. Matron knew that there was something very wrong. My head was splitting in half with the pain as if someone had stabbed it. I looked at the crisp, white linen on an empty bed and longed to lie down, completely still and surrounded by darkness. Just long enough for the pain to ease, and the pounding to stop. Quietness for a few moments. Perhaps then I could carry on . . .

Back in my room I was so sick in the basin that my stomach hurt as well as my head. I found some relief sitting on the floor with my temple pressed hard against the cold, porcelain bowl. I cried with the pain and with the guilt too. I felt I had let down my colleagues and all my patients who needed me. When I finally stood up and saw my sunken eyes reflected in the mirror, I was truly horrified at how grey and ill I looked. Some of those in my care had looked healthier than me!

I slept all that night and all next day. When I reported for duty that evening the pain had gone, but I felt that my head was filled with cotton wool. I struggled with my work. It was several days until I felt well again. I tried to put the headache out of my mind. But then it happened again.

How I coped with my headaches

What I know now, but didn't know then, was that I was having severe migraine attacks. I didn't realize that you needn't have bright lights in your eyes for it to be migraine. My headaches had become much worse and I thought they might be killing me. Like many nurses in training, I had often mistakenly diagnosed myself with brain tumours and other nasty illnesses. It was time for me to get help, and I went to my doctor.

For me, the important first step in coping was getting help when I needed it and identifying the headache, which came as a relief. The next steps were to learn about my migraine, discover my own triggers and make changes to aspects of my lifestyle that were not helping me at all. As a young nurse I was always anxious, making sure that I was doing my best, and the wards could be hot, stressful places for both staff and patients. Irregular hours were another problem outside my control. I would barely recover from one week of night duty before it was my turn again.

I had to make changes. I discovered that infrequent meals and lack of fluids were significant personal triggers that I could do something about. I forced myself to drink more water even when I wasn't thirsty and had regular snacks. I also stayed awake on my first day off night duty, so that I could recover my sleeping pattern more quickly. These simple strategies made a real difference to the frequency of my attacks.

Learning to cope with my migraine has been a journey that has taken many years. It was a happy coincidence that I worked at the City of London Migraine Clinic. It is a subject very close to my heart. I only wish I had known then what I know now. I could have understood earlier that migraine is more than just headache and is really a whole process. Our doctors and patients often described migraine as kind of body 'power cut'. No wonder I would always feel ghastly for days!

My migraine attacks still happen from time to time, despite my best efforts. So, importantly, I've had to find treatments that work for me. These have changed a few times, and working at the Clinic has helped me know what to do for the best. Keeping one step ahead is ongoing. You can't forget that you are prone to migraine attacks – they don't let you. However, by understanding my own migraine and triggers and by finding effective treatments, I have gained more control. I have eventually learned to cope with my attacks. Although they occasionally stop me in my tracks, I usually know why. I no longer live in fear of migraine, as I have done at times in my life.

Coping with headaches

Although there are no miracle cures for migraine or other kinds of headache, there are effective treatments and so much you can do to help yourself. A combination of approaches can really make a difference.

I believe that it is important to try to recognize what type of headaches you have. This can be difficult because even experts argue over names, and more than one headache type can occur at the same time. However, the reassurance of knowing what you are dealing with will stop you from worrying about it. You can then concentrate on how best to deal with the headaches. These are the first steps to assuming control and learning to cope. Unfortunately, there are no quick fixes. It isn't easy – often it is a process of trial and error, and sometimes there can be relapses. You will still have to make allowances for your headaches, but aim never to allow them to control you, because you control them. I know this because it is what I am doing myself.

The global burden of headaches

People who have troublesome headaches understand the major impact they can have on family life, social life and employment. Not only do they stop you from doing what you want, but even when you haven't got a headache, you can be living in dread of the next one. They can also be very disabling and blight the lives of you *and* your family.

We are not alone with our headaches. Estimates suggest that up to ten million people in the UK regularly have migraine and other headaches. Headaches account for about 20 per cent of days off sick from work. The cost to the UK economy could be more than £1.5 billion per year, because on any single day 100,000 people are absent because of a migraine attack. Additionally, we all know that even if you do go to work with a headache you will not be very productive.

This isn't confined to the UK. The initiative 'Lifting the Burden: the Global Campaign Against Headache' (see Useful addresses at the end of this book) recognizes all headaches as a global issue. Reflecting this, migraine is ranked by the World Health Organization as being in the world's top 20 most disabling diseases. For women it is ranked number 12. If other types of headache were included, the ranking could be even higher!

If more people were helped to manage their headaches, they would miss less time from work and home life, reducing the burden for both individuals and society. However, despite being the most common neurological disorder, headache is not a priority. Doctors and people who don't have disabling headaches (or know someone who does) often regard headaches as trivial. Perhaps this is because nearly everyone gets a mild headache from time to time and thinks nothing of it. Perhaps it is also because common headaches are intermittent and not usually life-threatening or catching. As a result, migraine and headaches are often not properly diagnosed or treated, specialist headache services are still not as widely available as they need to be and research funding is inadequate.

Your own headache burden

People with headaches do not help the situation. Because of the stigma of having 'just a headache', many of us try to ignore headaches, pretend we don't have them or simply rely on too many over-the-counter medications that don't work. Sometimes we spend money on treatments, hoping for cures that just don't exist. Also, like me, many people fail to recognize that they could have migraine, or simply don't visit their doctors to find out. Because medical treatments are available for most kinds of common headache, I encourage you to seek help if you need it and to keep looking until you find it. There might not be cures, but most people can find relief. By combining effective medical treatments with healthy living, complementary therapies that work for you and a positive approach, you really can lessen your burden.

How this book can help you cope with your headaches

I understand about trying to cope with headaches because of my own experience, but I was also privileged to work with leading headache doctors. Dr Nat Blau and Professor Anne MacGregor, the former Medical Directors at the City of London Migraine Clinic, and their dedicated team of doctors worked tirelessly every day to help people who have headaches. We listened to patients' problems and helped them to find coping solutions through care, effective treatments and new research.

In this book I would like to share with you some simple ideas that may help you to cope better with your headaches. I have learned these over the years through my own experience and from talking to people with headaches about what works for them. These are the kinds of things that I would have liked to have known when I first discovered that I had migraine. It isn't just about going to the doctor and taking tablets – far from it. It is more about listening to your body and what it might be trying to tell you when you get a headache.

Throughout the book I have indicated where there is scientific evidence for ideas and treatments and where there is not. Surprisingly little robust evidence is available. For those of us battling with our headaches, it isn't about research (although do consider taking part in a study if you can). Instead, it is about finding what helps you best to live your life with as few headaches as possible and without living in dread of them. When a headache does come, as it will from time to time, you need to be able to deal with it effectively.

This book aims to help you cope better in the following ways.

- Helping you to recognize your headaches. What kind of headaches do you have? Could they be serious and when should you see your doctor?
- Helping you to understand more about your headaches. This includes what they are, who gets them and the likelihood of improvement.
- Showing you how to cope with and without drugs. You need to find a strategy that works for you. Combining strategies may help you to cope better.
- Providing specific advice for headaches in women. By virtue of hormones, women have more headaches and migraine than men at different stages in their lives.

- Showing you how to help yourself. Looking after your health and your diet and being willing to help yourself can make a real difference to coping.
- Helping you know what to expect from medical help. By being prepared you can get the best out of medical help, because sometimes you can't cope by yourself.

I hope you will find useful ideas to help you to cope with your headaches. Sometimes the smallest changes can make the biggest difference. I know lack of fluids is a strong trigger for my migraine. As I used to tell our research trialists, new drugs aren't everything – I must drink the water on my desk and not just look at it.

Coping with Headaches and Migraine

1

Recognizing your headache: is it serious?

Headaches are so common that only about two per cent of people claim never to have had one. For the majority, headaches occur once in a while and are not too troublesome. They could be due to tension, a cold or flu, or just over-indulgence in alcohol – a hangover headache. One or two painkillers are enough to ease them.

These headaches are manageable and, apart from occasional inconvenience, they don't worry us too much. But what if your headaches are a sign of something serious? Having a stroke or a brain tumour is what people worry about most, especially if headaches are severe or frequent.

Fortunately, brain tumours are rare. More importantly, fewer than ten per cent of brain tumours present with just a headache. A serious underlying cause represents less than one per cent of people who go to their doctor with headache. This is all reassuring, but it is important to know when you *should* see your doctor.

When you should see your doctor

Sometimes a doctor's reassurance is as helpful as any therapy you might try, so see your doctor if you are worried about your headache for any reason. Headaches on their own without any other symptoms are rarely a cause for concern. The following headaches and symptoms are prompts to seek medical advice. They do not necessarily mean that you have serious headaches, just that you should seek a proper diagnosis.

- Headaches beginning after the age of 50.
- A new headache in a child under the age of 12.
- Sudden onset of a new or 'worst ever' headache, especially if very severe, abrupt or explosive, which peaks within minutes. 'Thunderclap headache' is a fitting description.

- Worsening of headache and/or associated symptoms over days or weeks.
- Physical problems that are not typically associated with headaches or continuing in the absence of headache. These include changes or loss of consciousness, fits, severe confusion, blindness, vision problems, red eye, weakness of limbs, loss of sensation, and pains in the face, jaw or mouth.
- Headache with a fever not caused by something obvious like having a cold or flu.
- Headache with prolonged nausea and vomiting or vomiting without another obvious cause.
- Headache brought on by exertion, including coughing, trying to breathe out with nose and mouth blocked (valsalva), sneezing, stooping, exercise or straining on the toilet.
- Headache that changes with posture; for example, it is better when you lie down.
- Headache associated with sexual activity, before or during orgasm.
- New or unusual symptoms or a change in pattern in your longstanding headaches, such as greater frequency, intensity or duration.
- A new headache if you do not normally have headaches.
- Onset of headache if you have cancer, HIV/AIDS or immune deficiency.
- Onset of headache following a head injury.
- Headache at the same time as high blood pressure.
- Headache with an aura lasting for longer than 1 hour or associated with weakness of your arms or legs (see Chapter 2).
- An aura without a headache if you haven't previously been diagnosed with migraine with aura.
- An aura for the first time if you are using a combined hormonal contraceptive.
- Psychological changes associated with headaches, such as marked changes in behaviour or personality, or failure to cope at work or school.

Different kinds of headaches

Doctors group headaches for the purposes of diagnosis, treatment and research.

Primary headaches

A primary headache (and associated symptoms) is the term used when the headache is the disease itself, as opposed to a headache that is caused by (or secondary to) another illness, infection or injury. Sometimes described as benign headaches, primary headaches on their own are not life-threatening, although they have all been described as 'quality of life-threatening'. They include migraine, tension-type headache (TTH) and cluster headache.

Secondary headaches

These headaches are caused by another process, injury or disease of the head and neck, including blood vessels, bones, sinuses, eyes, ears, nose, teeth, mouth and face. They include stroke, brain tumour or infection (e.g. meningitis). Substances such as drugs and alcohol, or withdrawal from them, are also causes.

Secondary headaches are excluded by a doctor before a diagnosis of a primary headache is made. They are outside the scope of this book because they need specific medical treatments, rather than self-help measures.

Recognizing headaches

Migraine

Migraine is a common, primary headache. It is not always recognized. The main feature is a severe 'sick' headache that lasts from a few hours to several days. You are usually well between attacks, which are episodic weekly or years apart. If your headache occurs every day, then you may be having migraine and another headache. Treatments you are taking may be causing more frequent headaches. (See Chapters 10, 11 and 12.)

People wonder whether there is a difference between a headache and a migraine. A migraine attack is much more than just a headache, which is only one of the symptoms. If you are not sure whether or not you have migraine, answer the I-D Migraine Test™

questions. There is more information about recognizing and coping with migraine in Chapters 2–5.

> ### The I-D Migraine Test™
>
> During the past 3 months, did you have any of the following symptoms together with a headache?
>
> - You felt nauseous/sick?
> - Light bothered you (a lot more than when you didn't have a headache)?
> - Your headache limited your ability to work, study, play or do what you wanted to for at least one day?
>
> If you answered 'yes' to at least two out of three questions, then it is likely that the headache was migraine. (Reference: Lipton and colleagues, 2003.)

Tension-type headache

More common than migraine, TTH is the 'normal' kind of headache that happens from time to time, caused by muscular tension or stress. Sometimes described as a tight band or squeezing around the head, there are no distinguishing symptoms and you don't usually feel sick. If you need to treat TTH, one or two painkillers are normally effective. It can become troublesome if it starts to happen more often or if painkillers lose their ability to control the pain. You can read more about TTH in Chapters 6 and 7. Also look at Chapters 10, 11 and 12 if your headaches are happening on most days.

Cluster headache

Unlike migraine and TTH, cluster headache is a rare primary headache. It is not widely recognized, properly diagnosed or treated, but in its typical form it can be identifiable. Some people visiting the City of London Migraine Clinic have told us that they recognized their headache from information on our website. Another sent a colleague to us because he recognized symptoms that were identical to his own!

Not to be confused with migraine, which can 'cluster' together in days of severe attacks, cluster headache is different. It has several distinguishing features. The headache is excruciating and is described as 'suicide headache'. Short attacks of pain lasting minutes to hours occur in bouts of one to eight per day. These bouts can persist for 6 to 12 weeks, and can happen once or twice in a year. During attacks you may be very restless or agitated. On the affected side you may notice eye changes and a blocked or running nostril. The other side is totally unaffected.

If you think you have cluster headache, then you need medical advice because self-help measures don't work. There are effective treatments and you can read more in Chapters 8 and 9.

2

Migraine: causes and triggers

Christine, 27
'People think that migraine is just a bad headache. That is only part of
it! I'm sick for hours on end, can't do anything except lie down and feel
awful. It takes me days to recover properly and I lose time out of my life.
I'm getting married next year and already I'm worrying about whether
I'll get a migraine on my wedding day . . . '

Tackling migraine requires a dual approach – prevention and treatment. Unfortunately, like me, many people don't even realize that
they have it! They miss out on effective management strategies
and fail to cope. Additionally, having other types of headaches at
the same time can confuse matters. Try the I-D Migraine Test™ in
Chapter 1 to find out whether you are a 'migraineur'. Recognizing
your migraine and understanding how it affects you can allow you
to cope better. Everyone is different and migraines vary between
attacks in the same person.

What is migraine?

Migraine is a primary headache, like tension-type headache and
cluster headache, and it may co-exist with them. There are no specific tests to identify migraine. It is diagnosed by a doctor based on
your headache description and symptoms.

The word migraine derives from 'hemicrania', meaning headache
on one side. The one-sided head pain is typically severe and pulsating. You can feel or be sick and become sensitive to sound, light
and smell. One of the features of migraine is that it is a disabling
type of headache. If migraine doesn't stop you from doing what
you were doing, it really slows you down – a 'power cut' process.

The migraine may or may not be accompanied by an aura, usually
involving distinctive visual disturbances – this is different from the
blurred vision that often accompanies a migraine headache. Most
migraineurs do not in fact have aura.

Migraine is a recurring disorder. It occurs on average every four to 6 weeks. Some people have migraine infrequently, with gaps of a year or more at a time. Others can have it much more frequently, with barely a week's respite during a bad run. Migraine lasts from four hours to 3 days. If the migraine goes away and returns less than 2 days later, it is part of the same migraine. This whole period is called a 'migraine attack'. Typically, people recover and are completely well in between attacks.

Phases of a migraine attack

In a migraine attack, the headache itself is only one of five phases. These are the warning phase, the aura, the headache, the resolution and the recovery. Understanding the phases will help you to cope with what is happening. During an attack, though, it is not always obvious which phase of the attack you are in.

Phase 1: warning symptoms of a migraine attack

This prodromal or premonitory phase is common, affecting two thirds of migraineurs. You may notice a few aches, especially around your neck, and may not feel quite yourself. Warning symptoms can be one extreme or the other:

- mood – feeling very happy or miserable or irritable;
- behaviour – over-active or lethargic and clumsy;
- appetite – not feeling hungry, feeling sick or craving certain foods, often chocolate;
- bowels – either constipation or diarrhoea; and
- fluid balance – feeling thirsty, wanting to pass more urine or water retention.

Neurological symptoms of migraine can begin as:

- yawning – sometimes more than usual, as if you cannot stop;
- inability to find your words;
- inability to focus your eyes or blurred vision (*not* migraine aura, which is a distinctive set of symptoms – see 'Phase 2: migraine aura');
- sensitivity to light, sound and smells; and
- feeling very tired and unable to concentrate.

These changes can be very subtle and develop for up to 48 hours before the headache even starts. You may not be able to recognize them at the time, but your family and friends might. More than once a doctor at the City of London Migraine Clinic has asked me whether I have a migraine. I've denied this, only for it develop some hours later! They noticed me looking paler, yawning, muddling up my words or being rather crabby. It was often a day when I'd missed my lunch and had no chance to slow down and eat and drink something. These are not symptoms I can always take notice of, but if you can avoid some of your triggers then you may be able to stop an attack developing.

Phase 2: migraine aura

A typical migraine aura is a distinctive set of visual, sensory and speech symptoms. You may have one or all of these neurological features, together or in succession.

- *Visual aura symptoms* account for 99 per cent of migraine auras. They take the form of blind spots, distorted vision like looking through a broken mirror, flashing lights, zigzags (fortification spectra) or an expanding shimmering dot with a jagged edge, like a crescent (scintillating scotoma). You may have a sensation of a visual disturbance marching across your field of vision, from one side to the other. It may appear to affect only one eye, but if you cover it you will find that the other eye is affected too. This is because 'visual' aura symptoms are from your brain. They have been reported in a woman with migraine who was born without eyes.
- *Sensory aura symptoms* account for a third of auras, usually occurring with visual symptoms. Typically, pins and needles, tingling or numbness starts in your fingers and moves up your arm to your face and tongue. The legs are not usually affected. The sensation is one-sided and is not normally associated with weakness or loss of power.
- *Speech disturbances* associated with aura cause temporary difficulty finding your words (dysphasia). This occurs less often and is usually in association with visual and/or sensory symptoms.

The aura symptoms are part of the migraine attack but start and stop *before* the migraine headache begins. You return to normal when they are gone. Onset is not sudden but gradual, over at least 5 minutes. They can last up to an hour in total, with an average of 20 minutes. The headache usually begins up to an hour or so later.

Although auras vary between attacks, most migraineurs become used to their typical symptoms. If you get an aura for the first time, if it lasts longer than usual or if symptoms do not return to normal, then consult your doctor. Persistent loss of strength in an arm or leg is not a typical aura, although it can occur in hemiplegic migraine.

Phase 3: migraine headache and associated symptoms

The headache is the same regardless of whether it was preceded by an aura. It usually pulsates or pounds. It can be around the temple or anywhere on one side of the head. Unlike tension-type headache, it is moderate or severe, not usually mild. Your neck can also be painful during a migraine and the build up of an attack.

Sometimes the headache isn't the worst symptom, as your whole body seems to shut down. Accompanying symptoms are nausea, and you can be very sick. You are also sensitive to sound, light and smell. They don't have to be particularly loud, bright or bad, but during a migraine they can seem intolerable. You seem overly sensitive to everything, and things that wouldn't normally hurt, like brushing your hair, can be painful. Feelings of depression during a migraine can be overwhelming. This is more than just being miserable because you have a headache, and may be related to brain chemicals involved in migraine attacks.

Routine activity and movement aggravate migraine; you just want to lie down in a dark room. You look pale, have no energy, can't eat, concentrate or do anything properly, and generally feel rotten.

Phase 4: resolution of the migraine attack

The way that a migraine attack resolves varies between people and between attacks in individuals. We don't know much about how or why attacks switch off. Some people sleep it off, feeling much better when they wake. Others, unfortunately, wake up and the migraine is still there. Some migraineurs, particularly children, find that once they have been sick (sometimes violently) they have a sense of relief, as though the pressure of the pain has gone. Other people need to take medication and some just let the attack run its course.

Phase 5: recovery from the migraine attack

This postdromal phase describes how you feel after the attack and can vary. Many migraineurs feel completely washed out and drained for at least another day afterward. They can feel quite low and lethargic. Others, though, can feel high – almost euphoric even – and they rush about, probably making up for lost time!

Types of migraine

Migraine can be described as episodic – when you are well between attacks – or chronic – when migraine occurs more days than not. The vast majority of migraine attacks are episodic and these account for the first three subtypes outlined below. In a very small minority of people migraine attacks can become chronic.

Migraine without aura

Previously known as 'common migraine', this affects about 70 per cent of migraineurs. Some women experience this around their period ('menstrual migraine'; see Chapter 13).

Migraine with aura

You don't have to experience aura to have a migraine attack. Previously known as 'classical migraine', this only affects about 30 per cent of migraineurs.

About 20 per cent of people with migraine experience both types of migraine attacks – that is, some with aura and some without. Only around 10 per cent of people have attacks exclusively with aura.

> *Michael, 46*
> 'I have had migraine since my early twenties. It always starts in my left eye with a bright spot of light, which gradually gets bigger and brighter. I can't see properly. I close my eyes and it is still there. Sometimes I get a prickly feeling in my fingers that spreads up my arm too. I now know it is the start of a migraine attack, and a headache will soon follow.'

Migraine aura without headache

This represents about one per cent of migraine attacks. It is more common in older people and those who have had migraine with aura in the past. You should discuss this type of attack with your doctor as other causes may need to be ruled out.

Chronic migraine

Migraine is an episodic condition and only about two per cent of migraineurs experience progression from episodic to chronic migraine. According to the current edition of the International Classification of Headache Disorders, if you have headache occurring on 15 or more days per month for more than 3 months, which has the features of migraine on at least 8 days per month, then you may be diagnosed as having 'chronic migraine'. The migraine can be with and/or without aura. The most common cause of chronic migraine is medication overuse, which accounts for half to three quarters of all cases. (See Chapters 11 and 12.) However, this cannot be confirmed until after drug withdrawal when headaches improve and migraine becomes episodic again. All treatments described for the more usual episodic migraine can be used for chronic migraine and recently botulinum toxin A (BOTOX®) has been licensed in the UK for preventative treatment. (See Chapter 4.)

Rare types of migraine

If you suspect that you have any of the following rare types of migraine, see your doctor. You may need to see a specialist too.

Migraine with brainstem aura

Previously known as 'basilar migraine' or 'basilar-type migraine', this is migraine with aura with additional symptoms before the headache. Symptoms arise from the brain stem. They include slurred speech, ringing in the ears, severe dizziness, temporary vision loss and occasionally loss of consciousness. Although triptans (anti-migraine medications) are not usually recommended for this type of migraine, other standard treatments can be prescribed.

Hemiplegic migraine

This is migraine with aura with episodes of weakness or paralysis of the arm and leg on one side of the body. The weakness or paralysis can precede migraine headache, or can continue for the duration of the attack. Your doctor must diagnose this type of migraine, because symptoms are similar to those of stroke. It can run in families, in which case it is called 'familial hemiplegic migraine'.

Retinal migraine

Temporary blindness, blind spots or bright lights in one eye only may be retinal migraine. Migraine headache may begin during the symptoms or for up to 1 hour afterward. Eye examination is normal, and your doctor will exclude visual disturbances caused by other factors.

Status migrainosus

This is when migraine lasts for longer than the usual 72 hours. It may last for several weeks. Occasionally, hospitalization is required if dehydration occurs because of persistent vomiting. Triptans are usually very effective at treating migraine, but sometimes the symptoms repeatedly return on consecutive days, resulting in ongoing symptoms.

Who gets migraine?

Migraine is common, affecting about 10–12 per cent of the population. In the UK, estimates suggest that six million people are affected and that 190,000 migraine attacks occur every day. Migraine typically first occurs during the teenage years or early twenties and usually before the age of 40. It can occur in children, with boys and girls equally affected until puberty. Over a life time about 25 per cent of women have migraine, as compared with 8 per cent of men. Migraine is usually worse for women in their thirties and forties, whereas for men it remains more constant over the life time.

In the Europe and the USA, migraine is more common in Caucasian people than in other races. We don't yet understand the genes involved in migraine but this is an exciting area of research. Genetic factors could be very important reasons why some of us have migraine. If relevant genes can be identified, treatments can be targeted and genes could also be used for diagnosis in the future. Specific genes have already been identified for the rare familial hemiplegic migraine, but we don't know how relevant this is to typical migraine with and without aura. Our work at the City of London Migraine Clinic, in collaboration with geneticists in

Australia, suggests that genetic variants in certain genes are related to menstrual migraine. Migraine does seem to run in families, with people inheriting a tendency to have migraine. However, genes are only a part of the reason why people experience migraine. Although genes increase a person's susceptibility to migraine, environmental factors play an important role to trigger attacks.

Causes of migraine attacks

The exact causes of migraine are still unknown and are the focus of considerable research and debate. We are not sure how attacks are switched on, maintained or switched off.

What causes the start of a migraine attack?

Migraine is now thought to be a disorder that primarily originates from neurological changes in brain chemistry. Blood vessels in the brain then constrict and swell, which the brain interprets as headache.

Current theories suggest that those of us with migraine have over-excitable brains, even when we don't actually have a migraine. An inherited low threshold makes us sensitive to migraine triggers, which act as stimuli to provoke migraine attacks in us but not in those without migraine. Changes in various chemicals within the brain, including calcium, magnesium and glutamate, have been implicated in the excitation process in migraine. This is when nerve cells (neurones) become over-active and we get a migraine attack.

The neurones transmit pain signals by sending electrical and chemical messages. One of many chemical messengers (neuro-transmitters) implicated in migraine is serotonin (also known as 5-hydroxytryptamine, or 5-HT). Serotonin could be important at the start of an attack, when levels are initially high and then drop. Before a headache even starts, fluctuating serotonin levels may change blood vessels and increase blood clotting as platelets in the blood clump together. Brain function in certain areas of the brain, particularly the brain stem and hypothalamus, becomes disrupted. As the hypothalamus controls appetite, thirst, sleep and mood, this could account for the warning symptoms before a migraine attack. Research is currently being conducted on parts of the brain stem to see how they might generate a migraine attack.

What causes a migraine aura?

A neurological process called 'cortical spreading depression' (CSD) has been proposed to account for migraine aura. We don't know whether CSD is important in initiating migraine, exactly how it starts and whether it is significant in those who don't have migraine aura.

The process is believed to begin when a stimulus provokes excitation of nerves to become more electrically active. A wave of decreased electrical nerve activity then spreads across a part of the brain called the cortex. This has many functions, including controlling your vision and senses. CSD could account for the various symptoms experienced during an aura at the start of an attack. CSD may be associated with blood vessel constriction and reduced blood flow in the cortex. It has been suggested that all of these changes are linked to aura, because the rate of CSD moving across the cortex is similar to visual symptoms moving across your visual field before a migraine attack.

What causes the migraine headache?

Many complex processes in the nervous system are likely to play a role. Release of serotonin initially causes blood vessels in the outer layer of the brain (meninges) to constrict and later they swell as serotonin levels drop. Serotonin binds to special receptors throughout the brain, including on the trigeminal nerve. Branches of this sensory nerve spread from the outer meninges to deep within the brain stem. They are responsible for the transmission of pain sensation that is relayed to the sensory areas of the cortex.

When the blood vessels swell, they irritate the surrounding nerves of the trigeminal system. Various inflammatory substances are released, including calcitonin gene-related peptide (CGRP). This causes more swelling of blood vessels and further activation of the nerves. These changes in blood vessels, blood flow and nerve sensitization could account for the pulsating pain of the headache, nausea and other migraine symptoms.

What causes a migraine attack to end?

The attack ends when pain and inflammatory processes subside, which can take several days. Painkillers and anti-inflammatory drugs can help to stop migraine attacks. Sometimes, anti-migraine medications that target the migraine process specifically are more effective. Direct injection of serotonin has too many blood vessel constricting side effects, but triptans are highly effective once a migraine headache begins. These serotonin receptor agonist drugs activate receptors and mimic the effect of serotonin. They are believed to switch off an attack by preventing swelling of the blood vessels and, importantly, by stopping release of inflammatory substances. Drugs that block serotonin receptors and drugs that influence serotonin levels (e.g. anti-epileptic drugs) can be effective as migraine preventatives.

Common triggers for migraine

A recent study showed that 76 per cent of migraineurs can identify triggering factors for attacks. Consistent differences between triggers for migraine with or without aura have not been established. It usually takes more than a single trigger. Here are some common triggers.

- Diet – missing meals, delayed meals, hunger and caffeine withdrawal.
- Dehydration – not drinking enough water.
- Alcohol – migraineurs are more susceptible to the effects of alcohol.
- Sleep – too little or too much can trigger migraine. Migraine typically occurs at the weekend when sleep patterns and routine change. Late nights combined with alcohol, late breakfasts and caffeine withdrawal are common factors. Lack of sleep for other reasons such as depression, exam pressure or menopausal hot flushes are also triggers.
- Environment – loud noise, smoke, bright or flickering lights, strong smells (especially chemical smells or perfume) and work environment.
- Travel – associated triggers include lack of sleep, stress of preparations, missed meals, dehydration, change to routine and crossing time zones. We don't know whether oxygen and pressure changes in aircraft cabins specifically trigger attacks, but loud engine noise, cramped seats and the smell of perfume in the duty-free shop certainly don't help!
- Weather – changes in barometric pressure during thunderstorms

can be associated with increased migraine frequency, but data are conflicting. Humidity and bright sunlight can trigger attacks.

- Hormones – natural hormone changes occurring during menstruation, pregnancy or menopause, or those from using the pill or hormone replacement therapy are triggers for migraine in some women.
- Exertion – this can bring on a migraine, or more usually makes it worse. It can include exercise, sexual activity, coughing, sneezing or straining on the toilet. If you have migraine or any headache associated with exertion, you should discuss this with your doctor to confirm the diagnosis. It is mostly not a reason for concern, but underlying causes should be excluded.
- Emotion – the mechanisms are unclear, but any emotion (e.g. stress, anger or even excitement) can be a trigger. You may get through the stressful time and get the migraine on relaxation afterward.
- Other illnesses – untreated or uncontrolled illnesses (e.g. coughs, colds and flu, or eye, sinus, jaw, teeth or neck problems) may trigger migraine.

Migraine and other medical conditions

There is an association between migraine and other conditions, including depression, anxiety, epilepsy and vertigo. This does not mean that having migraine causes these conditions; it is just that they are more likely to affect people who also have migraine. We need research to understand these connections. It may be more than a coincidence that anti-depressant and anti-epileptic medications can be very effective migraine preventatives, even if you don't have depression or epilepsy. Other medical conditions may influence the migraine medications prescribed by your doctor. If you have depression, then your migraine medication might help both conditions at the same time. If your depression improves then the migraine could too.

Migraine and particularly migraine with aura, may be a risk factor for changes seen on brain scans. White matter abnormalities, infarct-like lesions and brain tissue volume changes are more likely to be seen, compared to people without migraine. We don't know whether these changes are significant and research is ongoing.

We have no evidence that these abnormalities are associated with obvious symptoms such as cognitive decline or any other neurological problems, such as losing your balance. It is natural to be concerned that severe migraine might be damaging your brain but so far the changes don't appear to be associated with migraine duration, frequency, severity or the amount of medication taken. There is currently no suggestion that you will require a scan unless you have unusual symptoms. Your doctor's neurological examination should pick up any symptoms that warrant further investigation. (See Chapter 20.) The brain changes don't seem to predict the course of migraine or indicate that treatments are modified. Future research will inform us further and it may simply mean that the changes become recognized biomarkers for the inheritance of migraine.

Migraine with aura is a marker for being at a higher risk for stroke and, in women, for heart disease. The body of evidence suggests that risk is only associated with aura, not migraine without aura. There isn't much you can do about the tendency to migraine with aura, so don't be overly concerned. You'll already be trying to reduce attacks and this could reduce stroke risk, although significance of migraine frequency is unknown. It makes sense to concentrate on what you can do to reduce the risks for stroke and heart disease. This means giving up smoking, exercising regularly, maintaining a healthy weight and, for women, not using combined hormonal contraceptives. Also have your blood pressure and cholesterol checked regularly and treated if necessary.

Research on migraine and breast cancer has been reassuring, as migraine does not appear to raise the risk for breast cancer. Some studies hinted that migraine might actually have a protective effect, but that has not been shown in subsequent large-scale analysis.

Does migraine improve?

There is currently discussion about migraine being a progressive condition, in which changes in the central nervous system may cause a few people to develop frequent migraine attacks more readily. We need more research in this area. Fortunately, for most people who do not overuse their medications, migraine is an episodic disorder. Frequency of attacks varies considerably over a life time. You can have gaps of weeks, months or even years at various stages in your life. Migraine can be worse for women when their hormones change as they approach the menopause.

Usually, for both men and women, migraine generally improves with age. Migraine attacks tend to become both less frequent and less severe. Don't wish your life away though! Migraine isn't guaranteed to disappear, and you must always do what you can to reduce the frequency of attacks.

3

Migraine: coping with medication

Symptomatic (acute) medications are used to treat migraine symptoms of head pain and nausea when they occur. When you treat a migraine attack, try to use the right drug, at the right dose and at the right time. This gives it the best chance of working. This chapter outlines how to make the right choice of medication and suggests a simple two-step strategy to treat a migraine attack. It also considers preventatives, taken daily.

Some medications are purchased over the counter and others are only obtained on prescription. Not all suit everyone because of side effects, especially at higher doses or if you have other medical conditions. Always read the packet insert information carefully. If your medication is not working or you have concerns about how it is affecting you, then see your doctor or pharmacist.

Medications for migraine symptoms

The right drug is the one that works best for you, with a minimum of side effects. Recommended medications for migraine symptoms in adults are as follows.

Simple painkillers

These are available over the counter. Try aspirin 600–900 milligrams (mg; two to three tablets) to start. You can repeat the dose every 4 to 6 hours, to a maximum of 4 grams over 24 hours. These doses of aspirin are higher than the recommended over-the-counter doses because these are the effective doses in clinical trials. A good alternative is ibuprofen 400 mg (two tablets) to start, then repeated every 4 to 6 hours to a maximum of 1.2 grams per day. Paracetamol 1000 mg (two tablets) is well tolerated and works for some people, but it is less effective than aspirin or ibuprofen for migraine. It can be repeated every 4 to 6 hours to a maximum of 4 grams in 24 hours.

Anti-sickness (anti-emetic) drugs

Anti-sickness drugs help with nausea and vomiting. Prochlorperazine, sold in the UK as 3 mg Buccastem M® Buccal Tablets, is available from the chemist. The tablet should be placed high up along your top gum, under your upper lip, and allowed to dissolve slowly. The usual dose is one or two tablets twice a day, for a maximum of 2 days. Other anti-sickness drugs (e.g. domperidone and meto-clopramide, available on prescription) have a 'pro-kinetic' activity in addition to their anti-sickness effects. The stomach and gut shuts down during a migraine attack, meaning treatments taken by mouth may not work well. By keeping everything moving, the addition of a pro-kinetic anti-emetic can encourage rapid absorption of your painkiller or triptan. It can be worth taking these drugs even if you don't feel sick early in your attack.

Non-steroidal anti-inflammatory drugs

Non-steroidal anti-inflammatory drugs (NSAIDs) include ibuprofen, available from the chemist. Other NSAIDs such as naproxen and diclofenac tablets can be prescribed by your doctor. NSAIDs can cause stomach irritation, so additional protective medication may also be prescribed.

Triptans

These are a specific type of anti-migraine drug. They can alleviate headache and all associated migraine symptoms. They are discussed in more detail below.

Migraine medications to avoid

Using the right treatments means avoiding the wrong ones! These include morphine, pethidine, dihydrocodeine and combination painkillers that contain caffeine and codeine. These help other pain conditions, but when they are used to treat migraine they can make you feel more sick, cause your gut to shut down even further and be addictive.

Two steps to treat migraine

This is a two-step strategy to treat a migraine attack in adults. The first step may be sufficient, and the medications needed can be bought over the counter. If step 1 doesn't work, then proceed to step 2, for which you will need a prescription from your doctor.

Step 1

- At the start of a migraine when the head pain is mild, take a *soluble* preparation of your preferred simple painkiller.
- Combine this with an anti-sickness medication. This will help with any sickness, but importantly it can help painkillers to work better.
- Repeat doses as necessary, according to the packet instructions. Repeat the anti-sickness medication to help the painkillers to work, even if you don't feel sick.

If step 1 has not worked within an hour, then proceed to step 2.

Step 2

- Take your preferred triptan or an NSAID, such as naproxen, as prescribed by your doctor.
- Combine this with an anti-sickness medication. This will help with any sickness, but importantly it can help the triptans or NSAIDs to work better.
- Repeat doses as necessary but without exceeding the maximum daily dose allowed for the medication type.

If a moderate or severe migraine attack is present when you wake or if you always need to proceed to step 2, then start with step 2 and miss out step 1.

Treat symptoms early

The right time to treat your migraine attack is as early as possible. Clinical trials suggest that treating an attack when the head pain is mild works best. It is important to distinguish between migraine and a mild tension-type headache; otherwise you could be treating headaches that might go away anyway. Keep treatments near so that they are convenient when you need them quickly.

Get the dose right

The right dose is high enough to work well for you but with the fewest side effects. You may need to try different starting doses. Generally, use higher doses at the beginning of an attack and repeat as necessary. One aspirin (300 mg) might not do anything, but three (900 mg) could be enough to stop a migraine at its onset.

It is not a problem to use high doses over a few days (within the maximum daily limits and in the absence of troublesome side effects) if you are treating migraine infrequently, such as once a month. If you are treating migraines most weeks, then you might be at risk for side effects and medication overuse, and a preventative may be more helpful. Remember – it is not the doses that are important but the number of days treated. Don't use triptans or combination tablets for more than 10 days in a month or pain-killers for more than 15 days in a month.

Find a medication type to suit you

Medication should ideally get into your blood stream quickly. If you are feeling or being sick and your stomach and gut are shutting down, this can be difficult. Different formulations of medications are available to help. There are tablets, mouth dispersible preparations, suppositories, injections and nasal sprays. You may need to experiment to find what suits you best. Try to use the soluble pain-killers or ones that dissolve on your tongue, which are more rapidly absorbed. Dissolve them in a sweet fizzy drink to help absorption and give your blood sugar level a boost.

Triptans – specific anti-migraine drugs

Triptans are a class of anti-migraine drugs that work on serotonin receptors in the brain. Clinical trials have shown that they are all effective at stopping migraine symptoms. Milligram dosages vary between the different triptans and cannot be compared. It is finding one that works well for you that is important.

The first triptan developed, sumatriptan, is now available over the counter (50 mg tablet) if you complete a form checked by the pharmacist. The other triptans and different formulations of sumatriptan are only available on prescription.

Types of triptans available

There are seven different triptans available in the UK. Some are in different formulations, making them more convenient to take. The formulations available are as follows:

- tablets (almotriptan 12.5 mg, eletriptan 20 mg and 40 mg, frovatriptan 2.5 mg, naratriptan 2.5 mg, sumatriptan 50 mg and 100 mg, rizatriptan 5 mg and 10 mg and zolmitriptan 2.5 mg);
- mouth dispersible, which dissolve in the mouth and do not require water (rizatriptan 10 mg and zolmitriptan 2.5 mg and 5 mg);
- nasal sprays (sumatriptan 20 mg and zolmitriptan 5 mg); and
- injection, provided in a preloaded auto-injector device for simple self-use (sumatriptan 6 mg).

Side effects of triptans

Side effects include a feeling of throat and chest tightness or pressure, nausea, tiredness and a heavy sensation in the limbs. Some side effects are difficult to distinguish from migraine symptoms, but if one triptan does not appear to agree with you then another might. The chest pressure symptoms in otherwise healthy people are not a cause for concern unless you feel pain rather than pressure. If you develop pain having not experienced it before with your usual triptan, then seek medical advice.

Triptans are not recommended for children, those over 65 or pregnant women. If you are at risk for heart disease or stroke or had these in the past, you will not be able to use triptans because they constrict blood vessels. You may be able to use triptans if you have had high blood pressure, but only if it is well controlled by medication.

Relapse with triptans

Relapse is when a migraine attack initially responds to a triptan but returns within 48 hours. A second dose is usually effective, but relapse can continue over several days. If relapse occurs repeatedly when treating your migraine, then discuss changing the triptan with your doctor. Combining triptans with NSAIDs and an anti-sickness medication at the start of an attack may be helpful.

Tips for using triptans

The triptan your doctor prescribes may depend on other medications that you are currently taking, because triptans can interact with some antibiotics, blood pressure tablets and anti-depressants.

- Take triptans with or without food, except rizatriptan, which should be used on an empty stomach.
- Use your triptan at the onset of migraine headache. They don't work if they are used during the aura phase of a migraine attack.
- Only use your triptan when you know that the headache is a migraine.
- Repeat the starting dose after 2 hours if the migraine goes away and comes back. Don't repeat if the first dose did not work. With the exception of zolmitriptan, which can be repeated after 2 hours, research shows second doses are unlikely to work.
- If your usual starting dose of a triptan is not effective, your doctor may suggest a higher starting dose. This can increase side effects and is not recommended for all triptans.
- Try a triptan for at least three separate migraine attacks when you have been free of migraine for at least a week. Sometimes an individual migraine might not respond, so it is worth trying again.
- If a triptan does not work or has side effects, try an alternative (or the same one in a different formulation) because another one may be effective.
- If the triptan needs to work very quickly or if nausea and vomiting are a problem, then your doctor may consider zolmitriptan nasal spray or sumatriptan injection.

Medications for migraine prevention

A preventative (prophylactic) medication is one that you take every day to reduce the number of migraine attacks. Used in addition to painkillers or triptans for migraine symptoms, research evidence suggests that the following drugs can be useful preventatives.

Beta blockers

These drugs are commonly prescribed for treatment of high blood pressure and angina. They are not suitable if you have certain medical conditions, including asthma. A course of propranolol

twice daily can be helpful to prevent migraine. Metoprolol or atenolol are also used, and it is worth trying a different beta blocker if
one is not effective. Side effects are tiredness, cold feet and hands,
and dizziness.

Amitriptyline

Amitriptyline is a tricyclic anti-depressant that can help to prevent
migraine, particularly if you also have tension-type headache, other
pain conditions or disturbed sleep. Note that your doctor does not
think you are depressed if he or she suggests this medication. More
information on amitriptyline is available in Chapter 7.

Anti-epileptic drugs (or neuromodulators)

These are used at lower doses than for epilepsy control. They are not
recommended during pregnancy, and so adequate contraception is
advised. Clinical trials have shown that taking topiramate once or
twice daily can help to prevent migraine attacks. The doses are built
up gradually. Side effects of topiramate include pins and needles,
weight loss and changes in mood, which usually settle with continued use. Sodium valproate twice daily can also be helpful; its side
effects include nausea, tiredness, weight gain and hair loss. There is
less evidence that gabapentin is effective. Side effects of gabapentin
include dizziness and sedation.

Other drugs

Other drugs such as pizotifen and clonidine have been used for
migraine prevention, but the drugs mentioned above are more
effective.

Why use a preventative?

Preventative medications don't cure migraine, but they are useful if
you have frequent migraines because they can reduce the number
of attacks by up to half. They can also help if migraines are severe
and disabling or if they don't respond well to symptomatic treatments, even if they are not very frequent. Regularly losing 2 or
more days a month to severe attacks can prompt consideration of
preventative treatment.

If your migraines always respond to treatment for symptoms,

then preventatives may not be necessary. If your migraines have increased and you are using symptomatic medication on 2 or 3 days each week, then you are at risk of developing a medication overuse headache. A short course of a preventative could be enough to break the cycle.

How long to use preventatives

If the medication works well, then the plan is not for you to stay on daily preventatives indefinitely, although some people do remain on them for long periods. Headache specialists usually recommend that you stay on the effective dose for about 6 months and then gradually reduce the dose over 2 or 3 weeks. If migraine returns during this time, then the dose can be increased again. Typically, when you stop preventative medication the improvement is maintained.

If a preventative does not appear to be working, it is best to continue for a minimum of 2 to 3 months at the required dose to give it the best chance of success. The only reason to give up is unacceptable side effects. These can sometimes be reduced by lowering the dose for a while and waiting before increasing again. If you have given the preventative a proper trial and it doesn't work, then your doctor can usually suggest alternatives.

Tips for using preventatives

Although none of us wants to take tablets every day, sometimes a short course can break the cycle of troublesome migraine. Here are some tips.

- You should feel willing and motivated to use medication daily. If you keep forgetting or changing your mind, then it won't have a chance to work properly.
- Discuss with your doctor why you need to take the medication and what to expect. The choices might be influenced by other medical conditions.
- Usually, doses are built up slowly to give your body a chance to get used to the medication. If you follow the instructions carefully, you are less likely to get troublesome side effects. This slow dose increase can mean that medication takes longer to start working. This can be 2 to 4 weeks, and so you do have to be patient.
- Remember not to give up too soon, especially if you experience side effects – they are often transient.
- Keep a diary to assess whether treatment is working. Sometimes it isn't the frequency of the migraine that improves, but the severity, duration or even the response to symptomatic treatments.

4

Migraine: coping strategies and other treatment options

Apart from using medications, how else can you cope? Having a healthy lifestyle and a positive approach can really make a difference, and we look at this in the last chapters of the book. This chapter focuses on understanding migraine triggers and your migraine threshold. It also outlines potential new treatment options, such as surgery for migraine.

Identifying migraine triggers

You may be able to identify your migraine triggers by keeping a diary or by thinking about factors that led to an attack during the 2 or 3 days beforehand. You might have recognized the migraine triggers listed in Chapter 2 or found that that none seem particularly relevant. Disappointingly, that is the nature of migraine triggers. They are different for everyone, and even your identified triggers won't be the same for every attack, because their effects are not always predictable.

Understanding migraine triggers

It would make coping with migraine so much easier if it were as simple as avoiding known triggers. However, we don't understand how triggers work. It appears that people with migraine react in an over-sensitive way to environmental or chemical triggers such as loud noise, bright lights or specific foods. Triggers may work directly to cause migraine attacks, but not necessarily. Exposure to a trigger can mean a migraine at one time but not at others. This is because triggers work together in more complicated ways to cause migraine attacks and to affect your threshold for developing them.

Trigger factors and warning symptoms

Prodromes or warning symptoms of a migraine are easily mistaken for triggers in the early stages of an attack, before the headache begins. You crave chocolate, the migraine begins and chocolate is regarded as the trigger. Actually, the food craving was a warning of an attack that had already begun. Likewise, over-activity can be regarded as a trigger, when your behaviour change was really a pre-headache symptom.

Recognizing what might be happening with triggers and pro-dromes is important. If you can have something to eat and drink at this stage, perhaps have a lie down or at least a few minutes to relax, then you may be able to stop an attack developing. If the migraine headache does begin, then ensure that you have your medication ready to treat it early.

Your migraine threshold

The threshold theory of migraine is a useful way of thinking about migraine triggers. Your threshold is the level at which there are sufficient triggering influences of any kind to provoke a migraine attack. At the City of London Migraine Clinic we asked people who had migraine to think of *how many* triggers they needed to start a migraine attack, rather than which one might cause it.

Imagine a ladder of triggers. With each trigger you climb up a rung of the ladder. Once you reach a certain level you cross your threshold and develop a migraine attack. For example, you may be tired, have had a stressful day at work, not drunk enough water *and* had your lunch late. On their own, these triggers might not have started an attack, but together they add up to tip you over your threshold.

Raising and lowering the migraine threshold

Your individual migraine threshold is determined by your genes and your tendency to have migraine. This means that people who are prone to frequent migraine have lower thresholds for devel-oping attacks – that is, they have fewer rungs of the trigger ladder to climb. The threshold for developing a migraine attack may be made higher by taking daily preventative drugs. This could mean that you need more triggers to get an attack.

Triggers such as illness or a menstrual period in women can act in two ways. They may act directly to cause a migraine attack but they can also have the effect of lowering your threshold so that other triggers are more likely to provoke an attack. Stress, late nights or a glass of wine can trigger a migraine in a woman at period time, but at other times these same triggers don't provoke an attack.

By recognizing how triggers can build up, you may be able to do something about the trigger that actually tips you over the threshold. This is especially if you think that triggers might be working to lower your threshold. These principles work for me and are an important part of how I cope with my own migraine. It is now rare that I have a migraine attack without knowing why. I know that at times of stress, tiredness or ill health I have to drink plenty, eat regularly and make allowances. Otherwise, I will almost certainly get a migraine attack.

Coping with triggers for migraine

Not all attacks have an obvious cause, and you cannot avoid triggers all of the time. Don't allow triggers to become an additional worry. See if you can identify what, if anything, is a trigger for you. Triggers are important, but not necessarily significant for everyone, because they do not just 'turn on' an attack. The most important thing is to work out what is relevant for you. If you cannot identify triggers then don't be overly concerned – some of them you can't do much about anyway. Only avoid triggers if you notice a pattern. Otherwise, it is too easy to start avoiding favourite foods (such as chocolate), an alcoholic drink or evenings out with friends. Life can then become rather dreary and you feel that you are really missing out – all because of migraine!

If you want to eliminate a suspected trigger, then do so systematically. Keep a diary to see whether it really makes a difference and just change one thing at a time. Small changes are much more manageable anyway. As a migraineur you must recognize that you may be very sensitive, but don't become a slave to trigger avoidance.

Lifestyle trigger factors

Try to make sure that your lifestyle prevents your migraine and does not trigger attacks. These are the trigger factors over which you have most control.

- Diet – eat regularly and don't miss meals.
- Fluids – drink at least 2 litres of water throughout the day.
- Sleep – get into a regular sleep pattern and make sure that you get enough rest. Try to maintain it at weekends and when you are out of your routine, such as holidays.
- Exercise – get active and exercise regularly. Keep hydrated and eat regularly to keep blood sugar levels stable.

Environmental trigger factors

You may have little control over your environment, so concentrate on the factors that you can do something about.

- Noise, smoke and strong smells – these are sometimes difficult to avoid, but leave the environment if you recognize a trigger. If you have to be exposed to triggers (e.g. going to a loud concert), then get some early nights beforehand, remember to eat regularly and keep drinking water.
- Weather – although you can't change the weather, you can avoid other triggers such as dehydration if the weather is humid. A large sun hat and sunglasses can help if bright sunlight is a trigger.
- Travel – it is impossible to avoid some potential triggers when travelling, but minimize those you can. Get enough sleep and break up journeys if possible. Ensure that you eat regularly and keep hydrated – remember that air travel is very dehydrating. Avoid alcohol while flying, because its effect is more potent. Be organized in your preparations and allow plenty of time so that travelling is no more stressful that it needs to be.
- Visual stress – if bright or flickering lights from the TV, computer screens or school whiteboards are triggers, then take regular breaks from the screen, try to avoid tension build up in your neck and shoulders, and keep hydrated. There has been concern about compact fluorescent integrated light bulbs causing migraine. Newer bulbs are now supposed to emit a constant flicker-free

light and no longer emit the blue light that some migraineurs are sensitive to.

- Work environment – work brings many migraine triggers. Poor lighting, ventilation, shift patterns, overtime, poor ergonomics at your computer workstation, no regular meal breaks, impossible management targets, telephones and computers are just a few. Poor posture can cause muscle strain. Identify whether these could be making your migraine worse. Regular breaks and a few small changes may make a difference.

Psychological trigger factors

These can play an important role in migraine.

- Stress – challenging, unpleasant or threatening events, varying from major life events to minor daily hassles, can be impossible to avoid. Research has indicated that both occurrence and perception of stressful events are higher for those with migraine and other headaches, than for those who do not have headache. Of course having rotten headaches are additional stressors in their own right. The influence of stress appears strongest in people under the age of 60, suggesting that older people have learned to cope better. Some theories suggest that increased perception of stress may be a premonitory symptom of an attack and could even be due to changes in the brain as a result of headaches. Finding ways to cope with stress is therefore essential for migraineurs. Avoid it where you can and don't underestimate the importance of regular breaks and time for hobbies and relaxation. Additionally, notice the impact that stress has on the other migraine triggers, such as missing meals and sleep. It lowers your migraine threshold so that other triggers more quickly build up to an attack.
- Other emotions – anger, excitement and relaxation after stress are also difficult to avoid. Try to prevent controllable triggers from building up to cross your migraine threshold.

Hormonal trigger factors

Natural hormone changes can be significant triggers for migraine, or alter the threshold for getting them, at various stages in a woman's life.

Other illnesses

Get illnesses treated. Any illness can act as a trigger or lower your threshold for developing a migraine attack.

Rachael, 20

Rachael is a police officer. She shares a flat with friends. She has had migraine with aura since she was 18. Rachael remembers the first attack very clearly because it occurred after an important police examination.

On the bus home Rachael noticed an odd zigzag pattern of shimmering light in her left eye. It moved across from left to right and lasted for about 15 minutes. Rachael had felt tired after her examination, but by the time she arrived home she was feeling sick. She then developed an extremely severe headache. It was on one side of her temple and it pounded. She recalls being violently sick and then going to bed. Her flatmates were concerned because her face was so white. The next morning the headache was gone, but it was another few days until she felt well again.

The police occupational health doctor diagnosed the headache as migraine with aura. Rachael has had several similar episodes, with and without the visual symptoms of migraine aura. Rachael was advised that she should not use the combined oral contraceptive pill because of a slight increased risk for stroke in young women who also have migraine aura. She was prescribed a triptan to take at the start of a migraine headache. Rachael visited us at the City of London Migraine Clinic because she felt that her medication no longer worked and she wanted further advice. Her migraine attacks had increased in frequency and her senior officers were concerned about her having to go off duty.

The specialist confirmed typical migraine with and without aura and recommended a triptan nasal spray. This would be quick and easy to take on duty at the onset of the head pain, after the aura phase. If possible, the addition of an anti-sickness drug such as domperidone or metoclopramide would help with the sickness and with absorption of the triptan, because even nasal sprays are mostly absorbed from the gut.

The doctor discussed why Rachael's migraine attacks might have increased. She was currently on a new work placement that meant that she was working irregular hours. The shift patterns had affected her sleep, and meal breaks on duty were often many hours apart. Although Rachael could do little about the shifts, she was told to try to drink plenty of water, cut down her ten coffees a day and to eat regularly, taking snacks with her if necessary. She was also encouraged to eat more proper meals when she was off duty, because she admitted to living on takeaway food with her flatmates. Rachael needed more time for relaxing too. The new post was demanding, and Rachael said that she sometimes spent her days off just catching up on sleep. She never felt refreshed. It was suggested that she should keep to a regular sleep pattern, even on her time off.

At her follow-up visit Rachael had kept migraine diaries, which showed significant improvement. The nasal spray and anti-sickness combination worked quickly and effectively. Importantly for her, Rachael was able to continue working during an attack. The diary showed that she should try to take her medications as early as possible when the head pain started, including migraine attacks without aura. Early treatment would mean that any attack would be less likely to develop.

It had been difficult to eat regularly and drink enough water, but it had become part of Rachael's routine and she thought it helped. She had also tried to improve her overall diet and go to for a run on her days off. This was enjoyable and relaxing. It gave her more energy rather than less and she slept better too. Rachael felt more positive about coping with her migraine. She was more confident managing with her new treatments, and the small changes she made in her lifestyle had helped make her attacks less frequent.

New treatment options for migraine

In recent years various new strategies for migraine prevention have been studied and introduced. Current research is developing new medications that block the action of substances such as glutamate, calcitonin gene-related peptide (CGRP) and other neuropeptides. Trials using Telcagepant, a CGRP receptor antagonist drug, were shown to be effective for migraine prevention but there were concerns about possible liver toxicity. This resulted in the manufacturer stopping development. More recently trials of anti-CGRP antibodies are looking promising because they appear effective for migraine prevention and are well tolerated. Another neuropeptide, pituitary adenylate cyclase-activating polypeptide (PACAP), is also of current interest. It may have a role in the migraine process as it affects light sensitivity and blood flow through the outer brain layers. Its receptors in the brain may be new targets for future migraine treatments.

The approaches discussed below are still being studied to ascertain if they are consistently safe and effective and some are only considered if standard treatments have failed. Migraine Action and the Migraine Trust can advise on recent developments. (See Useful addresses at the end of this book.)

Neurostimulation devices

A range of non-invasive neurostimulation devices such as GammaCore®, Cefaly® and Spring TMS® are currently being tested for treatment and prevention of migraine and other primary headaches. They appear to be effective, generally well tolerated and could represent a new era in treating headaches. These devices may benefit those who cannot tolerate, or do not respond to, current treatments, those who prefer a drug-free approach (e.g. pregnant women) or those who want to supplement their current regimens.

In the UK, the National Institute for Health and Care Excellence (NICE) is encouraging further research on table-top or hand-held nerve stimulation devices which deliver transcranial magnetic stimulation (TMS) or vagus nerve stimulation (VNS). These devices are placed on the scalp or neck and either VNS, single (sTMS) or repeated (rTMS) magnetic pulses to the head or neck are delivered, depending on the device. The frequency, intensity, duration and interval times of pulses may be varied.

Research evidence is currently limited in quality and quantity, with uncertainty about the safety of long-term or frequent use. There is also uncertainty about the optimal dose of TMS for both treatment and prevention of migraine, and the optimal frequency of use for prevention. Studies have been small and it is difficult to achieve true sham-controlled (placebo) trials, as most devices induce noticeable effects during stimulation. NICE recommends that treatment it is carried out under the direction of specialist headache doctors. You should not expect a cure and any reduction in migraine symptoms may be modest. At present, VNS appears more promising in the treatment of cluster headache rather than migraine.

Greater occipital nerve block injection

The greater occipital nerves supply the scalp and are located on either side at the back of the head. They feed into the trigeminal nucleus in the brain stem and injections of local anaesthetic and steroids can block pain transmission along the nerve, reducing headache symptoms.

Who is this injection suitable for?

Greater occipital nerve block injections are used at some specialist centres for migraine, cluster headache and tension-type headache with varying temporary success. Research is limited but people with frequent, medication-resistant headaches may benefit. Most people are able to have a nerve block unless they are allergic to the medications used, use blood-thinning medication or if they have an active infection. Your doctor should be aware of medical problems now or in the past before having the nerve block.

What does the procedure involve?

The procedure lasts only about a minute. You will be seated or lying down while the greater occipital nerve is located by the doctor feeling the tender or painful area at the back of your head. The injection can be on one or both sides. A fine needle is used for the small injection and generally people describe a warm sensation with discomfort, rather than pain.

What are the risks and benefits of the injection?

Side effects can include temporary pain and numbness at the injection site and some people notice a lump which settles after a few days. Rarely, infection, prolonged bleeding or loss of hair can occur at the site. You may be allergic to the medications or briefly feel faint. Transient difficulty speaking and swallowing have been recorded due to the local anaesthetic. This isn't usual though and most people are able to carry on with their usual activities after the procedure. As the needle stays outside the skull there is no chance of brain or spinal cord leaks or injury and serious complications are very rare. Weakness or change in facial expression does not occur because the nerve does not connect to muscles.

Pain relief can last from several days to a few months and it isn't possible to predict who will respond. The scalp will go numb after the injection and pain may be relieved within minutes. This is due to the local anaesthetic and when it wears off after a few hours, pain may return for several days. By the third to fifth day after injection more lasting pain relief occurs as the steroids take effect. If you respond to the injections you may be offered repeat injections when the pain returns. They can be repeated every 2 months. If you do not respond to your first treatment within a week or two, you may offered a second one. If this does not work then it is best to consider another treatment.

Botulinum toxin type A injection

BOTOX® is the prescription name for botulinum toxin type A – a purified neurotoxin that paralyses muscles and blocks nerves affecting neuromuscular function. It is derived from the bacteria *Clostridium botulinum* which can cause severe food poisoning called botulism. In therapeutic uses it can be used in minute doses (a fraction of what causes botulism), directly into muscle rather than the blood stream. It has been used in medicine to help movement disorders and muscle spasms. In the cosmetic industry relaxation of the facial muscles can help reduce the appearance of wrinkles and frown lines. The discovery of botulinum toxin type A for migraine treatment was accidental – people who were using it for cosmetic purposes also reported improvements in migraine.

Who is this injection suitable for?

Early clinical trials were disappointing and BOTOX® is not effective for episodic migraine, tension-type headache or cluster headache. More recent studies have shown a modest benefit for prevention of headaches in adults with chronic migraine. That is, you have headaches on at least 15 days each month, with migraine on at least 8 of these days. In the studies, people treated with BOTOX® averaged 8 to 9 fewer headache days per month compared to their baseline versus 6 to 7 fewer headache days per month with non-active treatment (placebo).

We don't know how it works or why it is only effective in chronic migraine and not episodic migraine and tension-type headaches. While BOTOX® could decrease muscle contraction that may act as a trigger to migraine by blocking acetylcholine release, this is not thought to be the main mechanism of action in migraine. Botulinum toxin type A is able to repress calcitonin gene-related peptide (CGRP) release from activated sensory neurons and recently has been shown to block nerves from being activated by mechanical pain. This may be important in migraine which worsens with physical activity such as sneezing or bending over. By reducing overall pain messages, brain excitability may be diminished, thereby reducing migraine attacks.

In the UK, NICE approved BOTOX® as a preventative treatment for adults with chronic migraine who have already tried and failed at least three different drug treatments to prevent chronic migraine headaches. They should also be appropriately managed for medication overuse (i.e. not taking too many painkillers or using them too often). BOTOX® treatment for chronic migraine is now available on the NHS in the UK for people who have had their migraines carefully assessed. It is not currently available in Scotland as the Scottish Medicines Consortium advised NHS Scotland not to offer BOTOX® on the basis of value for money – this is an expensive treatment. The guidance may be reviewed in future. BOTOX® treatment is not suitable for women who are pregnant or breast feeding as we have insufficient data to know if it can harm your baby or pass into breast milk. You should advise your doctor of all your medical conditions and medications that you are taking. BOTOX® may not be suitable for people with neuromuscular disorders.

What does the procedure involve?

Administration of BOTOX® for chronic migraine is different from administration for cosmetic purposes and healthcare professionals must be specifically trained to administer it according to the chronic migraine protocol. BOTOX® is given as a series of 31 tiny injections (0.1 millilitres) into muscles divided across seven very specific areas in the forehead, above the ears, and the back of the neck and shoulders. The procedure takes about 5 minutes and the injections have a prickly, stinging sensation rather than being painful.

What are the risks and benefits of the injection?

The most frequent side effects are neck pain, headache, migraine, eyelid swelling or drooping, eyebrow drooping, musculoskeletal stiffness and muscular weakness. These usually occur within the first week following injection and, while generally transient, may last several months or longer. Possible allergic reactions include: itching, rash, red itchy welts, wheezing, asthma symptoms, dizziness or feeling faint. Although rare, it has been reported that botulinum toxin products may spread from the area of injection and cause various effects, the most serious of which are swallowing and breathing difficulties. If you notice any serious symptoms you should seek urgent medical help.

Pain relief is usually within the first 2–3 weeks of injection; however, you may require another set of injections to achieve maximum benefit. Injections are spaced at 12-week intervals and are repeated until chronic migraine changes to episodic migraine – defined as fewer than 15 days with headaches each month for 3 months in a row. BOTOX® treatment should be stopped if it clearly isn't working – i.e. the number of days you have a chronic migraine headache each month should reduce by at least 30 per cent after two courses.

Hole in the heart closure

A hole in the heart (patent foramen ovale – PFO) affects around a quarter of the general population. It occurs when the opening between the upper chambers of the heart (atria) fail to close completely at birth. Although most people do not suffer any ill effects, heart specialists may recommend PFO closure for medical reasons. This can be done under anaesthesia and involves the insertion of a small device into a large vein in the groin. This is then passed up into the heart and positioned to close the PFO.

Some people who have had their PFOs closed have found, coincidentally, that their migraines have improved. Therefore, research has been done to find out whether this procedure should be undertaken specifically for migraine prevention. People with migraine with aura are around twice as likely to have a PFO. The link is only with migraine with aura and we don't know why – it could be genetic. The mechanisms are unclear. Blood that goes through the opening has not been filtered by the lungs, and it is possible that it contains tiny particles or chemicals that reach the brain and could trigger the onset of migraine aura.

Recent research did not demonstrate that PFO closure is better at preventing migraine than standard preventative drug treatments. The negative outcome means that headache specialists do not recommend this procedure for migraine outside of clinical trials, because it is invasive and not without serious risk. It has been suggested that in the absence of good evidence it is unethical to perform this procedure on the basis of having migraine alone. In the UK, NICE recommends that use of this procedure should be restricted to people who are severely affected by recurrent, refractory migraine. The procedure should only be done by an interventional cardiologist and supporting team with specific training and carried out in units where there are arrangements for emergency cardiac surgical support in the event of complications.

Migraine and surgery

Surgical techniques such as deep brain stimulation and continuous stimulation of the occipital nerve via electrode have been used for cluster headache. They have been carried out in severe migraine cases under clinical trial conditions. Currently, all surgery for migraine is experimental. This includes any surgical manipulation of muscles, blood vessels or nerves in the head and face. We need more detailed, large-scale research studies, which will provide both short-term and long-term safety data and evidence about whether any improvement is maintained.

If you have severe migraine and/or other headaches, you may consider surgery in the hope of finding relief from your pain. This always needs to be carefully considered, because surgery and anaesthesia carry risks that need to be weighed up against any potential benefits. No surgical techniques have yet been shown to help migraine better than standard available treatments.

Tips for coping with migraine

- Identify migraine triggers that you can do something about and deal with them. Don't worry about those you can't change.
- Think about *all* aspects of your life, including home, work and leisure.
- Don't underestimate small changes.
- Remember the trigger ladder.
- Despite optimal trigger management, always be prepared if a migraine breaks through.
- Keep informed about new developments in migraine. New treatments and medications are being developed.

5

Migraine in children and older people

Primarily a disorder of men and women during mid-life, migraine frequently occurs in children, although it can take different forms. Many people grow out of migraine as they get older, particularly women after the menopause.

Migraine in children

Migraine occurs in children and teenagers, particularly if it runs in the family. It affects about ten per cent of children aged between 5 and 15. Migraine in children should always be assessed by a doctor. This is essential in children under 12 with a new headache, new symptoms or a fever. There is not usually anything else wrong, but other causes must be excluded. Brain tumours are rare and, as for adults, headaches are not usually the only symptom.

Typically, migraine in children tends to be shorter lasting than in adults – perhaps only 1 or 2 hours. The headache can be on both sides of the head, and severe vomiting is often a feature. Migraine aura may also be present. Children are good at drawing what they see during their aura, which can help to confirm the diagnosis! Aura may disappear in adulthood migraine and come back in later life without a headache. In young girls a monthly pattern of migraine without aura may begin to develop during pre-puberty and puberty. Keeping a diary could help in the early recognition of menstrual migraine (see Chapter 13). Migraine often recedes during teenage years to return during the twenties.

Abdominal migraine and childhood periodic syndromes

In young children under 12, head pain may not be the main problem. Children can complain of intermittent general stomach pain that may or may not be accompanied by nausea and vomiting.

This is called abdominal migraine and it can reoccur in attacks like migraine.

Other 'childhood periodic syndromes' of recurring symptoms are marked by the child being completely well between episodes. Symptoms may include nausea, vomiting, vertigo and tilting of the neck. Children don't have a headache, but they can be very pale and sensitive to light and sound. A doctor must always diagnose these syndromes because many other conditions such as bowel disorders and infections can give rise to similar symptoms. These syndromes are related to migraine in adults, and around half of young children will go on to develop typical migraine in adulthood.

Coping with migraine in children

Coping with migraine in children means involving them in their care as much as possible, as appropriate for their age. Even young children are often very good at keeping detailed (and beautifully illustrated) diaries when requested. This can help to identify avoidable triggers. In children these frequently include the following:

- not eating regularly (or enough, especially during a growth spurt)
- exercise
- lack of fluids
- irregular sleeping patterns
- exposure to flickering lights
- over-excitement
- travel and
- stress at school or home.

Most children do not require medication for migraine attacks, which tend to be short-lasting. Severe vomiting may mean that tablets can't be taken anyway. If symptom treatments are required, this is usually ibuprofen (aspirin should not be taken by under-16s). Your doctor can prescribe domperidone for sickness and nausea. None of the triptans are licensed for use in under-18s in the UK apart from sumatriptan nasal spray for adolescents aged 12–17 years. All medications should be discussed with the child's doctor, because not all are suitable for children, and doses may need adjusting according to weight and height of the child. Medication overuse headache occurs in children and teenagers as well as adults.

If simple strategies are not effective then a child should be assessed by a specialist children's doctor (a paediatrician) with an interest in headache.

Migraine can be disabling in children and mean frequent time lost from school. If necessary, parents should seek help for migraine in a child, because it can be a source of family stress. Often it is the parents who need most reassurance! Take time to inform your child's school about their migraine. The school may not be sympathetic unless they understand how migraine affects the child and how they can help. Fluids and a lie down in the first aid room may be enough to stop an attack developing. At home it is very important to maintain regular routines for sleeping, eating, getting up and getting dressed, homework and time on the computer. Try not to let migraine dominate your child's life. If possible they should be strongly encouraged to continue all the activities they enjoy, such as sport, hobbies and seeing their friends.

Migraine in older people

If you are not lucky enough to grow out of migraine, like the majority, this doesn't mean that there is anything wrong with you. Generally, though, migraine attacks are less severe with fewer accompanying symptoms as you get older. Some people who have had migraine with aura find that they experience the aura without a headache as they get older. You should discuss this with your doctor, to exclude the possibility of stroke or transient ischaemic attack, which are more common with advancing age as arteries fur up.

Migraine rarely develops for the first time in someone over 50, so your doctor will usually look for other causes for headache. These include dental issues, jaw and neck problems, facial pains (trigeminal neuralgia) and inflammation of the arteries (temporal arteritis).

Coping with migraine in older people

If troublesome migraines persist then you will need to take extra care to try to reduce attacks and treat them appropriately. This means eating enough, drinking plenty of fluids and avoiding overusing medications to treat migraines. You should chat with your doctor if you have any concerns, your headache changes, you develop a new headache or symptoms, or you have other medical problems. Various factors can adversely influence migraine in later life. Ill-fitting dentures make proper nutrition difficult, and resulting unstable blood sugar levels could trigger migraine. Social isolation may contribute to depression and emotional triggers.

If you are on a tight budget and only heat one room using a gas appliance, you are at higher risk for carbon monoxide poisoning if the appliance is faulty. Headaches and nausea at home that improve outside in the fresh air are an early sign, although this warning does not always occur. Carbon monoxide poisoning from this odourless, colourless gas can cause unconsciousness and death. The flame should burn blue, not yellow, and there should be no soot deposits. Regular checking of appliances and fitting a carbon monoxide detector are important.

Having migraine does not appear to increase your risk of high blood pressure or cognitive impairment as you get older. However, migraine may more readily co-exist with these and other illnesses. These may impact on both the migraine itself and the treatments your doctor prescribes.

As you get older you are much more sensitive to the side effects of all medications, some of which can cause headaches. Ageing affects our blood vessels and causes our digestive, liver and kidney functions to be less efficient. You and your doctor should watch out for side effects of all of your medications, including those for migraine. Sometimes doses need to be reduced or changed because of another medical condition. Manufacturers don't recommend the use of triptans in people over 65 because they can constrict diseased blood vessels in the heart. Your doctor or specialist may consider prescribing triptans 'off-label' (p. 143) for infrequent use if you are a healthy non-smoker with normal blood pressure.

6

Tension-type headache: causes and triggers

Tension-type headache (TTH) is a 'normal' kind of headache. The most common primary headache, and usually successfully self-treated, it is little more than an occasional inconvenience. You only need help from healthcare professionals when headaches either increase in number or no longer respond to painkillers.

TTH has previously been known as tension headache, muscle contraction headache, stress headache, ordinary headache and psychogenic headache. These names give clues as to possible causes. Mild and often featureless, TTH lacks the distinguishing symptoms that characterize migraine or cluster headache. However, TTH can exist with other headaches and may be mistaken for migraine without aura. Recognition is important because, ideally, different headaches should be dealt with separately if management is to be successful.

Although usually less disabling than migraine, the low impact headache of TTH can still be a real nuisance. If TTH becomes chronic rather than episodic, it can have a severe impact on your life.

Symptoms of tension-type headache

Apart from a headache, you may notice no other symptoms with TTH. Pain may be pressing, tightening or squeezing. TTH is usually only mild or, at worst, moderate. It does not throb and tends to be on both sides of the head. This is unlike migraine, in which pain is severe, one-sided and pulsating. The pain can start from or spread into the neck. Tenderness in head and neck muscles may be noticed when pressed with the fingers.

TTH lasts anything from 30 minutes to seven days in the episodic form, but it is often just a few hours. Unlike migraine, the headache doesn't worsen with routine physical activities. You don't often have to stop what you are doing, but you may be aware that you are working less effectively. Nausea is not usually a problem, although there can be loss of appetite. There may be heightened sensitivity to loud noises and bright lights, which is one of the reasons why TTH can be confused with migraine.

Paul, 38

'I get a dull kind of pain like a tight band or vice around my head. It tends to come on in the later part of the day and my neck also feels stiff. I don't feel sick and I can carry on working. I take a couple of paracetamol and it goes. I'm a bus driver and I don't think that sitting all day helps. Recently, I've started swimming twice a week and I think that eases the tension in my neck.'

Different kinds of tension-type headache

There are three categories of TTH, based on how often the headache occurs. *Infrequent episodic TTH* occurs on average less than 1 day per month and has little impact on individuals. These are the kind of headaches that occur now and again and do not bother us too much. The other two types, however, occur much more frequently and may require medical help. They can be very disabling and debilitating. *Frequent episodic TTH* occurs between 1 and 14 days per month for at least 3 months. TTH is classified as *chronic TTH* when it occurs on 15 or more days per month on average, for more than 3 months. Chronic TTH starts as episodic and in some people evolves over a period of time to the point at which pain becomes almost daily or even continuous. We do not know why this happens in some people and not others.

Who gets tension-type headache?

On average about half of adults have experienced an episodic TTH, but some studies suggest that this could be nearer 80 per cent. Chronic TTH is rare and affects about three per cent. TTH can occur at any age – including in children – but is most likely to occur in the forties, with women being more affected than men.

Causes of tension-type headache

TTH has not been well defined. Because it doesn't have any specific symptoms other than head pain, it has been difficult to quantify and research. Causes were previously considered psychological, but recent studies suggest a neurobiological basis (e.g. biology of the nerves involved in pain transmission and perception). Although we are gaining new knowledge, underlying causes remain uncertain. We don't know whether the pain originates in the scalp and neck muscles and is referred (i.e. felt elsewhere), or whether there are disturbances in pain processing in the brain itself. It is possible that both mechanisms are important. Over-excitable nerve transmission from head and neck muscles may play a role in episodic TTH, and abnormalities in pain processing and generalized increased pain sensitivity could become important in chronic TTH when the headaches are more frequent. Studies suggest an increased genetic risk for frequent episodic and chronic TTH, but not for infrequent episodic TTH.

Triggers for tension-type headache

Emotional tension and physical tension in scalp and neck muscles are the two main triggers associated with TTH. Mental tension and stress often, but not always, aggravate TTH. Also, people with frequent episodic and chronic TTH are more likely to be anxious and depressed than those with infrequent episodic TTH. Whether low mood is a cause or a result of the headaches is unknown. Physical tension and sometimes tenderness in the muscles of the scalp and neck are also implicated. These can occur from musculoskeletal abnormalities or for other reasons, such as poor posture or muscle strain (e.g. when lifting heavy objects or carrying heavy bags on a regular basis).

Josephine, 59
'I had a fall last year and broke my ankle. It took a long time to heal. I couldn't do the part-time work I really enjoy which gets me out of the house. I remember feeling really low. I'd only ever had occasional headaches during my life, but at this time I seemed to be getting them once or twice a week. There were just a dull ache and didn't stop me from doing anything. I got even more fed up as they were just something

else to deal with. My daughter suggested I told the GP about them. He gave me a thorough check over, which was reassuring. He didn't prescribe anything, which I thought he might. He just said it was probably because I was much less mobile and not really myself. Once I got back to work, started moving again and feeling better, the headaches disappeared as quickly as they came. I hardly ever have one now.'

Does tension-type headache improve?

Episodic TTH often improves over time. In one recent study nearly half of adults with chronic and frequent episodic TTH were in remission at a 3-year follow up. It is important to identify and treat any causes and additional problems such as migraine, medication overuse, musculoskeletal disorders, depression and sleep problems. This is because if these issues are not tackled first, then they may be underlying contributing factors to TTH. Unless they are properly managed, TTH is unlikely to respond well to any management strategy.

7

Coping with tension-type headache

Despite being an ordinary kind of headache, tension-type headache (TTH) can be a real blight on your life. If your headache responds to an occasional painkiller, then it is not too much of a problem. But what if the painkillers stop working or the headaches start happening frequently? In this chapter we look at ways in which you can help yourself and the treatments you can take.

Coping with tension-type headache without medical treatments

Although clinical studies don't show the benefit of particular non-drug management strategies on TTH, lifestyle changes can be worthwhile. Sometimes, keeping a diary and taking a step back to think about what could be influencing your headaches is revealing.

Simple coping strategies

If you feel a TTH developing, simple strategies (e.g. application of hot or cold packs) can be very soothing and surprisingly effective if done in the early stages. Massaging aching neck and shoulder muscles – even on yourself if there is no one to do it for you – can ease muscular tension. Having something to eat or drink is always a good idea. Sometimes with vague kinds of headaches that are difficult to identify, it might just be a headache caused by hunger or dehydration.

Physical therapies

If you have musculoskeletal problems – particularly with your back, neck or shoulders – then physical therapies such as physiotherapy, osteopathy or chiropractic may be helpful. Make sure that your therapist is aware of your headaches in addition to any other problems, because this may influence their approach. Working with your therapist to improve your posture can also help TTH.

Complementary therapies

Some people report benefit with complementary therapies such as acupuncture and homeopathy.

Stress management

If you are feeling stressed as the headache is developing, try a change of environment; for instance, get away from your computer or go out for a breath of fresh air. Because stress-related issues may play a role in TTH, any lifestyle changes to reduce stress may be helpful.

Exercise

TTH appears to be more common in sedentary people. Regular exercise can be beneficial.

Coping with tension-type headache using medical treatments

Drug treatments may be helpful, but in the long term it is better to identify and treat any underlying contributory factors first. These include muscular problems, sleep problems, depression or medication overuse.

Symptomatic (acute) drug treatments such as painkillers are appropriate for episodic TTH, occurring on no more than 2 days per week. More frequent use increases your chances of developing medication overuse headaches. Usually, no other treatments are needed. You can use maximum doses when the headache starts to stop it from developing. With episodic TTH this is normally all that is required, and the headache often responds to a single dose.

Frequent episodic or chronic TTH is a different matter. These often require prescription preventative drug treatments taken daily to gain relief from relentless headaches. Achieving this becomes much more difficult in longstanding chronic TTH. If medication has been over-used, this must be recognized and tackled. Otherwise, it hinders headache diagnosis and stops any other treatment strategies from working properly.

Therefore, treating chronic TTH with symptomatic treatments is not usually recommended. If you have frequent headaches you should see your doctor, who may prescribe a short course of the non-steroidal anti-inflammatory drug (NSAID) naproxen, taken regularly over a 3-week period. This can break the cycle of frequent headaches and the habit of always reaching for painkillers. If you have tried many different treatments, your doctor may refer you to a pain management clinic.

Medication for episodic tension-type headache symptoms

Clinical studies suggest that oral aspirin (600–900 mg) has the best effectiveness. Children under 16 should not use aspirin. Generally, the NSAIDs work well. Ibuprofen (400 mg) may be bought over the counter. Naproxen and diclofenac may be prescribed by a doctor. Stomach irritation and ulceration can sometimes be a side effect of all of these medications. Paracetamol (500–1000 mg) appears less effective but can be helpful for some, especially if other medications are not tolerated.

Opioids such as codeine or other strong analgesics and sedative hypnotics, including drugs like diazepam (Valium), are not recommended. This is because they make you drowsy and can be addictive.

Medication for prevention of tension-type headache

The best time to start preventatives is not clear, but because the risk of developing more headaches increases when they occur weekly, this may be the time to consider. If medication overuse with symptomatic treatments is occurring, then these treatments may have to be stopped before starting preventatives. It is not known whether preventatives can prevent or delay the transformation of episodic to chronic TTH that occurs in some people.

Amitriptyline

Amitriptyline is the treatment of choice, and there is evidence of its effectiveness in clinical studies. It is a tricyclic anti-depressant and is used in lower doses in TTH prevention than in depression. Your doctor prescribes it because it reduces pain and muscle tenderness and aids sleep, not because it is an anti-depressant. If you are depressed, then your doctor will usually prescribe a newer type of anti-depressant.

Dose regimens for amitriptyline vary. You start with a low dose at night, gradually increasing at 1-week to 2-week intervals. The final dose will depend on when you feel benefit and how well you tolerate the drug. When improvement has been maintained for about 6 months, you can gradually reduce. It can be restarted if the headaches come back. The plan is usually to have a short course of the drug to break a headache cycle, not to stay on a daily drug for an indefinite period of time.

Side effects are typically minimal, provided doses are low and increases are gradual. Common side effects include dry mouth, constipation and blurred vision, but they usually improve with continued use. By taking amitriptyline 2 hours before bedtime, sedation the next day can be minimized. Remember that you can get side effects before the drug has started working, so it is important not to give up too soon. Amitriptyline can be very effective, so it is worth persevering for at least 3 months.

Other treatments

There is less evidence from clinical trials for TTH preventatives other than amitriptyline. Mirtazapine, alternative tricyclic antidepressants and tizanidine (a muscle relaxant) may be helpful. Clinical studies have not shown effectiveness for botulinum toxin injections into head and neck muscles.

Janice, 29

Janice is an accounts assistant for a large company. She attended the City of London Migraine Clinic because her headaches were increasingly frequent. Janice has always had the occasional headache, and two paracetamols usually resolved it fairly promptly. Now paracetamol had stopped working, so she no longer took it. The headaches were occurring up to 4 or 5 days a week. Janice is single, having split up with her boyfriend, who moved out of their flat. Janice is managing to pay the mortgage on her own but is finding it a struggle and is doing overtime to make ends meet.

Janice described the headaches as the same as she has always had, just more of them. The pain was mild and had more of a pressure quality rather than a throbbing or pulsating sensation. It spread from her neck and felt like a band of muscle tightness across the back of her head on both sides. Her neck muscles felt slightly tender. She didn't feel sick and had no other symptoms. Headaches could come on at any time of day and last from a couple of hours to all day. They didn't usually stop her from doing anything, but she felt that she was not performing as well at work as she could be.

After examining Janice and assessing her headache diary record card, the doctor diagnosed chronic TTH. This can sometimes evolve from an episodic form. In Janice's case this was not migraine, which can co-exist with TTH or be mistaken for it. Headaches due to over-using medication were excluded in Janice's case by the careful diary record that she kept. The doctor considered that Janice's stress with the break up of her relationship, coupled with extra hours of overtime spent mostly at a computer, contributed to increasing headaches. Janice agreed this was likely.

As Janice's headaches were frequent, not responding to medication and really troubling her, she started amitriptyline as a preventative to help with pain and muscle tenderness. Janice started at a low dose 2 hours before bedtime to minimize sedative effects the next day, and gradually increased the dose. She tolerated the medication well and, apart from a dry mouth and sleepiness at first, didn't notice any troublesome side effects. Janice was advised not to treat her headaches as they occurred unless she felt it was necessary, and in any case not on more than 2 days a week. Aspirin or ibuprofen was suggested. Janice did not feel that she could cut down her working hours because she needed the income, but she did agree to take more regular breaks from her computer, get advice about improving her posture and workstation set up, and try to get more exercise.

Janice was reassured that her headaches had no serious underlying cause. After 6 months Janice was able to stop taking the amitriptyline. Her headaches reduced rapidly because of the combination of preventative medication and more exercise in the form of swimming and a regular gym class. She still gets occasional headaches but these respond well to aspirin.

Tips for coping with tension-type headache

- If you are anxious about your headaches this can make them worse. Seek help if you need it.
- TTH can be difficult to recognize and co-exists with other headaches. Get a proper diagnosis if headaches are troublesome.
- Look after yourself and remember to eat and drink regularly.
- Keep a diary card to identify possible underlying factors.
- Focus on non-drug ways to cope and find new ways to relax and deal with stress.
- Get depression and anxiety treated. These make TTH worse and resistant to treatment.
- Become more active and do more exercise.
- Don't treat headaches on more than 2 or 3 days a week; otherwise a medication overuse headache may develop.

8
Cluster headache: causes and triggers

Jason, 35
'My worst ever experience. It is an excruciating, stabbing pain behind my right eye like a red-hot poker. I feel that my eye is being pushed out of my head. I can't sit still. I have to pace about. I scream and swear – I just can't help myself.'

Barbara, 42
'The pain is off the scale. The pain of every single attack is much, much worse than being in labour when I gave birth to my two children. Imagine giving birth four times a day and that might give you some idea of what I go through.'

These are some of the ways people with cluster headache have described their attacks. It is one of the most painful conditions known to mankind. In our City of London Migraine Clinic newsletter, Alan summed it up by telling us,

'It is difficult to describe the severity of the pain of cluster headache to those who have not experienced it. Imagine the pain if you slam your fingers in a door or hit your thumb with a hammer. Severe as the pain might be initially, it does not continue at that level of severity for long. The intense pain of a cluster headache is even worse and it can go on and on . . . sometimes lasting for several hours.'

I was shocked when Sean confided to me,

'If you put ten of us having a cluster headache attack in the same room as a shotgun, we would all be tempted . . . I would not be surprised if you opened the door to find at least one dead person.'

No wonder that cluster headache is called 'suicide headache'. This isn't an exaggeration, because some people have been driven to take their lives. It is hard to imagine their pain and the total despair.

Cluster headache is a rare primary headache belonging to a class of headaches called trigeminal autonomic cephalalgias or TACs. Other headaches in this group are even less common. It has been aptly noted that the shorter and more frequent the headache attacks, the longer the name of the syndrome. So, short-lasting unilateral neuralgiform headache attacks with conjunctival injection and tearing (SUNCT) and short-lasting unilateral neuralgiform headache attacks with cranial autonomic features (SUNA) are much more frequent and shorter in duration than episodic paroxysmal hemicrania, cluster headache or hemicrania continua. All these headaches are associated with very severe one-sided head pain and one-sided symptoms. As cluster headache is the most common TAC, it will be the focus of this and the next chapter.

Although it may co-exist with migraine, cluster headache requires specific diagnosis and treatment, usually by a specialist. Cluster headache should be distinguished from the other TACs if possible, because treatments vary. A magnetic resonance imaging (MRI) brain scan may be performed to eliminate other reasons for symptoms, such as a pituitary gland tumour. Sometimes people say they have 'cluster migraines'. Certainly, during a bad run migraine days can group together, but cluster headache is a separate kind of headache.

Despite having distinctive features in its typical form, cluster headache is not always recognized. In the past it could take up to 10 years for a proper diagnosis to be made! If you (or someone you know) may have cluster headache, it is important to get medical advice and access to effective treatments. Over-the-counter painkillers and self-help treatments are of no value in this incredibly severe headache.

Features of cluster headache

These vary from person to person and even attack to attack. You may not have every feature every time, but here are some of the main ones.

Intense, excruciating pain

This is felt on one side of your head only. Pain is never mild. It is often on the right side but can vary between attacks. It usually occurs in and around your eye. Sometimes it moves from behind your eye, feeling as though the eye itself is being pushed out. It can be in the temple region or spread to another part of the head. Pain feels like stabbing or boring like a knife, rather than having a throbbing quality. Pain comes on quickly with no warning and peaks within a matter of minutes. There is no gradual worsening, as seen with other types of headaches.

Intermittent, short pain attacks

These last between 15 minutes and 3 hours, if they are untreated. This is relatively short compared with migraine pain, which typically lasts 4–72 hours. They occur from once every other day to up to eight times a day. This can also happen at night, often waking you soon after falling asleep. It is easy to become exhausted.

Predictable attacks

The attacks often occur at exactly the same time each day or night. Likewise, bouts can start at the same time once or twice a year. Sometimes with the changing of the seasons, some people can also predict the onset of their bouts with amazing accuracy. How often they occur distinguishes the type of cluster headache you have.

One-sided accompanying symptoms

The symptoms occur just on the affected side of your head. This can seem very odd, but the other side is completely normal. Symptoms include a red eye, tears from the eye, a blocked or running nostril, a sense of fullness in the ear, and sweating and/or flushing on one side of the face or forehead. A smaller pupil, eyelid drooping and eyelid swelling can also occur on the affected side. They are difficult to observe on yourself. It may be your partner who notices changes during an attack, which can be minimal or quite marked and persist afterward. Symptoms such as nausea and light sensitivity associated with migraine are not typical in cluster headache, but they can occur. Sensitivity to light and sound may be just on the affected side. This is another difference from migraine.

Restless, agitated behaviour

Restless and agitated behaviour during an attack means you often cannot keep still. This is unlike migraine, in which the urge is to lie down. The need to pace about or rock back and forth can be uncontrollable. You may hold your head or bang it against the wall. Some people seek fresh or really cold air on their faces, which can help slightly. Severe pain can provoke unusually aggressive behaviour. Knowing that they cannot control themselves makes some people want to be left completely alone. You may not want to be touched or comforted, and this can be very difficult and disturbing for those trying to support you.

Neil, 43

'I have had clusters regularly twice a year for the past 4 years. They last for about 6 weeks. They always come around the same time in March and September. I never plan anything important at these times. I get about four attacks a day. Two of these are always during the night, and I always seem to get one about 3 pm in the afternoon. My colleagues know that that they should just leave me alone, and we never plan a meeting for then!'

Types of cluster headache

The two types of cluster headache are distinguished by how often the headache attacks occur.

Episodic cluster headache

This affects about 80–90 per cent of people with cluster headache. Headache attacks cluster in episodic bouts lasting from 2 weeks to 6 months, with an average of about 6 to 12 weeks. The bouts of daily or near daily headaches occur two or three times a year. The onset may be at the same time each year and you know when it is coming. Sometimes there are gaps of several years between bouts.

Chronic cluster headache

This affects about 10–20 per cent of people with cluster headache. The cluster headache attacks don't have distinct bouts with pain-free gaps (remissions). Any remissions last less than a month and there is often no obvious pattern to your attacks. Episodic can evolve to chronic cluster headache in around ten per cent of people but we don't know why and it cannot be predicted. Chronic cluster headache is more difficult to treat and control than the episodic type. Fortunately, about 30 per cent of people with chronic cluster headache switch to the episodic type.

Who gets cluster headache?

Although cluster headache is rare, it still affects around 3 people per 1000 in the UK. Cluster headache may be even more common but is under-diagnosed. Prevalence (the number of people who have it) in the UK is similar to that of multiple sclerosis, which is far more widely recognized. Anyone can develop cluster headache, including children, but it typically occurs in people between 20 and 40 years of age.

Unlike migraine and tension-type headache, cluster headache affects about five times more men than women. The proportion of women may be increasing. This could be due to better recognition, because women traditionally have been diagnosed with migraine instead. There is a type of headache similar to cluster headache that mainly affects women – paroxysmal hemicrania. Attacks are much shorter than in cluster headache, lasting for only seconds or minutes. Paroxysmal hemicrania does not respond to cluster headache treatments. However, it does respond – almost magically – to an anti-inflammatory drug called indometacin. Hemicrania continua, another headache in the TAC group, is also responsive to indometacin, but in higher doses. As the name suggests the severe pain of this headache is continuous.

Causes of cluster headache

Despite current research, we do not yet know the cause and mechanisms of cluster headache. The timing of cluster headache attacks is a fascinating phenomenon. The striking annual regularity with the changes of seasons and attacks at exact times each day during a bout suggest links with circadian rhythms or the body clock. Research has focused on this biological clock, which is controlled by a part of the brain called the hypothalamus. Recently, positron emission tomography (an imaging technique, also known as PET) has suggested that this area is abnormally active during attacks of cluster headache and may generate the pain. The inflammatory substance calcitonin gene-related peptide (CGRP) which is implicated in causing migraine, has also been found to be elevated during episodes of cluster headache.

Cluster headache may be inherited in about five per cent of cases. We are not sure how significant a genetic link is in relation to other factors such as environmental triggers.

Triggers for cluster headache

Triggers are mostly significant in chronic cluster headache or during a bout of episodic cluster headache. They do not tend to provoke new bouts. Here are the main ones.

- *Alcohol* can trigger an attack within half an hour in about 90 per cent of those with cluster headache. This is quite different from migraine, in which the effect is delayed. Alcohol is not usually a problem when you are outside a cluster bout. Some people recognize when they are emerging from a cluster episode by their tolerance to alcohol. Specific foods don't appear to trigger cluster headaches.
- *Smoking* is associated with cluster headache. Sixty per cent of people with cluster headache are smokers, and a further 20 per cent have smoked previously. Despite this association, smoking does not cause cluster headache or trigger individual attacks. Stopping smoking is not guaranteed to help but it is highly recommended for general health. There is some suggestion that heavy smokers are more likely to develop chronic cluster headache.
- *Sleep* is a definite trigger, with up to three quarters of attacks occurring at night. They often coincide with REM (rapid eye movement) sleep only an hour or two after falling asleep. You may dread the night because attacks often wake you. There may be an association with sleep apnoea, which is when breathing stops for short periods during sleep.
- *Elevated temperature*, either due to environmental temperature changes or to exercising, can provoke attacks.
- *Exposure to volatile substances* such as solvents, oil-based paints and other chemicals with strong smells can act as a trigger. Nitroglycerine, histamines and monosodium glutamate are also triggers.
- *Relaxation* can provoke attacks. Unlike migraine, stress is not a trigger with cluster headaches, which often start when you relax or go to sleep.
- *Air travel* is another potential trigger, possibly related to changes in altitude or changes in time zones, which upset the biological clock.
- *Head injury* 1 or 2 weeks before the first cluster headache occurs

in about one to two per cent. It is not regarded as a typical trigger and is difficult to assess, because head injury is common in the general population.

Does cluster headache improve?

Your pattern of cluster headache is impossible to predict. Some people have recurring attacks of pain, whereas others enjoy remissions for a decade or more. We don't know why episodic cluster headache evolves to the chronic form in a minority – about ten per cent. Fortunately, the general pattern for all cluster headache types is one of improvement over the course of a life time. Encouragingly, attacks can become much less frequent as you get older and often disappear altogether.

9

Coping with cluster headache

Cluster headache is an excruciating headache. It is called 'suicide headache', and with good reason. Unfortunately, self-help treatments don't work. Over-the-counter painkillers and tablets are not absorbed via the stomach quickly enough to provide relief. You can try a self-help and non-drug approach, because anything that promotes general health and well being may help you. However, we have no scientific evidence of specific benefits.

You need medical help to cope with cluster headache, and a visit to your doctor is important for diagnosis. It is best if your doctor understands your condition so that you can work together to find effective treatments. GPs are supportive, but few will have encountered cluster headache in general practice. If cluster headache is not recognized it can be mistreated as migraine. Do seek another opinion and referral to a headache specialist doctor if you need more help. Although there is no cure, medical treatments can help enormously.

Coping with cluster headache with medical treatments

Doctors use treatments in two main ways. Symptomatic (acute) treatments deal with cluster headache once it starts and preventatives are taken daily. The two types of treatment are used together to achieve maximum benefit. Preventatives are continued for at least 2 weeks longer than the usual duration of the cluster bout, to be confident that it has completely finished. The preventative dose is then tapered down slowly. Additionally, specialists may use a short-term course of preventatives such as steroids to abort the cluster headaches quickly while waiting for long-term preventatives to take effect. This is called a bridge therapy. Afterward a maintenance preventative therapy may be used until the end of the cluster bout, or continuously in the case of chronic cluster headache.

Treatments for cluster headache symptoms

Generally, tablet forms of medications are not effective because they don't work quickly enough.

Sumatriptan injection

Trials show that sumatriptan injection is effective in about 75 per cent of people with cluster headache. It can stop cluster attacks in 15–30 minutes. Sumatriptan injection is licensed for use in cluster headache and is available on prescription. Although many people don't like injecting themselves, the auto-injector device is simple to use. Generally, the discomfort is minimal compared with the pain of the headache.

The injection can only be used twice in 24 hours, with at least 2 hours between doses, which is why it is combined with other treatments. It can be used long term in chronic cluster headache. Sumatriptan can't be used by people with heart problems or high blood pressure. Medication overuse headache can occur in the treatment of cluster headache and is more likely if you or your family have migraine.

Susan, 34

'The injections work well for me and the attack has usually gone in 15 minutes. I can feel it beginning to work before then, which is such a relief. I always carry the injection with me in case of an attack so I can use it at the start. It doesn't work as well otherwise. I use a lot of injections when I'm in a cluster. The last bout was the first one in 3 years and I only ever use the injections during cluster bouts. The injections are expensive, but my GP is very supportive, as he knows how devastating my cluster headaches are without them.'

Oxygen therapy

Oxygen delivered at 100 per cent with a high flow rate can stop cluster attacks within 15–30 minutes. It is not specifically licensed for use in cluster headache, being more commonly used at low flow rates for chest or breathing problems. However, recent research suggests that oxygen should be widely available for cluster headache. It can help more than two thirds of people and is safe to use without any side effects. Once your diagnosis is confirmed, your doctor can prescribe it 'off-label' (p. 143). Oxygen is easy to use but it is vital to obtain the correct equipment and use it properly if you are to gain benefit.

Tips for obtaining and using oxygen therapy

- Your doctor can send a Home Oxygen Order Form (HOOF) to your regional supplier. If an initial form is completed as an emergency order, the oxygen should be delivered to your home on the same day. The doctor can complete a second non-urgent request at the same time, to ensure ongoing supply.
- Make sure you are using oxygen at a high enough rate. You need 100 per cent oxygen at 7 to 12 litres per minute with a non-rebreathe mask. Experiment to find the effective rate. Adjust the head strap for a snug fit. Masks with holes are not effective.
- Sit upright and lean slightly forward, if possible. Follow the safety instructions and remember not to smoke near the cylinder.
- Try to use oxygen early in an attack. This gives the treatment the best chance of working. It can work quickly within 5 to 10 minutes, but you may need to experiment. People often use it for about 15–20 minutes. Keep using the oxygen until the attack has gone completely – otherwise it can come back.
- If you find oxygen to be effective, ask your doctor for a standard oxygen cylinder for home use and a portable one for elsewhere. Both types come with built in regulators so that you can obtain the high flow rate.
- An oxygen cylinder may not last long if your attacks are frequent, so ask your doctor for a second cylinder. Always have the empty cylinder replaced promptly, so that you are not caught without a supply.
- Oxygen concentrator machines that provide 1 to 5 litres per minute are insufficient and ineffective for treatment of cluster headache.

Daniel, 31

'Oxygen was a great discovery. I didn't think it worked at first, but then I realized I was not using the right mask and the flow rate was too low. My GP got that changed, and I now have a cylinder in my office and at home next to my bed. I am never far from one if an attack comes on. I can feel it working within a few minutes and I usually continue the oxygen for about 15 minutes until the attack goes completely. It is helpful at night and means I can get some sleep instead of getting exhausted with the pain.'

Other acute treatments

Sumatriptan or zolmitriptan nasal sprays can work well although not usually as quickly as oxygen and sumatriptan injection. Other drugs sometimes used are octreotide by subcutaneous injection, intravenous dihydroergotamine (DHE), and lidocaine in nose drops or a spray. In terms of self-help techniques during an attack, most people are too agitated to think about relaxation or deep breathing exercises. No complementary therapies have been shown to be an effective alternative to medication. Application of hot or cold packs and biofeedback may help to reduce the pain in addition to standard treatments.

Preventative treatments for cluster headache

Most people with cluster headache will require headache prevention therapy and different regimens are often used at the same time. Currently, the most effective preventatives are verapamil and steroids, given in tablet formulation with specially tailored dose plans.

Verapamil

The first choice is often verapamil. This is used in low doses to treat high blood pressure and heart conditions, including angina, but it is also effective at preventing cluster headache. Do not be alarmed that high doses may be required to control your cluster headache. The doses start low and are gradually increased as necessary. The effective dose is maintained for the anticipated duration of the cluster and then gradually reduced over 1 to 2 weeks. It can be increased if attacks recur and may be used long term in chronic cluster attacks. We don't have any evidence that long-term use in episodic cluster headache can stop further bouts.

At high doses verapamil can affect the heart in some people. So heart tracings called ECGs (electrocardiograms) are done regularly to monitor any changes. Other side effects include constipation and gum problems, and so a high-fibre diet and good dental hygiene are important.

Steroids

A 5-day course of prednisolone in reducing doses is effective at rapidly stopping cluster attacks. This short-term prevention can be helpful while waiting for other longer term treatments (e.g. verapamil) to take effect. Unfortunately, headaches usually recur when treatment is stopped, and the long-term side effects of possible infection and bone loss limit ongoing steroid use. Short-term side effects such as gastric irritation can be lessened by using a special tablet formulation called 'enteric coated'.

Other preventative treatments

Other preventative treatments include lithium, which can be moderately effective. Blood levels need monitoring to ensure that levels of the drug are adequate and to avoid toxic effects.

A half or a whole ergotamine suppository was a standard cluster headache treatment for many years, used for short bouts of cluster headache. Taken at bedtime, ergotamine may stop some night-time attacks. There is little evidence from clinical practice or research to suggest that pizotifen, sodium valproate, gabapentin, melatonin and botulinum toxin A (BOTOX®) are effective treatments for cluster headache prevention.

Small-scale studies of a nasal spray form of capsaicin called civamide suggest moderate benefit. There is interest in studying topiramate, an anti-epileptic that is helpful in preventing migraine. Some people have experienced benefit from greater occipital nerve injections of steroids or anaesthetic.

Other treatments for cluster headaches

Other treatments for cluster headaches may be regarded as invasive or non-invasive. Surgical treatments are invasive and are only considered for those with frequent cluster attacks (usually the chronic form) when standard medical treatments don't work. There is no guarantee of benefit and all surgery can have risks. We need much more research in this area and so far only small numbers of people have been treated.

Continuous stimulation of the occipital nerve at the back of the head, via an electrode placed under the scalp, can be of benefit in reducing painful attacks. This is known as occipital nerve stimulation. Because the hypothalamus has been shown in brain scans to be a possible origin of cluster headache, there is also interest in stimulating this area directly. This is called 'deep brain stimulation' and has shown some success in a small number of people with chronic cluster headache. This highly invasive procedure has the potential for devastating side effects such as stroke or even death.

Non-invasive treatments are likely to have fewer and less severe side effects. A recent study on a small number of people who have episodic and chronic cluster headache has suggested that vagus nerve stimulation (VNS) may be beneficial for both treating and preventing cluster headaches. A hand-held GammaCore® device which produced a mild electrical signal was held against the skin of the neck to stimulate the vagus nerve. Although much more research is needed, this study is exciting because the device is portable, convenient and is not associated with significant side effects like those from drugs or surgery.

James, 44

'My cluster attacks always start with slight "niggles" before a full-blown cluster begins. This is now the signal for me to start verapamil. I have used it for two previous bouts and it really helped. I still had some attacks in the early weeks, but somehow they didn't take hold. I was able to start reducing the verapamil after 6 weeks and they didn't start up again. Previous bouts tended to last 12 weeks, so this was a great improvement.'

Tips for coping with cluster headaches

- Get medical help and referral to a headache specialist. It is important that you find and work with a supportive doctor.
- A diagnosis of cluster headache can feel devastating and you may feel isolated. You are not alone and help is available.
- Get in touch with the Organisation for the Understanding of Cluster Headache (OUCH). This excellent charity provides useful information about coping with cluster headache. (See Useful addresses at the end of this book.)
- Report any side effects and changes in health to your doctor. Some treatments used for cluster headache need to be monitored.
- Keep a diary of headaches and associated symptoms. Diaries are helpful to assess whether the treatments are working.

- Use symptomatic treatments as early on in an attack as possible. Be prepared with your treatment for the next attack.
- Begin preventatives early in a cluster bout. They are more likely to prevent headaches quickly and may help symptomatic treatments to work better.
- If you sense that a bout of cluster headache is about to start, see your doctor to obtain your prescriptions and oxygen supply.
- Identify triggers if possible and avoid them if you can (e.g. alcohol). You don't need to stop exercising unless this is a trigger for you. If getting over-heated is a trigger, then take care to keep the central heating turned down low and take cool, rather than hot, baths and showers.
- Don't take naps during the day if you get night-time attacks. Naps may trigger daytime attacks too.
- Give up smoking. Although this may not affect the pattern of cluster headache, it reduces chances of other illnesses such as heart disease and you may not have to stop other treatments in the future.
- During a cluster bout, make allowances for how you feel. Don't plan activities that you don't need to do.
- Tell friends and colleagues about your cluster headache. During a bout you may just be concentrating on getting through the pain – those close to you will not understand what you are experiencing. Colleagues are more likely to be supportive (especially if you miss time from work) if you have explained what is happening.
- Let others know if there is anything that they can do to help. Your loved ones will be horrified at what you endure. Your colleagues will be scared of what they may have to witness. Everyone will feel terrible that there is little they can do. If there is something they can do – perhaps getting the hot and cold packs – then tell them. If it is best for them to simply stay away, then gently explain that too.

10

Daily headaches

Pauline, 42
Pauline rang me to volunteer for a clinical study on menstrual migraine. She had severe migraine at period time and less severe weekly attacks that she treated with triptans. I asked her about any other headaches. She told me that she also got fuzzy headaches every day and took painkillers for them most days. All her headaches were really getting her down.

Daily or nearly daily headache affects about four per cent of the adult population, mainly women. More than three quarters have had episodic headaches previously. Few people seek help from their doctor, and by the time they do they may have endured pain for a long time.

Reasons for developing daily headaches

Daily headache is a label (not a diagnosis) for headache of any type that regularly occurs on more than 15 days each month. We don't know why some people develop daily headaches and others escape, but several factors contribute.

Overuse of painkillers or triptans

Overuse of these medications can lead to medication overuse headache if you are regularly treating yourself on 2 or 3 days each week.

Changes in other headache

Changes in other headache such as migraine, tension-type headache and cluster headache from episodic to chronic forms can result in daily headaches. Development of additional headaches can be due to overuse of drugs and the most common cause of chronic migraine is medication overuse (see Chapter 11).

Underlying trauma, diseases and infections

These include sinusitis, neck and jaw problems, and temporal arteritis (a form of inflammation of arteries that is more common in older people). Frequent unchanged headaches for many years make a brain tumour unlikely. If headaches become progressively worse or are accompanied by other symptoms, see your doctor.

Rare daily headaches

These can be caused by high or low pressure in the brain. Other rare headaches (e.g. hemicrania continua) and new daily persistent headache can be of sudden onset. These are best assessed and treated by a specialist.

The influence of other risk factors

A combination of risk factors can influence any of the other reasons, and these include:

- poor sleep, including snoring and other sleep disturbances
- caffeine intake
- obesity
- genetic factors
- thyroid problems
- anxiety and depression
- stressful life events and
- being divorced, separated or widowed.

Other unknown reasons

Not everyone who has daily headaches will be over-using medications or have an identifiable cause for their headache. Other biological and psychological mechanisms that we do not yet understand may be the reason.

Coping with daily headaches

If your headaches are most days you are not alone. Here are the key aims as you cope with your headache.

Get help from a headache specialist

Do not put off seeking help. Daily headaches are more difficult to treat the longer you have had them. Sometimes, experts find it hard to distinguish headache types, especially if medication overuse is present. However, you can get help to prevent some headaches and to treat properly those you cannot avoid.

Identify your headache

You may have more than one type of headache. Keep a diary. Migraine, tension-type headaches and medication overuse headaches can all co-exist. If headaches can be identified and tackled separately, then it may be that by improving one type of headache the other(s) will benefit too.

Treat non-migraine headaches first

Tension-type headache and medication overuse headache typically make migraine worse and less likely to respond to any management strategies. The result is different types of headaches on most days and a tendency to overuse medication.

Deal with other medical issues

Any uncontrolled problem is likely to worsen headache. Consider all your health issues and tackle them separately, but remember that they affect you as a whole person.

Identify and avoid overuse of symptomatic treatments

Medication overuse is discussed in Chapters 11 and 12.

Identify and avoid other risk factors

This is not always possible but maintaining a healthy weight, getting enough sleep and cutting down on caffeine intake may help.

Find different ways of coping with the pain

You may need specialist help from a pain centre or clinic to deal with chronic pain. Combinations of physical and psychological approaches may be used to help, and your doctor may refer you (see Chapter 20).

11

Medication overuse headache

Penny, 35

'I have headaches all the time and I almost rattle with the amount of pills that I am taking. They don't really help, but if I don't take them every day then the headache is worse.'

Painkillers and triptans are part of our weaponry in the war against headaches and migraine. They are important to help us cope. However, use must be limited and appropriate, otherwise – instead of helping – the treatment makes the problem worse. This is called 'medication overuse headache' (MOH). Anyone with tension-type headache (TTH) or migraine who treats their headaches regularly with medication is at risk of developing MOH. Medication overuse is the most common cause of chronic migraine, although this cannot be confirmed until after drug withdrawal when headaches improve and migraine reverts to the episodic subtype.

What is medication overuse headache?

Symptomatic medications taken on 2 or 3 days each week on average, over several months, can cause MOH. Medications prescribed and taken daily to *prevent* headaches and migraine are not the problem. The issue is with medications used to *treat symptoms* of headache when it occurs. *All* symptomatic treatment may cause MOH. These include:

- opioids (e.g. codeine and dihydrocodeine)
- combination painkillers (paracetamol with codeine or aspirin combined with caffeine)
- ergotamine
- triptans used for migraine (e.g. almotriptan, eletriptan, naratriptan, rizatriptan, sumatriptan, zolmitriptan and frovatriptan)
- non-steroidal anti-inflammatory drugs (NSAIDs) (e.g. aspirin, ibuprofen, naproxen and diclofenac) and
- paracetamol.

Amount of medication needed to cause medication overuse headache

Low doses of symptomatic treatments on frequent days causes greater risk of MOH than large doses infrequently. The number of days of dosing in a month are important – not the number of doses in a day. This means that you can treat severe headache confidently using maximum daily doses of medication if necessary, but not too often. The guidance is as follows.

- Triptans, opioids such as codeine, combination painkillers and ergotamine should not be taken on 10 or more days per month.
- Simple painkillers such as aspirin, paracetamol and ibuprofen should not be taken on 15 or more days per month.

Features of medication overuse headache

Studies suggest 65 per cent of people with MOH have migraine, 27 per cent have TTH and the rest have both or other headaches. The MOH may be similar to your usual headache and/or it may be an oppressive dull ache that is constant or may wax and wane.

MOH is not progressive. It occurs most days and is often worse in the morning when medication levels in the blood are lowest. It can be aggravated by mental or physical effort such as exercise. Medication for symptoms or prevention and other treatments have little effect on it. If you try to stop medications your headache gets much worse.

Other symptoms may include tiredness, lethargy, irritability, forgetfulness, difficulty sleeping and constipation. Nausea and vomiting are less of a problem. Your daily activities may or may not be badly affected.

Who gets medication overuse headache?

Studies show MOH affects about two per cent of the general population. It affects five times as many women than men and also may occur in children and teenagers. Recent research suggests that MOH is more common in people who are overweight, depressed, have sleep disturbances or are smokers. MOH is frequent, increasing and happens worldwide, although the medications used vary.

MOH is common in those who seek help for their headaches. It is reported in at least ten per cent of those attending headache centres in Europe and up to 70 per cent in the USA. People often say that they have tried every medication and nothing works. They may have been to many doctors or therapists and none was able to help. Frequently, they are depressed about their headaches.

MOH develops in headache-prone people. People who do not have TTHs or migraine do not tend to develop MOH if they use painkillers for other conditions such as arthritis or back pain. People with these conditions who also have migraine should take particular care. MOH is less common with cluster headache, but may occur in those who have migraine or a family history of migraine.

Mechanisms of medication overuse headache

Addiction, a craving or a physical dependence is not usual with simple painkillers or triptans. It can happen with codeine and other opioids, caffeine, ergotamine, dihydroergotamine, barbiturates and sedatives. Psychological factors are important because you expect pain relief by taking medication, and this can be a hard habit to break. This can even be learned in childhood if your parents readily took painkillers.

The predisposition to MOH in those with migraine and TTHs could be genetic or due to biological changes in the brain. Specific mechanisms are unknown and may vary. Regular and repeated exposure to a drug could affect biochemical or nerve function and change pain receptor activation in the brain. Pain receptors may become switched on to give you a permanent sensation of headache pain or they could have a low threshold to produce pain.

Tips for preventing medication overuse headache

Medication overuse is often overlooked. You may be treating headaches with over-the-counter medications and doctors may not warn you in advance of prescribing drugs. Prevention while a headache is intermittent is best. Here are tips to help you.

- Limit triptan use for migraine to a maximum of 10 days per month.
- Limit painkillers to a maximum of 15 days per month.

- Remember that it is the number of days that you treat that is important – not the number of doses in a day.
- Avoid any drugs containing caffeine, codeine or other combination painkillers.
- Avoid barbiturates and tranquillizers.
- Avoid changing one drug for another. This is just as risky for developing MOH.
- Treat migraine early and with high-enough doses of medication. Add in anti-sickness medications to help nausea and – importantly – to prevent your gut from shutting down.
- If your usual medication is not very effective, or becomes less so, then check that you are using it correctly (i.e. at the right time, the right route and the right dose). Change your treatments if necessary.
- Keep a diary. Record all headaches and *all* medications you take, even on days that you do not have a headache. A bad month or two can happen from time to time – the concern is month after month of frequent headaches and frequent treatments.
- Distinguish migraine from other headaches. You may be treating headaches that would otherwise have gone away and therefore taking more treatments than you need to.
- Don't take treatments for headaches just in case one might develop. People often do this. It does not work and can increase your risk of MOH. It is much better to take a step back and assess your triggers, ensure that you have treatments that work if a headache develops and use preventatives if necessary.
- Be aware of the potential for MOH to develop quickly – even over weeks in some people.
- Don't delay seeking help if you think you need it. The longer that MOH continues, the more difficult it is to treat.
- Be honest with your doctor about the amount of medication you are using. Repeat prescription and over-the-counter purchases must all be discussed.
- Start preventatives and other strategies when headaches are becoming frequent but before you start over-using your medications. Preventatives are more likely to work and may reduce your risk of developing MOH.
- You could be at higher risk of MOH if you have other medical conditions. Get proper treatment if necessary. Be especially careful if you have to take painkillers for other conditions, which will often be made worse by MOH.

12

Treating medication overuse headache

If you have medication overuse headache (MOH), continued overuse of medications to treat symptoms will make your headaches worse and not better. Preventative medications and any complementary strategies you try are unlikely to be very successful. The only way to change this is to break the cycle and to stop the medications. If you can do this then there is a very good chance of significant improvement. Studies show that in the first 6 months around 70 per cent of people will have at least half the number of headache days. Many have even fewer. So it is really worth aiming for.

Tackling your MOH does not mean that you can't use medications for headache symptoms again, but in the short term you must stop. Most people find when their headaches become less frequent, medications – if used carefully and cautiously – become effective again.

How to stop medications

Stopping medications completely may be the best and quickest way for triptans, ergotamine and painkillers that do not contain codeine. Talk to your doctor if you are using codeine-containing medications or other types of drugs. A gradual withdrawal programme may be recommended, depending on the amount of codeine and type of drug you are over-using. You could start by taking your medication daily at fixed times only and then reduce the amount gradually over several weeks.

Drug withdrawal can usually be done as an outpatient with the support of your doctor and family. Referral to a specialist may be helpful, and sometimes hospitalization is advised to give you extra support over the first week, depending on what drugs you have been using. Drinking lots of water is particularly important.

What to expect when you stop medications

Because your body has become used to regular medications, you are likely to experience some 'withdrawal' symptoms when you stop the drugs. These include:

- aggravation of your headache, which temporarily can be severe;
- nausea and vomiting within a couple of days, which should gradually improve; and
- anxiety, restlessness, nervousness, insomnia and/or racing pulse.

Some people may worry about having fits and hallucinations when they withdraw from triptans and over-the-counter painkillers; fortunately, this has not been reported.

At their worst, severe symptoms last an average of 4 days. They usually start within 2 days of stopping the medication and begin to improve within 7 to 10 days for triptan overuse, 2 to 3 weeks for painkiller overuse, and 2 to 4 weeks with opioids such as codeine. If you have been using combination painkillers or mixing painkillers with triptans, then the whole withdrawal process can take 6 to 12 weeks. You should start to feel better during this time though, especially when the daily headaches begin to lift.

Supportive medical strategies

All over-used painkillers and/or triptans must be stopped completely – otherwise supportive strategies will not help. Research doesn't indicate which are best strategies, and they may vary between specialists.

- Naproxen can be used to aid recovery from MOH and replace your usual method of pain control. This non-steroidal anti-inflammatory drug (NSAID) is prescribed in a 6-week reducing regimen. It is taken daily at fixed times with food. If it irritates your stomach, then your doctor can prescribe additional medication.
- Amitriptyline can help to ease pain. It is prescribed over 3 months, starting with a low dose at night and increasing gradually.
- Anti-sickness medications such as domperidone or metoclopramide can be helpful.

- Migraine preventatives, including beta blockers (such as propranolol), topiramate, or botulinum toxin type A (BOTOX® – for chronic migraine) may be used. We need further studies to assess the best time to consider these. Some specialists commence before medication withdrawal whereas others wait. Preventatives are not lifelong therapies and the need for them will be reassessed regularly. They are typically tapered or discontinued after 6 to 12 months of successful treatment.
- Steroids such as prednisolone may be used in a reducing dose over 6 days.
- Greater occipital nerve injections of lidocaine and steroids may provide some relief of headache severity over 2 weeks to cover the worst period of withdrawal.
- Triptans may be prescribed by your doctor to treat severe migraine attacks soon after withdrawal, providing it was *not* triptans that you were over-using.

Dealing with headaches in the future

Headaches that remain after withdrawal are usually more obvious. A properly diagnosed headache and not a fuzzy, daily MOH is more likely to respond to medications, if they are used properly. Preventative treatments may be started and, although they have failed in the past, they may now be successful. Ongoing, regular follow up with your doctor and maintaining a diary is recommended, because your recovery will continue for some months. Studies show a relapse rate of up to 40 per cent within 5 years, so you must be on your guard. This is most likely during the first year, especially if you had a mixture of migraine and other headaches and/or combined your medications. We need more studies to find out why some people relapse and others don't.

If you are not taking medications and your headache didn't improve after withdrawal, your doctor may refer you to a headache specialist to confirm the diagnosis.

Coping with medication withdrawal

Stopping medication is never easy but it will be worth it. You won't get a 'miracle cure', but hopefully you can return to less frequent headaches, which respond to treatment. The daily headache should disappear and you can look forward to headache-free days. It seems unfair that you must prepare for even worse headaches during drug withdrawal. Remember, though, that it will only be for a relatively short time. Compared with the months and perhaps years that you may have battled with your headaches, the worst will be over quickly.

An awareness of what to expect can increase your ability to cope with withdrawal. The withdrawal may disrupt your life temporarily, so – apart from your willpower – gather whatever support you need to help you. The tips provided in the information box should increase your chances of success. Good luck!

Tips for coping with medication withdrawal

- Choose a time to suit you, so that you have the best chance of success and can ensure that support is in place. Also, try to choose a time of low stress if you can, but especially not when you are about to move house or have a big change at work. You might need some annual leave.
- If you are finding reasons not to do this, then deal with those reasons first. There may never be a perfect time!
- Plan to stop *all* painkillers or triptans *completely* unless you are on a medication-reducing schedule from your doctor. If the medication withdrawal is not complete, then you are more likely to relapse.
- Do as little as possible *or* keep busy. *Definitely* pamper yourself. There is no right or wrong way. Everyone is different. It will depend on how you feel.
- Ask for help if you need it; for example, help with childcare.
- Tell your family and friends. You will need their support and encouragement. Also inform colleagues at work.
- Discuss your medication withdrawal with your doctor. You will need support and perhaps some prescriptions, so plan a regular review. If you do not have a supportive doctor, seek a different one. Also consider going to a specialist headache centre.
- Find non-drug strategies to cope that are not painkillers. Some people find acupuncture, counselling or the principles of cognitive behavioural therapy helpful. Start relaxation and stress management therapies early on in the process. This will put you in a stronger position for coping in the long term.
- Keep a diary, even if it makes horrid reading. Even daily headache changes from day to day. After the medication withdrawal you will see how far you have come. It is always encouraging to see headache-free days, patterns become more obvious and it is easier to target treatment.
- Don't be ashamed. It is better to be open and honest about what is happening – both with yourself and those who are trying to help you.
- If frequent headaches don't go or they disappear and return again, have a chat with your doctor.
- Be positive and believe that you can do it. Even if you don't succeed you will be in a better position for success next time, because you will know what to expect and how medication withdrawal affects you.

13

Headaches, hormones and periods

About 80 per cent of people who attended the City of London Migraine Clinic were women. This is because of the influence of women's hormones on migraine. Oestrogen and progesterone rise and fall to create menstrual cycles during your reproductive life. At the menopause, when periods stop, these fluctuations dwindle. If you are sensitive to these normal changes you can get headaches and migraine. There does not have to be anything wrong with either you or your hormones! This chapter looks at hormones and headaches in relation to menstrual migraine, premenstrual syndrome and contraception.

Women, hormones and headaches

There is plenty of evidence suggesting female sex hormones have a lot to answer for. Perhaps you recognize yourself in the following.

- Until puberty boys and girls are equally affected by migraine. After puberty, when hormones change, more girls are affected.
- Migraine is three times more common in women during their reproductive years. It affects up to 25 per cent of women and only around eight per cent of men. It peaks in women in their forties when their hormones are changing.
- Fifty per cent of women with migraine notice a link with their periods.
- Many women notice headaches and migraine during the pill-free week when they are on the oral contraceptive pill.
- Around two thirds of women find that migraine improves during pregnancy.
- Migraine usually stops or improves after the menopause.
- Hormone replacement therapy can either help migraine or make it worse.

The burden of coping is difficult for women if headache patterns alter as hormones fluctuate. These fluctuations can be caused by your own hormone cycles or by external hormones you take for contraception or hormone replacement therapy. However, hormones are unlikely to be the sole headache trigger, so it is important to keep a perspective and not to forget non-hormonal triggers and lifestyle management, and to avoid medication overuse.

Menstrual migraine

This is migraine without aura specifically at period time. Although a small number of women report migraine in the middle of their cycle, we have no evidence supporting an association between migraine and ovulation. Menstrual migraine attacks start either 1 or 2 days before bleeding or on the first, second or third day. The attacks occur in at least two out of three menstrual cycles on average. Menstrual migraine is only properly diagnosed with diary records kept for at least three cycles. These are also essential for assessing response to treatments and the best timing for them.

Types of menstrual migraine

There are two subtypes.

- In pure menstrual migraine, attacks occur exclusively around the first day of the *period* and at *no other time* during the cycle. It is rare and affects less than ten per cent of women who have migraine.
- In menstrually related migraine, attacks occur around the first day of the period and *additionally* at other times during the cycle. This type affects up to 40 per cent of women who have migraine.

Women attending headache clinics often report that menstrual attacks are more severe than non-menstrual ones. Associated with more disability, nausea and vomiting, they are often less responsive to treatments, last longer and recur over several days.

Causes of menstrual migraine

The causes of menstrual migraine are unknown. Migraine triggers including environment, genetic tendency and changes in brain chemicals may combine with the additional trigger of hormone changes. There is no evidence of abnormal changes or levels in your hormones, which is why doctors do not do blood tests. You are just likely to be more sensitive to the normal hormonal changes.

There are two main hormones produced by the ovaries: oestrogen and progesterone. Studies in the 1970s suggested changes in oestrogen are most important for migraine. More recent work supports the 'oestrogen withdrawal' theory for some but not all women. This is the gradual drop in oestrogen that naturally occurs before a period. Oestrogen is unlikely to be the only factor, and the release of other chemicals called prostaglandins can also be associated with painful, heavy periods and menstrual migraines.

Treating menstrual migraine symptoms

There are no medications specifically for treating the symptoms of menstrual migraine. Clinical studies show that all of the anti-migraine drugs (triptans) can help with menstrual migraine. Some women find that standard painkillers and anti-sickness medications will suffice. Make sure that you are using your treatments optimally.

Preventing menstrual migraine with non-hormonal strategies

Menstrual migraine attacks are stubborn – you may eliminate most migraine attacks to find that the menstrual one still remains. There are no specifically licensed preventatives and research evidence is limited. Here are the main approaches used, and they may need to be combined.

- Non-drug approaches, including lifestyle management and trigger avoidance, are important. Menstruation is another step on the trigger ladder that can tip you over the migraine threshold. (The migraine threshold is discussed in Chapter 4.)
- Standard preventative treatments such as amitriptyline or propranolol may be helpful for both menstrual and non-menstrual attacks.
- Non-steroidal anti-inflammatory drugs (NSAIDs, e.g. mefenamic acid), started several days before the period and continued throughout (or on the days of heavy flow), can help by stopping release of prostaglandins. If your periods are unpredictable, you can start on the first day of the period. Naproxen is an alternative, but it does not help with heavy bleeding. These medications

can irritate the stomach so your doctor may prescribe additional protective medication.

- Preventative triptans have been used in research trials with some benefit. The best evidence is for frovatriptan. Specialists may recommend short courses, but additional triptans should not be used simultaneously.
- Magnesium taken daily can be effective but diarrhoea may be a side effect.

Preventing menstrual migraine with hormonal strategies

Severe menstrual migraine does not necessarily mean that hormonal treatment is required. Whether hormonal treatment is the best option for you depends on your individual circumstances, including need for contraception, other medical conditions (e.g. depression or high blood pressure) and how well your symptomatic treatments work. Hormonal treatments may work better if non-hormonal triggers are eliminated, but we do not have scientific evidence for this. Hormonal strategies that may be considered are as follows.

- Combined hormonal contraceptives, used by 'tricycling' or continuous pill dosing (see the section entitled 'Effect of hormonal contraception on headaches and migraine', p. 89), may be options if you do not have migraine with aura at other times in your menstrual cycle.
- Progestogen-only contraceptives such as depot medroxyprogesterone acetate injections which 'switches off' the ovaries might be useful. Periods are likely to stop and the oestrogen withdrawal trigger is lessened. This effect is less likely to happen with the desogestrel progestogen-only pill or implants, which allow the ovaries to continue to produce oestrogen.
- The Mirena® intra-uterine system is helpful in some women. It reduces the heavy period trigger by making the womb lining thinner. After some spot bleeding with early use, periods usually become lighter and may stop. The prostaglandin trigger for migraine is also reduced.
- Oestrogen supplements may stop the oestrogen withdrawal trigger. Supplements are not hormonal replacement therapy, in which additional progestogens are required to protect your

womb from oestrogen. Your doctor or specialist may prescribe supplements 'off-label' (p. 143) as gel or skin patches to be used around your period. Short courses of treatment are usually well tolerated but migraine may occur on stopping. You can only use this strategy if there are no contraindications for your use of oestrogen, you have predictable periods and you are ovulating regularly. This can be checked by blood tests. A home-use fertility monitor may be helpful to check ovulation and predict optimal timing of treatment.

- Gonadatrophin-releasing hormone analogues (e.g. goserelin), cause a reversible 'medical menopause' and are occasionally used by specialists for resistant, severe menstrual migraine. They are not widely used because they stop ovarian activity and cause severe oestrogen deficiency. This requires additional hormone treatments to prevent loss of bone density and hot flushes.

Preventing menstrual migraine with surgery

Surgery might seem the obvious solution to menstrual migraine. Unfortunately, it is not that simple, and hysterectomy is not recommended for migraine alone. Limited data suggest that hysterectomy with or without removal of the ovaries can actually aggravate migraine. In one study two thirds of women found that migraine worsened. This is because hormone cycles are controlled by a part of the brain called the hypothalamus. Hysterectomy removes only the end organs, or the last part of the process, and it does not tackle the root of the problem in the brain.

If you need a hysterectomy for other medical reasons (e.g. fibroids – growths in the womb), hormone replacement therapy may be recommended. There are some formulations of hormone replacement therapy that are less likely to aggravate your migraine attacks. (See Chapter 15.)

Denise, 44
Denise – a secretary and single mother of two – had been having migraine without aura since around the age of 12, when her periods began. Her daughter had started having headaches, and Denise was hoping that they would not follow her own pattern of severe migraines with her periods. Denise's mother also had migraine, which improved when her periods stopped at the menopause. Denise used to feel that this could not come soon enough for her and had

been wondering whether she should just get everything over with and have a hysterectomy.

Migraine was always worse for Denise at stressful times such as starting a new job and the terrible time when she got divorced. She remembers excruciating migraines during the pill-free week when she was using the oral contraceptive pill, but in contrast she was migraine-free during both pregnancies. Denise always noticed a link with migraine and her periods, and this has become worse in recent years. Her periods, still regular, had become heavier and more painful. Migraine attacks were usually much more painful during her periods, lasted up to 3 days, and were often associated with vomiting. She had to go to bed and miss work. Grandparents and neighbours were called at short notice to look after the children, making her feel guilty, which only makes things worse. Her GP, who diagnosed migraine, prescribed a triptan – a specific anti-migraine medication. Denise came to see us the City of London Migraine Clinic when the medication stopped working and she lived in dread of her period each month.

The specialist confirmed the diagnosis of migraine and reassured Denise that there were various strategies worth trying. The doctor advised that hormone tests, brain scans or operations would not help, and asked her to keep a diary for 3 months. In the meantime, Denise was encouraged to be strict about non-hormonal trigger factors and lifestyle issues. At her follow-up appointment, her diaries confirmed menstrually related migraine. Although non-menstrual attacks were greatly reduced and better controlled using aspirin and metoclopramide (an anti-sickness drug), menstrual attacks always needed a triptan repeated over several days. The doctor suggested changing the triptan to a longer-acting triptan and taking treatment earlier in the attack. Mefenamic acid (a non-steroidal anti-inflammatory drug; NSAID) was added for a few days only around period time to help both the migraine and also the heavier, painful periods.

These strategies, combined with Denise's efforts at managing non-hormonal triggers such as missed meals, overtiredness, dehydration and stress meant that she has regained control of her migraines and her life. She no longer lives in dread of her next period. If migraine occurs, her medication usually works well and she no longer misses time from work.

Premenstrual syndrome

Premenstrual syndrome (PMS) describes a range of symptoms in the week or so before your period, which usually subside when it starts. They often include tension-type headache and migraines. PMS is common and affects around two thirds of menstruating women. Although you might think that you are imagining things, this is a recognized syndrome. Symptoms include:

- tiredness
- difficulty sleeping
- irritability
- being tearful
- depression
- poor concentration
- breast tenderness
- abdominal bloating
- appetite change
- muscle and joint pain and
- acne.

Headaches and premenstrual syndrome

Headaches and migraines may be linked to the other PMS symptoms but we are not sure how. Migraine does not necessarily have the regularity and specific timing of menstrual migraine and the mechanisms may be different. We do not know whether specific changes in the hormone cycles cause PMS symptoms in some women. There are no hormone tests to diagnosis PMS, because the fluctuations are part of the normal menstrual cycle.

Coping with headaches and premenstrual syndrome

Some evidence suggests that the worse the PMS, the worse the headaches. So if you can reduce your PMS symptoms, your headaches may also improve. Diet and self-help measures may help both. The following measures may particularly help with PMS:

- reduce salt and sugar in your diet;
- take multivitamins and supplements such as vitamin B complex, calcium and magnesium;
- take herbal supplements such as evening primrose oil and *Agnus castus*.

If you need medical help to deal with PMS symptoms, then your doctor may suggest one of the contraceptive pills that stop ovulation. In some women this can lessen the symptoms.

Headaches and contraception

There are three groups of contraceptives: combined hormonal, progestogen-only and non-hormonal.

Combined hormonal contraception

Combined hormonal contraceptives (CHCs) include pills, patches and vaginal rings that contain both oestrogen and progestogen. They are safe and effective for the majority of women, even those with migraine. However, studies of combined oral contraceptive pills show an increased risk of ischaemic stroke (in which the brain is deprived of its blood supply) in young women. The risk increases with higher-dose oestrogen preparations. Overall, the chances of getting a stroke are low. An annual estimate is up to four per 100,000 healthy women who do not smoke. This is doubled to around eight if women are using combined oral contraceptive pills.

Studies have shown that migraine *with* aura (but not migraine *without* aura) is a marker for an individual at increased risk of stroke. So, if you have migraine with aura you must not use any of the CHCs for contraception, because this will potentially further increase your risk of stroke. See Chapter 2 for a description of aura, but talk to your doctor if you are unsure. If you develop your first aura while you are using a CHC, you must stop the CHC immediately. Get medical advice and use an alternative contraception method. Many of the progestogen-only methods are actually more effective at preventing pregnancy than CHCs.

Women with migraine without aura can use CHCs provided that they do not have other risk factors for stroke. These include heavy smoking, high blood pressure, high cholesterol, diabetes and obesity. You can continue to use all of the anti-migraine medications, including triptans, which do not appear to increase the risk further. Only ergots are not recommended. Your doctor will advise you if you use topiramate – it may reduce the effectiveness of some contraceptive pills.

Progestogen-only contraception

This type of hormonal contraception includes progestogen-only pills (POPs). There are two types of POPs – desogestrel POP and the traditional 'mini-pill' – which act in different ways.

Desogestrel POP primarily acts to prevent the monthly egg release (ovulation) while the 'mini-pill' has a local effect to thicken the secretions from the neck of the womb and create a physical barrier to sperm. These are taken daily. There are also injections of progestogen given every 3 months. Alternatively, an implant under the skin or a device inserted directly into the womb (intra-uterine) will release progestogen slowly and may be kept in place for several years.

We have evidence that progestogen-only contraceptives are not associated with an increased risk of stroke. They can be used if you have migraine, including migraine with aura.

Effect of hormonal contraception on headaches and migraine

Headaches and migraines may initially worsen during the first cycles of use but then improve with each cycle. Three months is a usual minimum, and headaches will often completely settle by 6 months. If they persist on CHCs, then changing to a progestogen-only or non-hormonal method may help.

Headaches and migraine typically occur during the hormone-free interval of the standard CHC pill regimen (21 days on/7 days off). The likely cause is oestrogen withdrawal – similar to that occurring in menstrual migraine. Some women may be sensitive to any drops in oestrogen. To avoid this, your doctor may recommend 'tricycling' (taking three pill packets back to back without a pill-free break). You then have only five withdrawal bleeds – and hopefully only five migraines – instead of 13 each year. Some specialists recommend continuous pill use (extended duration) without a break at all. There appear to be no health benefits of having the hormonal withdrawal bleed and this strategy can benefit menstrual migraine.

Non-hormonal contraception

Non-hormonal contraception includes coils, which do not release hormones, and barrier methods such as condoms and caps. They do not normally affect headache and migraine. However, the copper coil can increase bleeding, which may be associated with headache.

Tips for coping with hormonal headaches

- Keep a diary for at least 3 months to look for links between headaches and hormones. Include headaches, migraines and menstrual periods. Write down each time you take hormonal treatments (e.g. hormonal contraceptives and hormone replacement therapy) and any menopausal symptoms.
- Take time to get some exercise, adopt a regular sleep pattern and eat a balanced diet. Generally feeling healthier may mean that hormone fluctuations are less likely to trigger headaches.
- If simple strategies are not effective, if symptoms are very severe, or if your periods become heavy or painful or you have bleeding in between them, contact your doctor.
- Be informed about your body and try to become more aware of your own hormone cycles. By being 'in tune', you are more likely to cope with the headaches.
- Remember non-hormonal triggers. By reducing these first, sometimes a hormonal headache may be avoided altogether.
- If you decide to use hormonal treatments, give them a proper trial. It takes your body at least 3 months to adjust to additional hormones.
- Some hormone treatments have side effects of headaches, particularly with initial use. In a headache-prone woman, this can feel like a disaster. Don't expect too much too soon and hopefully you will feel the benefits when the headaches settle.

14

Headaches, pregnancy and breastfeeding

Having a baby is a special time but it can be overwhelming. With so much to think about, concerns about headaches can be an additional strain. Will my headache affect my chances of having a baby? What will happen to my headache when I am pregnant? I've just found out I'm pregnant – will headache medications have harmed my baby? Can I breastfeed and treat my headache? This chapter addresses these questions and offers ways to cope with headache before, during and after pregnancy.

The information is mainly related to migraine, but if you have tension-type headache, the advice is still relevant. If you have cluster headache then you are likely to be under the care of a specialist headache doctor. Some drug strategies should be stopped before you conceive and others started or continued in pregnancy under close medical supervision. Seek advice before you become pregnant, if possible.

Effect of headaches on having a baby

There is no evidence so far that women with primary headaches who are otherwise healthy are less likely to conceive. There is also no suggestion that you are at greater risk than the general population of miscarriage, stillbirth, birth defects or problems with growth and development of the baby. There is an increased risk of high blood pressure, blood clots, pre-eclampsia and eclampsia in women with migraine, especially if they are overweight. Midwives and doctors monitor all pregnant women very carefully for these potentially serious conditions, by checking blood pressure and urine protein levels. If you are a migraineur or develop migraine for the first time during pregnancy, let your healthcare professional know.

What happens to headaches in pregnancy?

Elizabeth, 41

'I have suffered from severe migraine with my periods since I was a teenager. The only time I ever had any respite was during my two pregnancies. It was bliss!'

For many women, especially those with migraine, headaches may be less of a problem during pregnancy. Around two thirds of women who have migraine notice improvement during pregnancy, particularly after the first trimester (3 months). Some women notice no change and a few get worse. Improvement is more likely with migraine without aura, which is linked to periods and can last during breastfeeding until menstruation returns. The reasons why this is so are unclear, because many changes occur in a woman's body during pregnancy. It may be related to higher or more stable levels of the hormone oestrogen, changes in blood sugar levels and higher levels of endorphins – the body's natural painkillers.

Non-hormonally related migraine and migraine with aura are less likely to improve. If women develop migraine for the first time in pregnancy, it is more commonly migraine with aura and may be just the aura without the headache. (See Chapter 2.) If you develop aura and/or any new headache while you are pregnant, it is important that you talk to your doctor, who will be able to reassure you or conduct further tests.

Tips for coping with headaches and preparing for pregnancy

Planning for pregnancy is a good time to think about your current headache coping strategies and optimize your general health before conceiving. This is particularly important if you use drug treatments, because these are more likely to affect a developing baby during the first 3 months, often before you know you are pregnant. Here are some ways to prepare.

- Ensure that your lifestyle is as healthy as possible. This will help you and your baby, and it may help with your headaches. This includes giving up smoking and alcohol, taking regular exercise and losing (or putting on) weight if necessary.
- Eat a balanced diet. Ensure that meals are regular. Avoid triggering a migraine by keeping blood sugar levels stable and avoiding dehydration.

- Take a vitamin supplement recommended for pregnancy that includes folic acid and iron.
- Try non-drug therapies to help headache. Migraine may improve during pregnancy and breastfeeding, and drug treatments – particularly preventatives – may no longer be required.
- Discuss with your doctor all medications you are taking, including herbal and over-the-counter treatments. Some may need to be stopped or changed.
- Limit drug treatments for headache symptoms to the first 2 weeks of your menstrual cycle if possible, because this is when you are least likely to be pregnant. These are the days of your period and approximately the next 10 days before you ovulate (release an egg from your ovaries).
- Medication overuse headache should be tackled before trying for a baby, if possible.

Coping without drugs during pregnancy and breastfeeding

There is a perception that any headache treatment that does not involve prescription drugs is milder, natural and therefore safer for your baby. It can be difficult to decide what is best for you and your baby. Ultimately, what you choose to do is a personal decision.

Physical and complementary therapies

Jane, 33

'I was keen to avoid all drugs when I was expecting my first baby so I tried a course of acupuncture. I told my acupuncturist that I was 6 weeks pregnant. My migraines stopped shortly after starting and so did my dreadful morning sickness. I felt well throughout the rest of my pregnancy and was really pleased that I did not need to take my usual migraine drugs.'

Physical and complementary therapies for headaches and migraine may be effective for some women while they are pregnant or breast-feeding. Simple techniques such as hot or cold packs on the head can be helpful, as can yoga, relaxation techniques, deep breathing and biofeedback. Acupuncture and massage, under the care of qualified practitioners, may be useful. Tell your practitioner that you are pregnant or breastfeeding, because this may influence the treatment. For example, some of the essential oils are not used in aromatherapy massage on pregnant women. The benefits of non-drug approaches may last beyond pregnancy and breastfeeding.

Herbal treatments and vitamins

Many women wonder about using herbs for migraine prevention during pregnancy. Unfortunately, these cannot be recommended. There's less information about safety for these products than for prescription medicines, which go through tough evaluation before they become widely available.

Of the herbs that have shown some effectiveness in migraine prevention, neither feverfew nor butterbur is recommended in pregnancy. Feverfew may cause bleeding problems and so should not be used. Ginger is reported to be helpful for treating morning sickness and may also be useful for the sickness associated with migraine attacks, although data are limited.

All pregnant women are recommended to take daily folic acid (400 mcg is the standard dose) in addition to vitamin D (10 mcg daily during pregnancy and breastfeeding). Vitamins B_2 and B_6 are sometimes used for migraine prevention, but the high doses required are not recommended during pregnancy and breast-feeding. A standard multivitamin preparation is a better option and may promote general health and wellbeing.

Coenzyme Q_{10} and magnesium have been shown to be beneficial for migraine prevention (see Chapter 18). Following discussion with your healthcare advisor, coenzyme Q_{10} and magnesium may be used during pregnancy with some limitations. They may help reduce the risk of pre-eclampsia in women at risk. Coenzyme Q_{10} (100 mg twice daily) may be used from week 20 of pregnancy onwards but not during early pregnancy or breastfeeding. Magnesium, at a reduced daily dose of 350 mg, may be used during pregnancy and breastfeeding.

If you decide to use herbs or diet supplements, minimize any possible risk. Read labels, purchase from a reputable source, use small amounts and ask your doctor, midwife or therapist for advice. New evidence on what is unsafe may become available. Evidence on what is actually safe is unlikely, because large-scale scientific clinical trials to provide evidence are not widely done.

Drug treatments for headache during pregnancy and breastfeeding

Sally, 28
'I was one of the unlucky ones as my migraines got much worse when I was pregnant. I was using paracetamol and my GP recommended a low dose of beta blockers for migraine prevention. I was worried about taking a tablet every day, but my attacks improved and I felt much better in myself. He explained that no medicines are "safe" in pregnancy but for the ones I was using, we did not have reason to think that they would harm the baby.'

Because it is unethical to carry out research trials to determine the safety of drugs in pregnancy and breastfeeding, we can't be certain how drugs will affect the growth and development of the baby. Information we have about safety is mostly circumstantial and very limited.

Your doctor and/or midwife will advise you on how to make the best decision for you and your baby. If you have been taking medications for migraine and discover that you are pregnant, then it is unlikely that you will have caused any harm. Even if drugs not recommended in pregnancy were accidentally taken, this in itself is not a medical reason to terminate the pregnancy. However, once you know that you are pregnant it is always best to use as few drugs as possible and in the lowest effective doses.

The lack of clinical trial data doesn't mean that you should not use medications at all, but it does mean that you need to make an informed choice by weighing up the risks and the benefits. Your doctor will carefully assess this for both you and your baby before he or she prescribes your treatment. Some cases of debilitating, severe headache may require effective treatment to avoid associated poor eating, poor sleep, dehydration and increased stress. All of these are unhealthy for both mother and baby.

Caution is still essential while breastfeeding because although medications are less restricted than during pregnancy, the drugs may pass from breast milk to the baby. This happens more readily with some drugs than with others.

Drugs to treat headache symptoms

Generally, paracetamol is the drug of choice. It may be used throughout pregnancy and breastfeeding because it does not appear to affect the baby. It is best taken in soluble form, ideally with something to eat. Aspirin is not usually recommended because it can cause problems with bleeding. It should always be avoided completely during the last 3 months of pregnancy and during breastfeeding.

Non-steroidal anti-inflammatory drugs (NSAIDs) are occasionally suggested in early pregnancy, but they should not be used during the last trimester. They may be used in breastfeeding as the concentration in breast milk is very low and unlikely to affect the baby. Codeine is not recommended for migraine because it can aggravate nausea. If you need it for other reasons, occasional low doses of codeine in combined painkillers are probably not harmful during pregnancy and breastfeeding. Ergotamine should not be used in pregnancy because it can increase the risk of miscarriage. It is not recommended in breastfeeding because it may stop milk production.

Triptans in pregnancy and breastfeeding

Healthcare professionals are encouraged to report pregnancy outcomes to databases of safety information on triptans used to treat migraine. The evidence, so far mainly from the Sumatriptan/Naratriptan/Treximet Registry, is reassuring but still limited. The number of women is small, data reporting is biased and there is little information from the later stages of pregnancy. Therefore, the general use of triptans in pregnancy cannot be recommended. Data suggest that sumatriptan can be used in pregnancy and breastfeeding but as this is 'off-label' (p. 143) it should only be taken under the guidance of a healthcare provider. Because there are fewer data for the other triptans, the current advice is to exercise caution in breastfeeding. In practice this means waiting for 24 hours before breastfeeding if you have used almotriptan, eletriptan, frovatriptan, naratriptan, rizatriptan or zolmitriptan for migraine.

Anti-sickness medications

Domperidone, buclizine, chlorpromazine, metoclopramide and prochlorperazine are not reported to cause harm during pregnancy and breastfeeding. Discuss with your doctor which is the best one for you. During breastfeeding, domperidone – which can increase milk production – is preferred to metoclopramide.

Drugs to prevent headache symptoms

Migraine often improves during pregnancy, so this is a good time to consider stopping daily preventatives. Occasionally, preventative drug strategies are commenced if headaches are frequent and severe or to reduce the amount of symptomatic medications.

The recommended preventative is the beta blocker propranolol, at the lowest effective dose. Although this has been widely used, it is usually stopped a few days before delivery because it can slow the baby's heart rate, cause low blood sugar levels in the baby and affect contractions. Other preventatives such as low doses of amitriptyline are sometimes used. In the absence of epilepsy, the anti-epileptics are not recommended because some may cause birth defects. We currently do not have published data regarding the use of botulinum toxin A (BOTOX®) for chronic migraine, during pregnancy and breastfeeding.

After delivery and breastfeeding

About 30–40 per cent of women have a migraine or headache within a few days of delivery. This can be very severe and may be due to hormonal changes such as a drop in oestrogen levels and endorphin levels returning to normal. Dehydration, extreme exhaustion and low blood sugar levels may also be significant. Their need for effective drug treatments for headache can make some women reluctant to start breastfeeding. Others give up prematurely for the same reason. However, headaches often settle down again, so if you do want to breastfeed it would be a shame not to. Breastfeeding provides complete nutrition for your new baby with protection from diseases and infections. It may also maintain a protective effect against migraine if your attacks improved during pregnancy. Although it can take a little while to establish, breastfeeding is highly recommended.

Tips for coping with headaches during pregnancy and breastfeeding

- If your headaches stay the same or get worse, this doesn't mean that there is anything wrong. Speak to your doctor for reassurance.
- You should always see your doctor if you develop any *new* headaches or unusual accompanying symptoms. He or she may run tests if necessary.
- Don't forget to avoid your usual headache triggers. Take extra care to avoid becoming dehydrated and eat little and often. This can be difficult if morning sickness is causing low blood sugar and dehydration. Ginger in tea or biscuits may be helpful. When you have had your baby and routines change, continue to avoid these triggers.
- Avoid overtiredness, which is a migraine trigger. This is important during the first and last trimesters (3 months) of pregnancy. It can be impossible with a new baby, but aim for a regular sleep pattern as soon as you can. Accept offers of help and get into a routine that allows you the rest that you need.
- Minimize additional stress if you can. Take exercise, have a massage, do things you enjoy and order shopping online. Don't feel guilty about making things easier for yourself. Avoiding headaches is better than treating them, but especially when options are more limited.
- Make time to continue with helpful non-drug treatments once you have had your baby.
- If you need medication for headaches, ask your doctor about those that are considered low risk during pregnancy and breastfeeding.
- Medication overuse can occur in pregnancy. Be aware of this possibility if you are regularly treating headache symptoms on 3 days a week.
- Anticipate the possibility of a severe headache in the early days after delivery and have potential treatments available. Discuss options with your healthcare team in advance.
- Try not to give up breastfeeding if you have headaches during the first few days after delivery. If you suffered from hormonally related headaches before pregnancy and they improved during pregnancy, they may settle down in the first few weeks. (Often when you stop breastfeeding and periods return, the headaches

come back, but by that time you will have more treatment options anyway.)

- Keep your baby's exposure to drugs to a minimum by considering the time at which you take your medication. Dosing immediately after breastfeeding or waiting until after the last feed of the day when the baby has a longer sleep can make a difference.
- Express and throw away breast milk while you are treating a migraine attack with non-recommended medications, such as triptans. Even though you feel unwell, it is worth doing to encourage ongoing milk production. It also helps to prevent your breasts becoming engorged and uncomfortable.
- Keep a supply of expressed breast milk in the freezer for use when you are unable to breastfeed, having taken medications. Alternatively, have a supply of formula milk ready to use.

15

Headaches, menopause and HRT

Sarah, 48
'My migraines got much worse in my early forties and have controlled my life in recent years. I can't wait for the menopause to arrive because I am hoping that the migraines will stop along with the periods. My mother's headaches got better after the menopause and I hope mine will too.'

The menopause

The menopause is the time of your last menstrual period and marks the end of your reproductive life. The average age for menopause is around 51 years, but it can happen from any time between 40 and 60. Medically, the definition of menopause is no periods for 12 consecutive months after the age of 50 or for 2 years under the age of 50. Until menopause is confirmed you should still use adequate contraception.

The perimenopause

The perimenopause is the time of change that leads to the menopause. Your hormone cycles begin to change and become disrupted. Menstrual periods are more erratic – sometimes closer together and at other times further apart. They may also become heavier and more painful. This time, the 'climacteric' or simply 'the change of life', can last up to 20 years.

Symptoms of the perimenopause

Hormone changes and fluctuations can be accompanied by many symptoms. Sometimes severe, they are mainly due to low oestrogen levels. These include more frequent and severe headaches and migraines, which are often linked to periods. Other troublesome symptoms can include:

- irregular periods – often shorter cycles and then missed periods;
- hot flushes and night sweats;
- mood changes – irritability, anxiety and depression;
- dry skin, hair and eyes;
- poor memory and concentration;
- weight gain;
- sexual problems – dryness and/or itching of the vagina, painful intercourse and loss of interest in sex;
- loss of energy and sleep disruption;
- muscle and joint pain;
- urinary problems – infections, urgent need to urinate and leakage when coughing or running; and
- heart palpitations.

The presence of some of these symptoms in a woman over 40 is enough to confirm the perimenopause, and so blood tests are not usually necessary.

Types of headaches around the menopause

Although migraine is strongly influenced by female hormones, not all headaches occurring around the menopause are migrainous in nature and tension-type headache can occur too. Fortunately, cluster headache is not only less common in women but it also seems to improve with increasing age. There appears to be no association with female hormones. Daily headaches made worse by daily medications can be a particular problem at this time of life.

Change in headaches around the menopause

If you have headaches related to oestrogen withdrawal, then you should be able to expect an improvement after menopause. This is because oestrogen levels decline in the first year after menopause and then remain low and stable. Although, we can't reliably predict what will happen, there is a good chance that migraine will improve. However, it can take between 2 and 5 years after menopause for the hormones to settle down and cease to be a trigger.

One study found that almost two thirds of women who had history of migraine noticed an improvement after menopause was established. Around ten per cent had worse headaches and 25 per cent did not notice any change. Another study found 53 per cent less migraine without aura in postmenopausal women. Migraine with aura may change less after menopause than migraine without aura. Interestingly, time since menopause was more important than having migraines with menstruation previously. This implies that it isn't just the reduced influence of hormonal factors that improves migraine, but retirement and reduced stress may also be involved. Neck stiffness or other ailments as you get older may contribute to worsening headaches.

Coping with headaches around the menopause

Despite the menopause being a natural change to your body, headaches and migraines are part of a range of menopausal symptoms that add up to make you feel really unwell. This has a negative impact on your whole life. Some women are not badly affected but others are severely incapacitated physically or mentally, or both. Recognizing this is important, and there are ways to improve how you feel that do not involve hormone replacement therapy (HRT). The better you feel overall, the better you will cope with your headaches. Unfortunately, if your menopause symptoms are troublesome, then you are more likely to be prone to them.

Don't tackle menopause symptoms in isolation and remember measures to cope with headaches too! Migraine triggers add up. If you are exhausted from broken sleep due to night sweats, then this tiredness could trigger an attack, regardless of your hormones. If many symptoms are combining to make you feel awful, sometimes an improvement in just one symptom can help.

Coping without drugs

Despite little scientific evidence, around half of women report that self-help and complementary measures benefit their menopausal symptoms. Although less effective than HRT, they are worth trying, especially if you don't wish to use HRT or can't use it for health reasons.

Exercise

Evidence suggests that aerobic exercise like swimming can be beneficial for menopausal symptoms, and all weight-bearing exercise is good for maintaining strong bones. Exercise may be helpful for your headaches, but eat enough and don't become dehydrated or this can be a trigger. Get into a sensible routine – overdoing it every now and then will make you feel worse.

Plant oestrogens (phytoestrogens)

These are also called isoflavones and are obtained from soy and red clover. This way of supplementing oestrogens may be helpful and is being researched. We don't have any long-term safety data. You should not use isoflavones if you have a condition in which oestrogen is not recommended (e.g. breast cancer). So far, data on whether they can help or trigger migraine is conflicting.

Diet and supplements

Try to eat a balanced diet and keep to a healthy weight. Hot flushes and night sweats may be reduced both in number and severity by reducing alcohol and caffeine. If you cut down on tea and coffee, do it gradually to avoid a caffeine withdrawal headache. Avoid headache tablets containing caffeine.

We have no evidence that supplements of vitamin E, vitamin C, selenium or evening primrose oil bring particular benefits. Although evening primrose oil may help with breast tenderness, it can cause headache as a side effect.

Agnus castus may help symptoms of premenstrual syndrome, but there is no evidence for its ability to help with menopausal symptoms. Dong quai, *Ginkgo biloba*, ginseng, St John's wort and black cohosh have all been widely used. Some women experience improvement but some of these are known to interact with medications and may have side effects, including headaches.

Complementary therapies

Although scientific studies have not demonstrated significant improvements and more long-term trials are needed, some women have found benefit from acupuncture and homeopathy. Tell your therapist about all your headaches and symptoms.

Ingrid, 53

'My migraines became more frequent as I got older. Broken sleep from night sweats made me really tired and I'm sure that made things worse. I felt like I could get a migraine at any time, all the time. I realized I would have to take more care of myself – I'd been too busy before! I started using red clover. I tried to eat regular meals, have more water instead of coffee and get more early nights. After about 6 months I felt much better. I think the red clover and a few changes made a difference to get me through a difficult time. I had my last period 2 years ago and hardly ever have a migraine now.'

Prescription drugs (non-hormone replacement therapy)

There are several alternatives to HRT, and some may have a positive influence on headaches and migraines.

Selective serotonin re-uptake inhibitors

Selective serotonin re-uptake inhibitors (also known as SSRIs) include fluoxetine and paroxetine and are widely used as anti-depressants. They have also been shown to help severe sweating and flushing symptoms associated with menopause and may help migraine and headaches. Another type of anti-depressant called venlafaxine can be helpful. To minimize the likelihood of side effects, doses are usually lower than for depression. Headaches can worsen in initial months, so don't give up too soon.

Gabapentin

This anti-epileptic has been found to reduce symptoms of flushes, aches and pains in many menopausal women. Although it is used in migraine prevention, there is no good scientific evidence of it working well. Doses are started low and increased gradually to minimize side effects, which can include dizziness and sedation.

Clonidine

Used to control blood pressure, clonidine may be helpful in reducing hot flushes in some women. Although it is licensed for migraine prevention, there are other more effective preventative treatments available. Side effects include dizziness, sedation and worsening of any depression.

Hormone replacement therapy and headaches

HRT is not recommended if your only menopause problem is headache. It is far better to use standard headache strategies, and for many women they are enough to cope well. However, if you are battling with severe menopausal symptoms in addition to your headaches, then HRT may be worth considering. It does not suit all women, but for others it can transform their life.

What is hormone replacement therapy?

HRT remains the best treatment and can improve menopausal symptoms for over 80 per cent of women. It is prescribed with the aim of balancing hormones. The main component is oestrogen, because many of the troublesome symptoms of the menopause are believed to be due to low oestrogen levels. If you haven't had a hysterectomy, you will also need to take a progestogen. This reduces the risk of oestrogen causing thickening and over-stimulation of the endometrium (lining of the womb). This is important because otherwise cancerous changes can develop. HRT doesn't always suppress the normal menstrual cycle, nor is it contraceptive.

Migraine, health risks and hormone replacement therapy

HRT has had bad press in recent years for all women, not just those who have migraine. There have been concerns over long-term safety, risks of breast and other cancers, heart disease, blood clots and strokes.

Although there are few data, no evidence so far suggests that having migraine with or without aura poses an additional health risk. This means provided that all your other risk factors have been taken into account by your doctor, having migraine alone will not stop you from taking HRT. You can continue your migraine treatments, including triptans and prevention medications, while you are using HRT.

Effect of hormone replacement therapy on headache and migraine

Few clinical studies have considered the impact of HRT on non-migraine headache and results have provided conflicting information. Some women notice an improvement, others no change and some find that their headaches get worse.

In theory, if you have hormonally related migraine then you should benefit from the stabilizing of oestrogen levels with HRT. Although some women do benefit greatly, this doesn't always happen. Data from questionnaire studies suggest that using HRT can aggravate migraines in some women, and this seems more likely if your migraines worsened during the perimenopause. We need more research on who might develop headache problems on HRT. There is some suggestion that if you had premenstrual syndrome then you may be more prone to the headache side effects of HRT.

In practice, we can't predict whether you will benefit or not. It is trial and error to find the HRT that suits you best. If your menopause symptoms are severe and affecting your life, find out whether HRT is an option and discuss the pros and cons with your doctor.

Best hormone replacement therapy for headaches

Joan, 50

'I had terrible hot flushes, which were so embarrassing. At night the sweats drenched me and I often needed to change the sheets. I was getting tired and depressed. Although the HRT tablets my GP prescribed worked wonders with the flushes and sweats, I got severe migraines all the time. The GP switched me to using HRT patches you wear on your skin. This suited me much better. The headaches have settled and I feel more like myself again.'

Despite a lack of clinical trial data, there are clues about which regimens and types of HRT may be less aggravating for headaches. Some types of HRT may even benefit hormonally triggered migraine. The aim of any HRT treatment is to reduce symptoms at the lowest possible dose of hormones.

Oestrogen component

Oestrogen fluctuations can be a trigger for migraine. Gels or skin patches, which provide more stable oestrogen levels, are better than tablets. Also, continuous HRT is less likely to cause oestrogen 'withdrawal' migraines than the cyclical regimens.

Oestrogen in too high a dose can cause migraine aura. Tell your doctor if you notice any changes in your headaches or accompanying symptoms. After other medical conditions are excluded, headache and aura symptoms are often resolved by lowering the dose or changing the way that it is taken.

Progestogen component

Patches, implants and injections are less likely to cause headaches because, unlike tablets, they maintain more stable levels of progestogen. Continuous progestogen is preferable to cyclical regimens, which are known to aggravate headaches.

Side effects of progestogen include headache and symptoms similar to those of premenstrual syndrome. These may be improved by changing the progestogen type or way in which it is taken. It is important that you do not stop taking the progestogen, which is needed to protect the lining of your womb.

We have no data on which type of progestogen may be better for women with headaches. Some women prefer progesterone derivatives to testosterone derivatives. A natural progesterone, Utrogestan®, is now available that is the same as your own progesterone and is available on prescription. The Mirena® intra-uterine system is a well tolerated way to take progestogen. It is contraceptive and can be helpful for women with migraine. Because it provides protection to the womb, your doctor can adjust the oestrogen dose and formulation to meet your needs.

Tips for coping with headaches around the menopause

- Keep a diary of your headaches and migraines to assess the effect of treatment strategies.
- Don't forget about non-hormonal triggers.
- Aim to optimize symptomatic headache treatments and consider preventatives if headaches increase.
- Report any treatment side effects and changes in health to your doctor. If you are unwell for any reason, this may make headaches worse.
- If you decide to use HRT, then give it a proper trial. It takes time for your body to adjust to hormones, so ideally use it for at least 3 months. Headache and migraine may worsen during this time before an improvement is noticed.

16

Helping yourself

Accepting that you have a predisposition to headaches is part of coping. The next part is doing something about it. Although medications and therapies have their place, you must decide to help yourself as well. This doesn't have to be difficult because small changes in your lifestyle can make big differences. It is about you taking ownership of the situation and not being a passive recipient of treatments and drugs. This chapter outlines very simple but effective ideas to help you cope better.

Learn about your headache

Reading a simple headache book like this one is a good start. There is a lot of information on headaches available on the internet, but you need to be sure that it is from a reliable source. Some websites only want to sell you a product. Always be selective and highly critical.

Research has shown us that people with headaches don't just want pain relief – they need to understand more about their headache. This is an important part of coping. If your headache is severe, being reassured and understanding that it is a proper neurological disorder is essential. You need to feel that it isn't just you who feels like this and to understand that you are not going mad. Because those of us with headaches may not often go to our doctor (and doctors are not always interested in headaches anyway), it is down to us to be informed and to ask questions about our headaches. We can then find out how to help ourselves, and what might be available to assist us. Think of this as ongoing – new ideas and treatments are always being developed.

Join a headache organization or group

Joining an organization is useful to learn about headache and keep up to date with new treatments and research. (See Useful addresses, at the end of this book.) The organizations have informative websites (even for non-members), newsletters and information days. They can tell you where to find headache clinics if you need more support. Information on finding or starting a local self-help group is also available. Some people find it helpful to talk to others who understand the impact of headaches on their lives and families. This isn't true for everyone but could be worth thinking about. People with cluster headache in particular may find it enlightening to talk to others. Because it is rare, they are unlikely to have met anyone else with it and can feel isolated.

Keep a headache diary

You do not need to keep a diary indefinitely – just while you are reviewing your headaches and treatments. Be honest and note *all* headaches and *all* medications. Include over-the-counter pain-killers and not just triptans for migraine. For cluster headache, record even the 'little niggles' before the bout starts. Understanding how they build up could provide valuable information on when to start preventative treatment next time. In short, everything counts!

Why keep a diary?

A diary is useful to track what is happening. It can help you, your doctor and your therapist to see whether strategies or lifestyle changes are having a positive effect. By considering 'before and after' headache patterns, this can be more obvious. If you didn't write it down, it is difficult to remember what was happening a few months ago. Sometimes when headaches have improved, but not gone altogether, you can forget what they were like. Remember that improvement takes various forms. It might not be headache frequency that improves – it could be severity, duration or perhaps taking fewer tablets and having fewer side effects.

Attack diaries provide information on frequency of headache and migraine, type and time when medication is taken, amount of medication taken, patterns at weekends, time the headaches started, changes in headache over time and the relationship to periods in women. All of this is helpful for checking diagnoses and optimizing treatments.

Trigger diaries for migraine encourage you to record food, drink, emotional state, sleep, daily activities and, in women, periods. This is to look for patterns, connections and possibly triggers to avoid. Don't get too obsessed with keeping these diaries other than for a short time – usually these triggers are fairly obvious.

Obtaining a diary

You can devise your own diary – whatever makes sense to you and is easy to keep. Various diaries are available from headache organizations and from the internet. (See Useful addresses at the end of this book.) You need to find one that is right for you. Diaries range from simple, downloadable paper diaries to novel, digital approaches to migraine management. You can use your computer, smartphone or tablet to track factors triggering or preventing your migraine and gain information that could help you manage it better.

Recognize and manage triggers

The relevance of triggers varies between headaches and individuals. If there are trigger factors for your headache, then it is up to you to avoid the ones that you can do something about. This can be alcohol for cluster headache or the build up of stress and muscle tension for tension-type headache.

Many triggers can affect migraine. Assessing and avoiding triggers requires commitment and an understanding of how they build up to tip you over your migraine threshold. One person at the City of London Migraine Clinic had two consecutive months of severe menstrually related migraine, lasting several days. She kept a detailed diary and we were surprised to observe that each one coincided with a business trip. It transpired that the short trips were so pressurized that she was completely out of her usual routine and had little time to eat or sleep properly. We suggested travelling at a different time in her cycle and not to forget about the non-menstrual triggers, which can add up. At her follow-up visit the menstrually related migraine still occurred, but it was more manageable.

Be prepared and get organized

Although this may seem obvious, you must be prepared to prevent headaches and to tackle them quickly. Depending on your lifestyle, this can take some organizing. It means renewing prescriptions before they run out; having treatments in your bag, jacket or car; and remembering them even if you change your routine. I had a severe migraine because I was away at a conference (embarrassingly, a headache one), didn't drink enough water, didn't eat regularly *and* left my medication in my hotel room, because I had a different bag with me.

If you often wake with migraine in the middle of the night, have your medications by your bedside with a glass of water. Jennifer, one of our clients at the Clinic, used tiny plastic pots with lids. She had her combination of tablets for each dose in each pot. Small pots like this are just the right size to keep ready for use by your bed but also in your bag or pocket. This saves valuable time because early treatment can stop the attack taking hold. Likewise, you need to be organized in your prevention by carrying a drink of water and planning to eat regularly. If you have migraine, being late for a meal by just an hour can trigger an attack. Plan ahead and carry a snack to be on the safe side.

If you have cluster headache you may not want to think about the next bout, but it makes sense to be prepared. Always have a current prescription and supply of your treatments so that you can start them immediately. Waiting days for a doctor's appointment causes unnecessary delay when you need pain relief.

Use over-the-counter treatments carefully

Over-the-counter treatments include a range of painkiller medications, herbs and supplements. These can be helpful to cope with headaches. Be cautious if you are using medications on 10 to 15 days per month because overuse can perpetuate the cycle of headache. Additionally, various gadgets and aids such as cooling strips for headache are available. Choosing to buy over the counter is a key part of coping and being in control of your headache. You can make choices about what you use and might find something that brings you relief. However, be wary of any promises of cure. If something sounds too good to be true, then it probably is.

The pharmacist

Your pharmacist can advise on coping, over-the-counter and prescription medications, and whether you need medical help. Always ask to speak with the pharmacist directly – not the counter assistants. You can purchase the anti-migraine drug sumatriptan over the counter in the UK by completing a form and discussing it with the pharmacist.

Take part in research

Scientific research projects on headache and clinical trials on drugs and treatments provide evidence that can increase our understanding. They help us to discover new and better ways of treating and preventing headaches. There is still so much to learn, so do find out about research and consider participating. The headache organizations advertise when volunteers are required or you can enquire directly.

It is potentially an opportunity to help yourself and others in the future. You may try new treatments before anyone else and have access to expert doctors. Even if the study doesn't help you directly, the information is still valuable.

Don't let placebos (dummy treatments) put you off taking part, because the chances of receiving one are often low. We need placebos to ensure treatments really work and are better than what we have already. Our brains release chemicals to improve pain on suggestion alone. A strong placebo effect may account for why some medications and therapies work for headache. Outside of research trials this doesn't matter, as long as it does no harm and you feel better!

17

Looking after yourself

Looking after your health is essential and is very easy to forget with the fast pace of modern life or if your headache dominates your health concerns. This chapter covers some of the issues that can have an impact on your health and could influence your headaches.

General health

Very simply, if your general health is poor and you are prone to headaches of any type, then you will not cope well. Poor health could contribute to making headaches worse too. A balanced diet, plenty of water and getting enough sleep will all help.

Exercise

You should exercise regularly. Research suggests that inactive people are more likely to have headaches. Exercise is particularly helpful for tension-type headache and need not provoke migraine if sensible precautions are taken. (See Chapter 19.)

Smoking

The connection with smoking and headaches is unknown. It can be a trigger for headache in a few people (even passive smoking), and those with cluster headache are often smokers. Smoking increases the risk of stroke and diseases of the heart and blood vessels. If you have migraine, then smoking increases your risk of stroke further. If you develop heart and or circulatory problems due to smoking, you will be unable to use triptans for migraine because they constrict blood vessels. Smoking also increases risk of many cancers, not just lung cancer.

Give up smoking if you can. It is the single best thing you can do for your general health and there is help available. (See Useful addresses at the end of this book.)

Eye strain

Surprisingly eye problems rarely cause headaches. Have regular check ups with your optician if you wear glasses or contact lenses or if you sense a problem with your eyes or sight. Opticians can check your overall eye health and detect potentially serious causes of headache. If you have migraine with aura, the visual disturbances are associated with changes in brain chemistry – not problems with your eyes. However, if you have eye strain, this may act as an additional trigger for migraine in some people, so it is worth eliminating.

Dental problems

Visiting your dentist may not seem very relevant to headache, but lingering gum infections or other teeth problems can cause head pain directly. They can also lower your threshold for developing headache and migraine, and so regular visits and good dental hygiene are important.

Medical problems

Although self-help plays a major role in managing many types of headache, you should recognize when you need medical help. That isn't just for headache (see Chapter 1), but also if there is something else wrong with you. If you have another illness or condition that is uncontrolled, then your headaches may worsen. If you have symptoms that seem minor but don't improve, visit your doctor. Headaches and migraine can improve dramatically when other conditions are recognized and controlled, including injuries; infections; back, neck, teeth, jaw, sinus or eye problems; period problems; depression and anxiety; fibromyalgia; thyroid diseases; insomnia; and even constipation.

Psychological health

Looking after psychological health might seem strange, because headaches are real disorders and are not 'all in the head'. However, in ways we don't fully understand, emotional factors play a part in headaches and how we deal with them. It has been suggested that people with migraine have certain personality types and are very driven and perfectionist. Although not proven, it isn't very helpful because we can't easily change our personalities! Here are some ideas about trying to feel better.

Help from family and friends

People offer help, but we don't always accept it and struggle on. Think about 'lightening your load', not just when you are experiencing debilitating headaches and can't do anything, but the rest of the time too. Organize family routines for household chores and cover from friends. Children are often surprisingly good at dealing with responsibility when a parent is unwell. Encourage everyone in the family to help in their own little ways.

Gather extra support so that everything continues if you are stopped in your tracks by a headache. By sharing everyday pressures and not allowing them to escalate, you may raise your threshold for developing headaches and particularly migraine. You don't have to feel guilty, because you know that you pull your weight when you don't have a headache. It isn't about giving into headaches – it is about living with headaches.

This of course is easier said than done. Lyn, who attended the City of London Migraine Clinic, told me that losing a leg is so visible that everyone can imagine what you might be experiencing. How different it is for people with migraine – everyone thinks it's just a bad headache and they have no idea how debilitating it is. This is part of the hidden problem of headaches – no one really understands what is happening, unless you explain and allow them to help.

Personal relationships

Lyn estimated that she lost about 20 per cent of her life to debilitating migraine attacks and couldn't get by without the support of her husband. Don't underestimate the impact of headaches on both you and your partner. You need his or her support. It is best to be open and communicate your problems and needs so that you deal with your headache together. You may feel guilty about letting your partner down if social occasions are missed and if headaches are an intrusion on family life. There may be times when you cannot take your share of the responsibility. This can be worse if you feel you have brought the headache upon yourself. Remember that this isn't true – it is a neurobiological disorder that you have a tendency toward. As long as you are doing your best to deal with your headache, there is nothing more that you (or anyone else) can expect.

Headaches and sex

Dealing with headaches has an impact on all areas of our lives, including our sex life. It is always a joke – even with people who don't have them – that a headache is an excuse not to have sex. It isn't a joke if your headache is affecting this aspect of your life.

Any long-term medical conditions, including headaches, can adversely affect your desire for sex (libido). It is easy for a partner to feel continually rejected and for your relationship to become strained. Supporting each other and good communication is important to deal with this.

For some people sex can actually cause headaches. They usually occur before or during orgasm. They are more common in men, people with migraine and those with high blood pressure. If you notice this for the first time, you should see your doctor. Occasionally sudden, severe, 'explosive' headaches occurring at orgasm have been associated with a stroke caused by bleeding in the brain. Headaches associated with sexual activity can be due to muscle tension in the head and neck as excitement increases. They don't usually have serious underlying causes, but your doctor should rule these out. Sometimes tests are required and treatments are available.

Relaxation and stress

Learning to relax and cope with stress is important for everyone, but particularly for those with headaches and migraine. If there are sources of stress in your life that you can do something about, then try to deal with them. Tackle issues one step at a time – sometimes just doing something positive is enough to make you feel better.

Take time for yourself, do activities you enjoy and – once in a while – allow yourself time to do nothing at all. You will need to decide to do this, plan time for it to happen and not feel guilty about it. Sometimes the only time people stop is when they are laid up with a headache!

Positive thinking

If thinking positively about headache is too difficult, try at least not to think negatively. Having headaches is a part of your life that you have to deal with, just like anything else. That means finding a treatment that works for you, being confident that you deal with headaches as best you can and not wasting energy worrying about a headache when you haven't got one. If you are having a bad phase, recognize it as just that – a bad phase that will pass. If treatments are not working as well as they were, find new ones.

Keep taking steps back and thinking about why you might be getting headaches. Is there something you can do about the situation? Has it changed? If you need extra help then get it – see your doctor, therapist or other healthcare professional. You do not have to battle alone. Whatever you do, don't give in. It is essential that you remain in charge of your headaches and that they don't gain control over you. If they do for a while, then try everything you can to shift the balance back again.

Depression

Some people naturally think positively, but others are the opposite and are real worriers. If headaches swamp your life it can be difficult to keep your perspective. If you feel that this is happening to you, then simple self-help measures might not be enough and you might need extra support. Depression readily co-exists with headaches and particularly migraine. If you feel you could be depressed, have a chat with your doctor.

Support at work

Many people don't admit to having headaches, particularly in their work, for fear of discrimination. Unfortunately, there is a stigma attached to having headaches, regardless of whether they are debilitating like migraine or cluster headache – as though they are not a proper illness.

If you can, explain to your colleagues. Having support from your peers and managers is an important part of coping. Explain about your headaches and how you are doing everything you can to help yourself. If you have migraine then ensure your work environment is not unnecessarily triggering your attacks.

A few people are so severely affected by their headache for prolonged periods of time that they are in danger of being overlooked for promotion or even of losing their job. If you need support to deal with your employer, the headache organizations can provide information on how to do this more effectively. (See Useful addresses at the end of this book.) Unfortunately, migraine is long term but intermittent, so you have a sickness pattern that occupational health departments flag up. Short notice illness puts strain on colleagues who have to cover for you. If you are not getting support at work to do your job effectively and you feel guilty, this can set up a cycle of stress that can perpetuate your headache problem.

18

Diet

If improving headaches were just about removing foods from your diet or adding a particular supplement, it would be so much easier to cope. It isn't that simple – many of you will have already eliminated all sorts of foods from your diet, only to find that your headaches are just the same. This chapter outlines diet considerations that can help. The dietary and herbal supplements most widely used for headaches and migraine are also discussed.

Avoid dehydration

This simple dietary measure can make a difference to the frequency of headaches and migraine. Our bodies are largely made up of water and changes in water balance affect the body's chemistry. For those of us with migraine, dehydration affects excitable nerve cells in our brains, triggering migraine attacks. If we lose more water from our body than we take in, dehydration can occur without us realizing it. I rarely get thirsty and find it difficult to drink enough. If you drink lots of water and still get migraines, don't stop. You are keeping your migraine threshold higher and might otherwise have more attacks. Here are some things to remember.

- Having a drink of water can sometimes stop a headache from developing.
- Don't wait to get thirsty to have a drink, because by then it could be too late.
- Drink plenty of water every day – aim for 2 litres.
- Keep water convenient and carry a small bottle. It is worth making the effort.
- Caffeine and alcohol are dehydrating, so tea, coffee and alcoholic drinks don't count in the allowance.
- Take extra fluids if you are exercising, the weather is warm or if you are ill with a fever, diarrhoea or vomiting.

Eat enough food

Eating enough is essential for good health and preventing head-aches, particularly migraine. Our brain derives energy from glucose (sugar) from our diet and is sensitive to changing blood sugar levels. If they drop (hypoglycaemia) because you have missed or delayed a meal, a migraine can develop quickly.

Lack of food and irregular eating are important triggers for migraine in children and for headaches associated with exercise. It is a major trigger for my migraine. Sometimes it can be less important than others, but remember how migraine triggers can add up. Here is some advice that we gave at the City of London Migraine Clinic, which I have found helpful.

- *Eat breakfast* to avoid a migraine attack later in the morning. Fasting overnight and not eating breakfast is too long for those prone to migraine.
- *Eat regularly* to avoid fluctuating blood sugar levels. This should be no longer than 4 hours, which can be very hard during a busy day. If you are watching your weight, eat healthy snacks (e.g. fruit, nuts or seeds). You don't have to eat a lot – little and often will be enough.
- *Eat lunch on time* to avoid a migraine in the late afternoon.
- *Eat food that will sustain you* and experiment with foods and combinations to find what suits you best. Food with a low gly-caemic index releases energy more slowly than food with a high index. I have been astonished to discover how I can keep going until lunchtime on a bowl of porridge or muesli, as compared with feeling hungry a couple of hours after eating toast. This is because oat-based cereals have a much lower glycaemic index than bread. Combining carbohydrate with protein in your diet also helps to stabilize blood sugar levels.
- *Eat a snack at bedtime* to avoid the long fast until morning. It can stop migraine waking you during the night. It doesn't have to be too much – another bowl of muesli can work wonders!
- *Eat a varied, balanced diet.* Avoiding too much of any one food group such as sugar, fats, carbohydrates or protein, particularly at one sitting, keeps your blood sugar levels more stable. Reducing sugar, fat, highly processed food and junk food is important for everyone. A healthy diet means dealing with stress better

and fighting off illnesses and infections more easily. This makes headaches and migraine much more manageable.

Maintain a normal weight

Being the correct weight for your height isn't just important for your general health. Research suggests that it could help your migraines and headaches too. Now you have another good reason to maintain your healthy weight or lose those extra kilos! Health professionals use a weight/height formula called the body mass index to indicate whether you are in the normal range or overweight or underweight. You can find out more about this from the Patient website which provides medical information and support. (See Useful addresses at the end of this book.)

Having headaches does not appear to be associated with being overweight. However, migraine attacks may be more frequent and increase the more overweight you are. The reasons are unknown. It could be increases in inflammatory substances such as calcitonin gene-related peptide (CGRP), which are known to be higher in obese people and are implicated in migraine attacks. Higher circulating levels of fats and fatty acids are also inflammatory substances and could be important. One study suggested that a low-fat diet could reduce headaches and the amount of medication required to treat them.

Eliminating specific foods

Many people think that they are 'allergic' to certain foods and that avoiding them will stop headaches, particularly migraines. The body develops antibodies to fight a true allergy, and research has not shown that migraineurs develop this in response to specific foods. Although some people may be sensitive or intolerant to certain foods, they rarely provoke a headache or migraine every time they are consumed. For this reason allergy and intolerance testing specifically for headaches is not usually helpful.

Apart from alcohol and the flavour enhancer monosodium glutamate added to Chinese food, there is little clear research evidence to support eliminating specific foods from your diet to help with headaches. If you find a specific trigger then avoid it, but generally most people find that eliminating foods doesn't help. Anyway, strict elimination diets are difficult to maintain and can make you miserable. More importantly, they may lead to not eating enough, and this is even more likely to trigger headaches and migraine. Additionally, fear and anticipation that something could bring on a migraine attack may be enough to trigger one.

Despite this, the list of postulated potential food triggers is substantial. Here are just a few of them:

- cheese, particularly aged cheeses
- chocolate
- citrus fruits
- pickled foods such as herrings
- preserved, cured or processed meats such as gammon, bacon, sausage, hot dogs and especially those with nitrites
- food additives including MSG (monosodium glutamate) and various E numbers
- artificial sweeteners such as aspartame
- dried fruits such as raisins, dates and figs
- peanuts, nuts and seeds
- smoked or dried fish
- vinegar
- fermented products such as soy sauce
- deep-fried food
- avocados
- bananas
- red plums and
- yeast.

Many of these items contain tyramine, which is naturally found in food from the breakdown of the amino acid tyrosine. The amount varies widely, but it is common in foods that are aged, fermented or have begun to decompose. Tyramine is the likely reason why cheese, chocolate and oranges are always blamed for migraine. Although some people are sensitive, research has not demonstrated a consistent link with tyramine, nitrites or any other food component. At the City of London Migraine Clinic we advised that chocolate is more likely to be a dietary symptom of a migraine attack, rather than a dietary cause. Dr Nat Blau, who founded the Clinic, once told a young boy that he could eat chocolate again, his mother having forbidden it because of migraine. The little lad's smile lit up the consulting room!

It is difficult to know what to do for the best, but some useful tips are provided in the information box.

Tips for identifying foods as a possible trigger for headaches

- Don't stop specific foods or food groups unless you strongly suspect that they contribute to your own headaches or migraines.
- Remember a true sensitivity to a food as a migraine trigger usually causes attacks repeatedly rather than occasionally.
- If you suspect a severe reaction to a food substance, which may include skin rashes and stomach upsets in addition to headache, then consult your doctor. Professional allergy and sensitivity testing may be appropriate.
- A doctor or dietician should monitor any strict diet. Don't commence one without advice if you are pregnant or planning a pregnancy.
- Consider diet triggers in the context of non-dietary triggers and your migraine threshold, rather than in isolation.
- Keep a food and headache diary for 2 months to see whether there are any recognizable triggers. Remember that the migraine process begins before the headache – so look 2 or 3 days *before* it begins.
- If you suspect that a certain food is a trigger, eliminate it for a month and see whether there is a difference. If there isn't, try eating it again and avoid another suspect instead. It is worth being systematic – otherwise you may be depriving yourself of foods in the mistaken belief that they are responsible for headaches.
- Don't make too many changes at once if you want to understand the triggers for your headaches. If you start a new migraine preventative and an elimination diet at the same time, you won't be sure which has helped.

Drink alcohol in moderation

Unlike specific foods, alcohol is a recognized consistent trigger for some headaches, particularly cluster headache. Almost 80 per cent of people with cluster headache reduce their alcohol intake during a cluster bout. The link is less clear with migraine, but migraineurs are much more likely to get a headache triggered by alcohol or succumb to a delayed headache – the hangover. One survey did not find any such sensitivity in those with tension-type headache, and 40 per cent of migraineurs avoided alcohol to avoid triggering migraines.

Type of alcoholic drink and migraine

Red wine and other dark-coloured drinks such as whisky, brandy, beer and port are more likely to induce migraine or lead to a hangover headache than white wine or clear spirits such as gin and vodka. Developing a hangover doesn't even have to be related to the amount you drink.

The exact chemicals responsible haven't been identified and sensitivity varies between people and even countries. The French are more likely to get a headache after white wine! Chemicals in dark drinks such as flavonoids, histamine and congeners are possible culprits. Congeners are natural by-products of alcohol fermentation and give colour, flavour and smell. They could affect blood vessels and encourage the release of inflammatory chemicals to give rise to a migraine.

Headaches and alcohol

Hangover headaches induced by alcohol are delayed, usually occurring when the blood alcohol concentration is falling. They can continue for 24 hours after the level is zero and we don't understand the exact mechanisms. The headaches are not necessarily the same as migraine but they are similar: severe, pulsating pain with nausea and vomiting, and made worse by movement.

Alcohol dilates blood vessels, affects blood sugar levels and increases the chemical prostaglandin – all of which cause headaches. It causes dehydration by affecting anti-diuretic hormones and it is broken down into acetaldehyde, which causes the skin flushing, nausea and vomiting associated with having a hangover.

Apart from avoiding alcohol, research doesn't show that there is anything that you can take to avoid getting a hangover. Treatment is simply rehydration and a couple of soluble painkillers. Coffee can sometimes help, but it is also dehydrating and can upset your stomach, so it may be best avoided. If you are going to drink alcohol, here are some tips to avoid headaches.

Tips for drinking alcohol and avoiding headaches

- Drink plenty of water and have something to eat.
- Drink alcohol slowly and in moderation.
- Avoid any drink that causes migraine quickly after a small amount – this may be a sensitivity rather than a hangover headache.
- Avoid top ups so that you can keep track of what you have had.
- Don't mix alcoholic drinks, which increases sensitivity in headache-prone people, regardless of amount.
- Beware of sparkling alcoholic drinks or even non-alcoholic mixers, which can speed up alcohol absorption.
- Avoid the risk associated with alcohol if you know that you are already vulnerable to a migraine attack because you are tired, have missed a meal or are stressed or excited.

Limit caffeine intake

Caffeine is a stimulant drug, found in coffee, tea, soft drinks and chocolate, which affects our brain by making us feel less tired and more alert. The relationship between caffeine and headache is complex. It can be added to paracetamol and aspirin tablets to enhance their painkiller effect. However, withdrawal from caffeine can cause severe headaches. For some people, caffeine intake is an additional risk factor for developing daily headaches.

Consider whether your caffeine intake could be contributing to your headaches. If you have more than 200 mg of caffeine daily and then stop or cut down, you can develop a caffeine withdrawal headache. Exact amounts of dietary caffeine are tricky to calculate. A cup of tea or can of soft drink may contain at least 40 mg, and a cup of coffee at least double that. It is more if the coffee is strong or you have a big mug! Add on 30 mg per chocolate bar and 30–65 mg *per tablet* of some of the combined painkillers, and you can see how easy it is for amounts to add up.

Research suggests that changes in brain blood flow account for caffeine withdrawal headaches. Anyone can have them – even people who don't normally have headaches. If you are very sensitive, then the difference in one cup of coffee a day is enough. If you drink fewer caffeinated drinks at the weekend than at work, weekend headaches may be due to caffeine withdrawal. They can be accompanied by restlessness, irritability and decreased alertness.

Tips for avoiding caffeine-related headache

- Minimize caffeine in your diet if you can.
- Choose decaffeinated options (only 5 mg per cup of coffee).
- Aim to keep low, stable levels of caffeine, even at weekends.
- Avoid caffeine in painkillers. Combination drugs with aspirin and paracetamol can lead to medication overuse more quickly.
- If you decide to cut down on your caffeine intake, do it very slowly over several weeks.

Dietary supplements

We have little evidence from clinical studies about what works and what is safe to use short or long term. Supplements have side effects, may interfere with other medications and should be discussed with your doctor.

Vitamin B$_2$ riboflavin

Some of the B-group vitamins have been postulated to be helpful in headaches and migraine. We have the best evidence for vitamin B$_2$ (riboflavin). This water-soluble vitamin is involved in releasing energy from the body's cells. Small research trials suggest high doses of 400 mg daily (this is at least 20 times the recommended daily intake) can be effective in preventing migraine. The dose should not be taken as part of a multivitamin preparation to avoid overdosing on other vitamins. Apart from bright yellow urine, side effects in the trials were minimal.

Magnesium

Magnesium has many functions in the body, including glucose metabolism, and it is one of the essential minerals. Research has shown some benefit for magnesium supplements in preventing migraine, particularly for women who also have premenstrual syndrome. The dosages range from 300 to 600 mg daily and ideally should be taken for a 6-month course. Diarrhoea can be a side effect.

Coenzyme Q$_{10}$

Coenzyme Q$_{10}$ occurs naturally in the body and speeds up the processes by which cells produce energy. Evidence from a small-scale study suggested that it could reduce the frequency of migraine attacks by up to half in some people. There were some side effects such as nausea, rashes and fatigue, but it was generally well tolerated. We need much more research but, if it is taken in single doses of up to 150–300 mg per day over several months, there may be some benefit. It can interfere with other medications such as warfarin and insulin.

5-Hydroxytryptophan

5-hydroxytryptophan (5-HTP) is an amino acid in the body that is used to make the chemical messenger serotonin. This may be implicated in migraine. There is no robust evidence from clinical studies for benefit from 5-HTP supplements. They should not be taken if you use triptans to treat migraine because of a risk of serotonin toxicity (serotonin syndrome). It may be possible to boost your serotonin levels naturally in your diet. Carbohydrate-rich meals can increase serotonin, and some foods such as turkey are high in tryptophan, which is converted into serotonin.

Melatonin

Melatonin is a hormone released from the pineal gland in the brain, which regulates our sleep cycle. We need more research to establish whether it is safe and effective in preventing migraine and cluster headache. It should not be used for headaches outside clinical trials. We have little information on side effects, and it could adversely stimulate the immune system.

Herbal supplements

Herbal treatments have been used for centuries and are the origins of some of our conventional drugs today. Some people find them helpful for headaches but they should not be regarded as safe just because they are 'natural'. Herbal medicines can be highly toxic and interact with other medicines. The Medicines and Healthcare Products Regulatory Agency (MHRA) in the UK increasingly register traditional herbs, but unlike conventional medicines there is no requirement to demonstrate that they work. If you take a herbal approach to coping with headache, ideally consult a qualified herbalist for professional advice. (See Useful addresses at the end of this book.)

If you are currently using herbal supplements or considering them, here are some tips.

Tips on selecting and using herbal supplements

- Obtain as much information as you can.
- Purchase from a reputable source.
- Look for products granted a traditional herbal registration (THR) by the MHRA, although remember that this relates to safety and doesn't mean that they are effective.
- Read labels so that you know what doses to take.
- Follow instructions carefully.
- Seek advice from your doctor, pharmacist or herbalist.
- Avoid taking several herbal medicines at the same time unless you are advised to do so.
- Use the lowest possible dose that works for you.
- Use herbal treatment for headache prevention for an agreed time and keep a diary to see if there is an improvement.
- Avoid long-term use because we do not have safety data.

Treatment with herbs can be by tablet, infusions, inhalations, warm compresses, massage oils and baths. Peppermint and lavender are commonly used for relief of headaches and migraine. Ginger, which is a spice, may help with associated nausea. It can be taken as tea, in biscuits or crystallized. The following herbal treatments have been used for migraine prevention.

Feverfew

Feverfew (*Tanecetum parthenium*) is part of the daisy family. Feverfew has been shown in some small trials to be better than placebo (dummy treatments) for reducing the number of migraine attacks. Other trials have not demonstrated an effect and larger studies are needed. We don't know exactly how it works, but it affects relaxation and contraction of blood vessels and stops release of serotonin from platelets, which could interfere with migraine mechanisms. The dose of tablets is 200–250 mg daily. It can also be taken as three or four fresh leaves daily, and the bitter taste can be disguised by eating it in a sandwich.

Let your doctor know if you want to use feverfew. You should not use it if you are pregnant, breastfeeding or taking aspirin or warfarin because of its blood-thinning effects. Side effects include digestive upsets and mouth ulcers. You should try feverfew for 3 months because it can take over a month to start working. Long-term use cannot be recommended because we do not have any safety data.

Butterbur

Butterbur petasin (*Petasites hybridus*) is a native European perennial shrub. We have some evidence from small clinical trials that butterbur can help to prevent migraine attacks. The active ingredients extracted from the root are called petasin and isopetasin. They are believed to act as anti-inflammatories and have effects on blood vessels.

Although in trials butterbur appeared to be well tolerated, there have since been 40 cases of liver toxicity associated with butterbur products. Two cases were severe enough to require liver transplantation. This has raised questions regarding long-term safety and whether the risks of taking butterbur outweigh any benefit. As a result many European regulatory authorities, including the Medicines and Healthcare Products Regulatory Agency (MHRA) in the UK, have withdrawn herbal registration for butterbur. In 2012 the MHRA urged the herbal sector to voluntarily remove butterbur products from the market to protect the public. Therefore butterbur is best avoided until we have clearer evidence regarding safety. In future, any supplements purchased must always be from a reputable source to ensure removal of the naturally occurring toxic components (pyrrolizidine alkaloids), which may be associated with liver damage and cancer.

St John's wort

St John's wort (*Hypericum perforatum*) is a perennial herb. Used to treat mild to moderate depression, it affects serotonin levels. There is some clinical trial evidence for improving depression, but not specifically migraine. The trial doses ranged between 300 and 1050 mg daily. St John's wort interacts with a number of medications, including the triptans (anti-migraine), anti-depressants, anti-epileptics, contraceptives, asthma drugs, heart drugs and blood-thinning drugs. You should not take St John's wort without discussing it with your doctor first. It is not recommended during pregnancy.

19

Non-drug strategies

Non-drug strategies are attractive because not everyone wants to use medications for headaches. Drugs don't always work, they have side effects and they can be over-used. It is also important not to think only of a conventional drug-orientated approach. You should consider how your whole body and mind work together to optimize your health and influence your headaches.

Sadly, various non-drug devices on the market promise cures and invariably disappoint. Try them and hope that you are not wasting your money. In contrast, simple heat pads, ice packs and cooling strips can be effective. There are also physical and psychological strategies, which may be beneficial. Some are termed complementary therapies, which is a useful way to think of them – complementing medical treatments. If you can combine and integrate approaches, this may give you a greater chance of success than either on their own.

We do not have any definitive scientific proof that any of the following approaches work for headaches, despite considerable research in some areas. We cannot state that any one strategy is better than another – it is a matter of trying and finding something that works for you.

Physical strategies

Physical strategies can be effective in chronic tension-type headache, migraine and headaches that occur following trauma such as whiplash injury. The brain stem at the top of the neck joins the brain with the spinal cord, and the nerves here link to the muscles and joints of the neck. It is possible that treatment of the neck and spine influences not just mechanical function but also nervous system function, which could influence headaches and migraine.

Specific differences between physiotherapy, chiropractic and osteopathy are debatable, and techniques overlap. The practitioner should always provide a thorough initial assessment and advice on your treatment plan.

Physiotherapy

Manual therapy by a physiotherapist can alleviate problems associated with the neck and spine. Treatments include massage, mobilization, manipulation and correction of posture. Improvement of your physical wellbeing can improve tension-type headaches and migraine. Some physiotherapists additionally offer acupuncture and lifestyle and stress management. This profession is allied to medicine, and physiotherapists in the UK are registered by the Chartered Society of Physiotherapy. (See Useful addresses at the end of this book.)

Osteopathy and chiropractic

These disciplines, like physiotherapy, are manual therapies that use various techniques such as manipulation of the bones and muscles. This manipulation ranges from gentle massage to short sharp thrusts to realign the spine and neck. The approaches are holistic, with the premise that good health is promoted when problems with the structure of the body are minimized. This can ensure good function of the whole body, including blood vessels and nerves.

Clinical trial evidence has not been conclusive. However, this approach may help migraine and especially tension-type headache, particularly if you have muscle spasm, pain, and tender points in your neck and shoulders that can trigger your headache. Osteopathy and chiropractic are the only two complementary therapies that are fully regulated, like medicine and physiotherapy. (See Useful addresses at the end of this book.) Some practitioners specialize in cranial osteopathy, which concentrates on gentle manipulation of the skull. This is controversial with no scientific basis. If therapists are not called osteopaths, then they will not necessarily be members of the fully regulated healthcare profession.

Exercise

There have been few studies assessing the benefit of exercise on headache and migraine. They have been small and did not last very long, so we do not know whether any supposed benefits were maintained. We need larger scale and longer term research. Exercise is good for your general health because it improves blood pressure, obesity, heart disease risk factors and physical fitness, and it reduces risk of diabetes and depression. How exercise may help prevent migraine and tension-type headache is not known. It could be due to increases in endorphins (the body's natural painkillers) and improved blood flow in the body.

Some people with migraine avoid exercise because it can be a trigger for headache. However, if you are strict about a proper warm up, exercise within a comfortable level for your own fitness, drink plenty of fluids and maintain blood sugar levels before, during and after exercise, then headaches can often be avoided. Joining a gym and having personal training sessions may suit some people but this can be expensive. Bouts of exercise – even just brisk walking for 10 minutes at a time, three times a day – all add up. If you can manage this 5 days a week then you can improve your general fitness. If you can incorporate this into your routine, it may be easier than going to the gym. It is best if you enjoy what you do, so that you can maintain it as part of your healthy lifestyle.

Alexander technique

This technique, formulated around 1900, focuses on your perception of your body's movement and posture through physical and psychological principles. Improvement of stiff and painful shoulders, neck or back, for example, may have a positive effect on your headache. It can be learned from a teacher in a group or individual session and takes commitment to learn and perfect.

Yoga

Originating in India, this incorporates physical and mental techniques, which can promote relaxation, stress reduction and ease muscular tension. There are many types and they may help prevent some headache triggers. Breathing exercises can be useful during an attack of migraine. You need to be taught by a qualified teacher and take time to learn at your own pace.

Pilates

This uses controlled breathing to align the spine and strengthen muscles. The movements aim to be controlled and precise. Gentle exercises, which can be performed at your own pace within a class, can promote a feeling of improved health and wellbeing.

Massage, aromatherapy and reflexology

Massage may reduce anxiety and muscle tension and promote better sleep, which could help with migraine and headache. Oils rubbed onto the skin during aromatherapy massage or inhaled must be used with care because strong smells can trigger migraine. Essential oils should be diluted in a 'carrier oil'. We have no idea of the safety and toxicity of strong oils used over long periods of time. So short term use of 3 to 6 months is sensible, and they should not be used if you are pregnant. Peppermint, lavender and eucalyptus are often suggested for treatment of headaches and migraine. Try one a time to see whether any are effective for you. In reflexology the foot is massaged to promote improvement in health. Although there is no scientific evidence for this therapy for any conditions, it can be very relaxing and people with headaches may respond positively.

Neurostimulation devices

Various non-invasive neurostimulation devices such as GammaCore®, Cefaly® and Spring TMS® are currently being tested for treatment and prevention of migraine and other primary headaches (see Chapter 4). Speak to your specialist headache doctor about obtaining a device or contact Migraine Action or the Migraine Trust to find out about any current clinical studies for which you may be able to enrol.

Transcutaneous electrical nerve stimulation

Transcutaneous electrical nerve stimulation (TENS) devices are used to control pain. They generate a small electric current, which can override pain message transmission to the brain. Studies have not shown significant benefits for people with headaches and migraine, but TENS may be useful alongside other therapies, particularly if you have back or neck problems.

Dental treatment

If you clench your jaw, grind your teeth (bruxism), or have an over-bite or a misalignment of your teeth (malocclusion), then these can cause jaw pain and muscular tension. Chewing gum can make problems worse. There is no robust evidence to suggest that splints or mouth guards can help with tension-type headache and migraine, although it may be worth asking your dentist for their opinion. Rather than treating symptoms of teeth-grinding, it might be best to look at the reasons for grinding teeth, such as stress or other psychological issues.

Psychological strategies

This approach focuses on positive thinking, reducing stress and anxiety, promoting relaxation and coping better with headache pain. These techniques and therapies are useful if you have depression and anxiety in addition to headaches, but they can benefit everyone.

Cognitive behavioural therapy

Cognitive behavioural therapy (CBT) is a psychotherapy approach that helps you to think about relationships between stress, headaches and coping. Learning how to change unhelpful thoughts and behaviours with CBT may enable you to control how you respond to stress, even if you cannot change the circumstances. This can be helpful to stop migraine triggers, change your lifestyle and reduce anxiety. It focuses on the present and challenges feelings of depression, helplessness and a 'just keep taking the tablets' approach. You can deal with your headaches in a more positive way and take more control. For example, rather than staying in worrying about developing a headache, you can learn to think, 'I might get a headache, but it isn't going to stop me from going out. If I get one I'll deal with it.'

There are some online programmes that you can work through, but ideally you should work with a qualified psychologist. Sessions last about an hour and around ten may be required. You can be referred by your doctor, or find a therapist yourself. It can be quite challenging but worthwhile.

Relaxation

Any relaxation technique that can help reduce stress and anxiety may be beneficial in preventing migraine and tension-type headache by raising your threshold for developing them. Relaxation exercises can also distract you from a headache that has begun. We don't know the exact mechanism underlying the relation between stress and headache. Stress rarely causes headaches but there is an association, and people often notice that migraine occurs with relaxation after a stressful event. Although we don't have much evidence, relaxation could mean lower levels of tension, which could make us more resistant to the stress response. That means that by being able to relax more, you reduce stress chemicals circulating in your body.

You can learn relaxation techniques such as deep breathing, meditation or visualization from CDs and DVDs. They can also be learned as part of disciplines such as yoga. Other relaxation techniques such as biofeedback and self-hypnosis are best learned from a therapist. All of these take commitment to learn and time to practice. If you can learn to relax more and balance some of the highs and lows of stressful everyday living, this could help with your headaches.

Biofeedback

Biofeedback training teaches you to control unconscious processes in your body that you are not normally aware of. These include hand temperature, heart rate and muscular tension. Techniques are taught by psychologists during several sessions using a computer to monitor your temperature, muscle activity or brain waves, depending on which biofeedback you are learning. With practice you can use the techniques at any time. There is some research evidence that the relaxation involved reduces stress, and the calming effect can help some people to control their headaches. Contact the headache organizations for details of where biofeedback is taught. (See Useful addresses at the end of this book.)

Hypnotherapy

Hypnotherapy or hypnosis achieves a deep relaxation state in which you subconsciously learn to change the way you feel about pain. Your body learns different ways of responding. Under the guidance of a qualified therapist you can learn self-hypnosis techniques. You may be able to reduce the frequency of headaches by raising your threshold or possibly stop headaches worsening when they start. We have no research evidence to prove that this therapy is effective, but some people may find it helpful.

Other complementary therapies

There are many complementary therapies available. The main ones that have been subjected to clinical study for headache are acupuncture and homeopathy.

Acupuncture

This is the traditional ancient Chinese practice of inserting fine needles into certain points of your body. The needles tap into energy channels with the aim of promoting healing and restoring balance. Western medical acupuncture uses needles at specific points to influence pain mechanisms. The body's natural painkillers (endorphins) may be released during the needling process. The benefits of acupuncture in headache prevention have been studied, but the results are debated and more trials are needed. Acupuncture may be helpful if you have a course with a qualified practitioner. (See Useful addresses at the end of this book.) You may need to repeat treatments to maintain any improvement. You can try acupressure yourself by pressing with your fingers on tender points such as your temple and neck.

Homeopathy

This method of therapy is based on principles of using substances in very dilute preparations to treat 'like with like'. A qualified homeopathic practitioner determines what is required based on individual needs. Clinical trials have shown very mixed results in headache. It may help some people and can be used alongside conventional medicine. A qualified practitioner is always preferable to trying over-the-counter remedies.

Tips for using non-drug strategies

- Do some investigating first. Read about likely effects of treatments so that you can ask informed questions.
- Be wary of any approach offering a cure. Some are based on testimonials from a few people gained by offering cut price treatments and are worthless.
- Consider carefully before parting with money. Many treatments are not available on the National Health Service because they have not been shown to work and can prove expensive over time.
- Choose your therapist with care. Ensure that they are registered or accredited if appropriate. (See Useful addresses at the end of this book.)
- Getting effective therapy involves working with your therapist. Do not commit before you are ready to.
- Tell your therapist about your medical history, including medications that you are taking. A holistic approach can help with your general health, not just with your headache.
- Have realistic expectations, because you cannot expect never to have a headache again. However, if your headache or general health improves, then that is an important benefit. Sometimes just taking time out from a busy life can be helpful.
- Keep a diary record of your headache to assess effectiveness.
- Ask your therapist whether headaches may get worse before they improve. This can happen and it is best to be prepared.
- Ask your therapist how long a course of treatment is likely to take. As with all prevention strategies, give it long enough to work.
- Don't try too many things at once – otherwise you can't be sure what works and what doesn't.
- Don't change medications without discussing with your GP and let them know what other strategies you are trying.

20

Help from your doctor

A supportive doctor is an ally, yet only around three per cent of us see our doctor specifically about headaches each year. Headaches are under-diagnosed and under-treated, and coping with headaches continues to be a burden that many people bear alone. If you can combine self-help strategies with the ongoing support of your doctor, you may gain better control over your headaches.

Do you need to go to the doctor?

If you have any of the signs or symptoms covered in Chapter 1, see your doctor to check the diagnosis. Aside from these features, you do not necessarily need to see a doctor unless you are concerned or need more help. Whether you choose to seek medical help is a personal decision. The doctor who gives you the support you need may not be the first one you meet.

Having a medical opinion helps you to understand your headaches. Information from a book or the internet cannot replace a personal consultation, and it is always reassuring when serious causes for a headache are ruled out. This can be therapy in its own right – it doesn't have to be about taking medications.

Your doctor can also help you with any other medical conditions that you might not connect with your headaches but could be making them worse. (See Chapter 17.)

Realistic expectations

It is important not to expect a cure for headache, because this is unlikely and will always be disappointing. Similarly, don't expect dramatic improvement after a single visit. It is more likely that several visits, months apart, will be required to optimize treatment. The reality is that headache management can be trial and error until you find something that suits you. Even then, don't be alarmed if your needs change and strategies require reassessment in the future.

You should expect your doctor to work with you and be able to discuss your expectations and concerns in an open way. These are different for different people. It might be about improving pain control, reducing frequency, stopping medication overuse or just reassurance that nothing is wrong. Your doctor should be sympathetic and explain your headache and possible management options in a way that you can understand. Together, you can make a decision about what is best for you.

Information the doctor will need

Apart from questions about other illnesses and general lifestyle, your doctor needs to find out about your headaches. There are different styles of consultation. Some doctors let you describe your headaches without interruption, but others ask you structured questions about each kind of headache you have. Obtaining this information is important for diagnosis and deciding whether further examination and investigation are necessary.

Before you see a doctor it is helpful to have an idea of the questions you may be asked or the information that you would like to give. Here are some ideas based on recommendations by the British Association for the Study of Headache. Think about them for each type of headache, if you have more than one.

Time questions

- When did your headache start? How long does it last? How often do you get it?
- Have you had a headache like this before?

Character of headache questions

- How severe is the pain? What is it like? Where is it? Does it spread anywhere else?
- Do you have any other symptoms before, during or after the pain?

Cause of headache questions

- Have you noticed any triggering factors, any aggravating factors or any relieving factors?
- Does anyone in your family have a similar headache or have they done so in the past?

Your response to the headache questions

- What do you prefer to do during the headache?
- Are your usual activities at home/work/school limited or prevented by the headache?
- Are you using medications now for your headache? Do they work? What have you tried in the past and did they work?
- What other treatments or strategies have you tried and did they help?

General health question

- Are you completely well between headaches or are there any persisting symptoms?

Other questions

- Why are you seeking help now?
- Has your headache become worse or changed?
- Do you have any concerns about the headache and its cause?
- Is there any other information that you would like to give about your headache?

Examination by the doctor

The first time you see a doctor or specialist about your headache, they will usually examine you. This is straightforward and undressing isn't normally necessary. People often wonder why doctors don't do more detailed examinations for headache. This is because they obtain most of the information required for diagnosis from your headache history. The examination allows your doctor to confirm the diagnosis, and is typically normal if you have a primary headache.

Your doctor will usually take your blood pressure. Although raised blood pressure isn't a usual cause of headaches, it may influence the choice of treatment. The doctor will examine your eyes using a torch-like device (ophthalmoscope). Increased pressure in the brain can cause headache and swelling, which may be seen in the back of the eye. The doctor will also assess your field of vision and eye movements to check that specific nerves in the brain are functioning correctly. Additionally, the doctor may feel your head and neck muscles to check for tenderness, which is often present in tension-type headache and migraine. They will also listen to your chest and neck using a stethoscope. This assesses your heart and blood flow to your brain.

The doctor may do various simple tests to check your co-ordination and reflexes, for example walking on your heels and toes and touching your nose with your finger. These are quick and easy but effective ways of checking different nerve pathways from your brain throughout your body – rather like a physical brain scan. These tests do not reveal any problem in most people with headaches. If your doctor is uncertain about the diagnosis then they may do further investigations.

Investigations and tests

There are no blood tests, radiographs (X-ray scans) or brain scans that show that you have migraine, tension-type headache or cluster headache. The results are normal. This surprises many people, who think a brain scan is essential – probably because their headache makes them feel so ill. Although a brain scan can be reassuring to both you and your doctor, it doesn't necessarily help him or her to diagnose the headache.

If there is doubt about the diagnosis and other causes of headaches must be ruled out, or you have a rare type of headache such as cluster headache, then your doctor may do further tests. If you have had a head injury, your doctor may order a skull X-ray scan. Blood tests may be useful if your doctor suspects headache due to infection or other diseases.

There are two main types of brain scans. CT (computed tomography) scans can detect bleeding, tumours and blood vessel abnormalities. MRI (magnetic resonance imaging) scans show all the blood vessels and brain tissue extremely clearly and may be used to detect strokes and very small tumours. If your doctor sends you for a scan, they are not necessarily sure that you have a serious cause for your headache, but they want to eliminate the possibility and confirm the diagnosis.

Headache specialist referral

Specialist referral for headaches is either to a neurologist (a doctor who specializes in disorders of the nervous system) or to a headache clinic. These are usually run by neurologists, GPs with a special interest in headache or specialist nurse practitioners. There are headache clinics in the UK that can provide advice on all aspects of headache management. (See Useful addresses at the end of this book.)

Your doctor may refer you if your headache diagnosis is not clear or if your response to standard treatment is not as expected. If you have cluster headache, then specialist referral is recommended to ensure that your treatment is optimized urgently. Early referral of troublesome headaches to a specialist is always best. Because it is possible to have more than one kind of headache, sometimes a specialist opinion is helpful. It is not always straightforward to determine whether you have one type or multiple types of headache – even for specialists. The specialist will liaise with your doctor with their recommendations.

Other referrals

Because headaches are influenced by many factors, your doctor may refer you to other healthcare professionals, including physiotherapists, psychologists or pain specialists. Pain clinics can help you to combine various techniques. This doesn't mean just medications, but includes CBT (cognitive behavioural therapy) together with TENS (transcutaneous electrical nerve stimulation). Combinations of strategies may be beneficial if you have had severe headaches for a long time or if you have other pain conditions as well.

'Off-label' prescriptions

If you need medication for headaches, your doctor can prescribe many more options than those available over the counter. These include medications that are specifically licensed to treat headaches and also those that are not but have still been found to be very effective. These include medications commonly used for blood pressure, depression, heart problems and epilepsy. If your doctor or specialist prescribes these medications 'off-label', then this will be explained to you and noted in your record. Their use is widely accepted in tackling headache and includes some of our useful treatments, such as amitriptyline in migraine and tension-type headache and verapamil and oxygen in cluster headache.

Tips for getting medical help

- Although many people don't go to their doctor with headaches (or have given up), seek help if you are unable to cope on your own.
- If your doctor is not sympathetic or providing support (despite your realistic expectations), then see a different one or go to a specialist clinic. Don't give up!
- If you don't understand, ask again. You will cope much better with new strategies if you understand what they are for and what to expect. Doctors are usually happy to write things down, give you a copy of letters or provide an information leaflet.
- Make some notes yourself. If your doctor is recommending combining or changing treatments, the regimen can be complex. You don't want to be wondering what you should be doing with your tablets in the middle of a migraine attack!
- Take your partner or a friend to the consultation. What one of you forgets, the other might remember. Involving your partner helps them to understand, so that they can support you.
- Prepare for the appointment by thinking about questions you might be asked.
- Take a headache diary to the appointment or keep a diary if requested.
- Be proactive in managing your headache. You may need to be prepared to make changes to your lifestyle and to try new treatments and give them a fair trial.
- Tell your doctor if you are working with other healthcare professionals and therapists or using other treatments. Even some over-the-counter preparations can interact with prescription medicines.
- Let your doctor know whether treatments are effective. If, after a proper trial, something doesn't work for you, then your doctor may suggest something else, rethink the diagnosis or refer you to a specialist clinic.

Useful addresses

Information and support for headaches

These charities provide excellent information on their websites and in their newsletters to help you cope with migraine and other headaches. They support and fund research and raise awareness of migraine and headaches.

Migraine Action
4th Floor, 27 East Street
Leicester LE1 6NB
Tel.: 0116 275 8317
Helpline: 08456 011 033
Website: www.migraine.org.uk

The Migraine Association of Ireland
Unit 14, Block 5
Port Tunnel Business Park
Clonshaugh
Dublin D17 WK24
Ireland
Tel.: +353 1 894 1280 or 1 894 1281
Callsave Helpline: 1850 200 378 (ROI) or
0844 826 9323 (NI)
Specialist Nurse Advice line: +353 1 797 9848
Website: www.migraine.ie

The Migraine Trust
52–53 Russell Square
London WC1B 4HP
Tel.: 020 7631 6970
Information and Enquiry Service: 020 7631 6975
Website: www.migrainetrust.org

National Migraine Centre (formerly **City of London Migraine Clinic**)
22 Charterhouse Square
London EC1M 6DX
Tel.: 020 7251 3322
Website: www.nationalmigrainecentre.org.uk

Organisation for the Understanding of Cluster Headache
OUCH (UK)
PO Box 62
Tenby SA70 9AG
Wales
Helpline: 01646 651 979
Website: http://ouchuk.org

145

Headache organization websites

The following organizations are dedicated to promoting a better understanding of headaches, and their websites provide useful information and links for the public and healthcare professionals. Membership of some is open only to professionals working in the headache field.

American Headache Society (AHS)
Website: www.americanheadachesociety.org

British Association for the Study of Headache (BASH)
Website: www.bash.org.uk

European Headache Alliance
Website: www.europeanheadachealliance.org

European Headache Federation
Website: http://ehf-org.org

International Headache Society (IHS)
Website: www.ihs-headache.org

Lifting the Burden: the Global Campaign Against Headache
Website: www.l-t-b.org

Migraine in Primary Care Advisors (MIPCA)
Website: www.mipca.org.uk

Health organizations

Curelator Headache
London office:
5A Colville Road
London W3 8BL
Website: http://curelator.com

Digital approach to migraine management using website and app to find out triggers and preventative factors.

Menopause Matters
www.menopausematters.co.uk

An independent, clinician-led website providing information about the menopause and all the treatment options.

Mental Health Foundation
London office:
Colechurch House
1 London Bridge Walk
London SE1 2SX
Tel.: 020 7803 1100
Website: www.mentalhealth.org.uk

National Association for Premenstrual Syndrome
41 Old Road
East Peckham
Kent TN12 5AP
Tel.: 0844 815 7311
Website: www.pms.org.uk

NHS Choices and 111 Service
Tel.: 111
Website: www.nhs.uk

NHS information and 24-hour NHS non-emergency telephone helpline for advice and health information if you are unwell.

Patient
Website: http://patient.info

An information resource on a wide range of health topics, including migraine and headaches.

Smokefree
Tel.: 0300 123 1044 (9 a.m. to 8 p.m., Monday to Friday;
11 a.m. to 4 p.m., Saturday and Sunday)
Website: www.nhs.uk/smokefree

Free NHS smoking helpline.

Therapy practitioner information

The following organizations provide information on various therapies and disciplines and have lists of registered practitioners.

Association of Reflexologists
5 Fore Street
Taunton
Somerset TA1 1HX
Tel.: 01823 351 010
Website: www.aor.org.uk

Body Control Pilates Centre
35 Little Russell Street
London WC1A 2HH
Tel.: 020 7636 8900
Website: www.bodycontrolpilates.com/shop

British Acupuncture Council
63 Jeddo Road
London W12 9HQ
Tel.: 020 8735 0400
Website: www. acupuncture.org.uk

British Association for Applied Nutrition and Nutritional Therapy (BANT)
27 Old Gloucester Street
London WC1N 3XX
Tel.: 0870 606 1284
Website: http://bant.org.uk

British Association for Behavioural and Cognitive Psychotherapies (BABCP)
Imperial House
Hornby Street
Bury
Lancashire BL9 5BN
Tel.: 0161 705 4304
Website: www.babcp.com

British Association for Counselling and Psychotherapy (BACP)
BACP House
15 St John's Business Park
Lutterworth
Leicestershire LE17 4HB
Tel.: 01455 883300
Website: www.bacp.co.uk

British Chiropractic Association
59 Castle Street
Reading
Berkshire RG1 7SN
Tel.: 0118 950 5950
Website: www.chiropractic-uk.co.uk

British Complementary Medicine Association (BCMA)
PO Box 5122
Bournemouth BH8 0WG
Tel.: 0845 345 5977
Website: www.bcma.co.uk

British Homeopathic Association
Hahnemann House
29 Park Street West
Luton LU1 3BE
Tel.: 01582 408675
Website: www.britishhomeopathic.org

British Hypnotherapy Association
30 Cotsford Avenue
New Malden
Surrey KT3 5EU
Tel.: 020 8942 3988
Website: www.hypnotherapy-association.org

British Medical Acupuncture Society
BMAS House
3 Winnington Court
Northwich
Cheshire CW8 1AQ
Tel.: 01606 786 782
Website: www.medical-acupuncture.co.uk

**British Psychological Society
(BPS)**
St Andrews House
48 Princess Road East
Leicester LE1 7DR
Tel.: 0116 254 9568
Website: www.bps.org.uk

**British Society of Clinical and Academic Hypnosis
(BSCAH)**
National Office
Hollybank House
Lees Road
Mossley
Ashton-under-Lyne OL5 0PL
Tel.: 07702 492867
Website: www.bscah.com/home

British Wheel of Yoga
BWY Central Office
25 Jermyn Street
Sleaford
Lincolnshire NG34 7RU
Tel.: 01529 306 851
Website: www.bwy.org.uk

The Chartered Society of Physiotherapy
14 Bedford Row
London WC1R 4ED
Tel.: 020 7306 6666
Website: www.csp.org.uk

Complementary and Natural Healthcare Council (CNHC)
46–48 East Smithfield
London E1W 1AW
Tel.: 020 3668 0406
Website: www.cnhc.org.uk

General Osteopathic Council
176 Tower Bridge Road
London SE1 3LU
Tel.: 020 7357 6655
Website: www.osteopathy.org.uk

The General Regulatory Council for Complementary Therapies (GRCCT)
Box 437 Office 6
Slington House
Rankine Road
Basingstoke
Hampshire RG24 8PH
Tel.: 0870 314 4031
Website: www.grcct.org

Institute for Complementary and Natural Medicine (ICNM)
Can Mezzanine
32–36 Loman Street
London SE1 0EH
Tel.: 020 7922 7980
Website: http://icnm.org.uk

National Institute of Medical Herbalists
Clover House
James Court
South Street
Exeter EX1 1EE
Tel.: 01392 426 022
Website: www.nimh.org.uk

Society of Teachers of the Alexander Technique
Grove Business Centre
Unit W48
560–568 High Road
London N17 9TA
Tel.: 020 8885 6524
Website: www.alexandertechnique.co.uk

**UK Council for Psychotherapy
(UKCP)**
2nd Floor, Edward House
2 Wakley Street
London EC1V 7LT
Tel.: 020 7014 9955
Website: www.ukcp.org.uk

Further reading

UK guidelines for management of headaches

British Association for the Study of Headache (BASH)
MacGregor EA, Steiner TJ, Davies PTG. *Guidelines for all Healthcare Professionals in the Diagnosis and Management of Migraine, Tension-type, Cluster and Medication-overuse Headache.* BASH, 2010.
(Available from www.bash.org.uk)

National Institute for Health and Care Excellence (NICE)
NICE guidelines CG150. *Headaches in over 12s: diagnosis and management.* NICE, 2012.
(Available from www.nice.org.uk)

Scottish Intercollegiate Guidelines Network (SIGN)
SIGN. *Diagnosis and Management of Headache in Adults. A National Clinical Guideline.* SIGN, 2008.
(Available from www.sign.ac.uk)

Journal articles

Bashir A, Lipton RB, Ashina S, *et al.* 'Migraine and structural changes in the brain: A systematic review and meta-analysis.' *Neurology* 2013, 81(14): 1260–8.

Becker WJ. 'Acute Migraine Treatment.' *Continuum* 2015, 21(4):953–972.

Burstein R, Zhang X, Levy D, *et al.* 'Selective inhibition of meningeal nociceptors by botulinum neurotoxin type A: therapeutic implications for migraine and other pains.' *Cephalalgia* 2014, 34:853–69.

Buse DC, Lipton RB. 'Primary headache: what's stress got to do with it?' *Cephalalgia* 2015, 35:844–849.

Cohen A, Matharu M, Goadsby PJ. 'Trigeminal autonomic cephalalgias: current and future treatments.' *Headache* 2007, 47:969–980.

Diener H, Limmroth V. 'Medication-overuse headache: a worldwide problem.' *Lancet Neurol* 2004, 3:475–483.

Diener H, Bingel U. 'Surgical treatment for migraine: time to fight against the knife.' *Cephalalgia* 2015, 35:465–468.

Evans EW, Lorber KC. 'Use of 5-HT1 agonists in pregnancy.' *Ann Pharmacother* 2008, 42:543–549.

Goadsby PJG. 'Recent advances in the diagnosis and management of migraine.' *BMJ* 2006, 332:25–29.

Hershey AD. 'Pediatric headache.' *Continuum* 2015, 21(4):1132–1145.

Hong SJ, Roberts DW. 'The surgical treatment of headache.' *Headache* 2014, 54(3):409–429.

Katsarava Z, Jensen R. 'Medication-overuse headache: where are we now?' *Curr Opin Neurol* 2007, 20:326–330.

Kurth T, Mohamed S, Maillard P, *et al.* 'Headache, migraine, and structural brain lesions and function: Population based Epidemiology of Vascular Ageing-MRI study.' *BMJ* 2011, 342:c7357.

Lipton RB, Dodick D, Sadovsky R, *et al.* 'A self-administered screener for migraine in primary care: the ID Migraine™ validation study.' *Neurology* 2003, 61:375–382.

Lipton RB. 'Risk factors for and management of medication-overuse headache.' *Continuum* 2015, 21(4):1118–1131.

Loder E, Rizzoli P. 'Tension-type headache.' *BMJ* 2008, 336:88–92.

MacGregor EA, Frith A, Ellis J, *et al.* 'Predicting menstrual migraine with a home-use fertility monitor.' *Neurology* 2005, 64:561–563.

MacGregor EA. 'Migraine in pregnancy and lactation: a clinical review.' *J Fam Plann Reprod Health Care* 2007, 33:83–93.

MacGregor EA. 'Headache in pregnancy.' *Continuum* 2014, 20(1):128–47.

MacGregor EA. 'Migraine management during menstruation and menopause.' *Continuum* 2015, 21(4):990–1003.

Newman LC. 'Trigeminal autonomic cephalalgias.' *Continuum* 2015, 21(4): 1041–1057.

Pavlovic JM, Buse DC, Sollars CM, *et al.* 'Trigger factors and premonitory features of migraine attacks: summary of studies.' *Headache* 2014, 54(10): 1670–1679.

Rodriguez-Acevedo AJ, Smith RA, Roy B, Sutherland H, Lea RA, Frith A, MacGregor EA, Griffiths LR. 'Genetic association and gene expression studies suggest that genetic variants in the SYNE1 and TNF genes are related to menstrual migraine.' *J Headache Pain* 2014, 15:62.

Schramm SH, Moebus S, Lehmann N, *et al.* 'The association between stress and headache: a longitudinal population-based study.' *Cephalalgia* 2015, 35:853–863.

Steiner TJ, Fontebasso M. 'Headache.' *BMJ* 2002, 325:881–886.

Steiner TJ, Scher AI, Stewart WF, *et al.* 'The prevalence and disability burden of adult migraine in England and their relationships to age, gender and ethnicity.' *Cephalalgia* 2003, 23:519–527.

Stovner LJ, Hagen K, Jensen R, *et al.* 'The global burden of headache: a documentation of headache prevalence and disability worldwide.' *Cephalalgia* 2007, 27:193–210.

Tepper J. 'Nutraceutical and other modalities for the treatment of headache.' *Continuum* 2015, 21(4):1018–1031.

Winter AC, Rice MS, Fortner RT, *et al.* 'Migraine and breast cancer risk: a prospective cohort study and meta-analysis.' *J Natl Cancer Inst* 2015, 107:1.

Books

Cantopher T. *Depressive Illness: The Curse of the Strong*. Sheldon Press, London, 2012.

Hutchinson S, Peterlin BL (eds). *Menstrual Migraine*. Oxford American Pain Library, Oxford, 2008.

Kernick D, Goadsby PJ (eds). *Headache: A practical manual*. Oxford University Press, Oxford, 2009.

MacGregor A. *Understanding Menopause and HRT*. Family Doctor Publications, Poole, 2010.

MacGregor A, Frith A (eds). *ABC of Headache*. Wiley-Blackwell BMJ Books, Chichester, 2009.

Index

acupuncture 50, 93, 103, 132, 137
age factors 1; cluster headache 59; migraine 12, 41–4; tension-type headache 46
alcohol: cluster headache 60; menopause and 103; migraine triggers 15, 30, 31; types and effects 123–5
Alexander technique 133
almotriptan 23, 72, 96
amitriptyline 25; medication overuse headache 77; menstrual migraine 83; during pregnancy 97; tension-type headache 51–2, 53
anti-depressant medications 16, 24, 25, 51, 104
anti-epileptic medication 15,16, 25, 66, 97, 104
anti-sickness/emetic medication 20, 21, 23; medication overuse headache 77; menstrual migraine 83; during pregnancy and breastfeeding 97
appetite 7, 13, 46, 87
aromatherapy 93–4, 134
arteritis 43, 70
aspirin 125, 126, 129; medication overuse headache 72, 73; migraine 19, 22, 42, 86; during pregnancy and breastfeeding 96; tension-type headache 51, 53
atenolol 25
aura: brain changes and 16; causes of 14, 15, 114; children 41; combined hormonal contraception and 88; experience of 33; hole in the heart and 39; HRT and 105, 106; menopause 102; migraine and 6, 7, 8–9, 10–11; older people 43; pregnancy 93; progestogen-only contraception and 89; serious headache and 2; stroke and 17; triptan use and 24

beta blockers 24–5, 78, 97
biofeedback techniques 65, 93, 136
black cohosh 103
botulinum toxin type A injection (BOTOX®) 37–9; chronic migraine 11; cluster headache 66; medication overuse headache 78; pregnancy and breastfeeding 97; tension-type headache 52
brain scans 16, 17, 56, 67, 86, 142–3
brain tumours 1, 3, 56, 70; brain scan for 142; children 41
buclizine 97
butterbur 94, 129

caffeine 119, 125–6; daily headaches 70, 71; medication overuse headache 72, 74, 75; menopause 103; migraine 15, 20
calcitonin gene-related peptide (CGRP) 14, 34, 37, 59, 121
cancer 1, 2, 3, 17, 105, 113, 129
capsaicin/civamide 66
carbon monoxide poisoning 44
children: cluster headache 59; medication and 23, 42, 51; medication overuse headache 73; migraine 9, 12, 41–3, 120; serious headaches 1; tension-type headache 46
chiropractic 49, 131, 132
chlorpromazine 97
clonidine 25, 104
clumsiness 7
cluster headache: being prepared for 111; bridge therapy 62; causes and triggers 59–61; coping with 67–8; definition of 4–5; experience of 55, 67; features of 56–7; improvement in 61; menopause and 101; occurrence of 59; pregnancy and 91; preventive treatments 62, 65–6;

Overcoming Common Problems

Coping with Headaches and Migraine

Second edition

ALISON FRITH

First published in Great Britain in 2009

Sheldon Press
36 Causton Street
London SW1P 4ST
www.sheldonpress.co.uk

Second edition published 2016

Copyright © Alison Frith 2009, 2016

The author and publisher have made every effort to ensure that the
external website and email addresses included in this book are correct and
up to date at the time of going to press. The author and publisher are not
responsible for the content, quality or continuing accessibility of the sites.

British Library Cataloguing-in-Publication Data
A catalogue record for this book is available from the British Library

ISBN 978-1-84709-411-7
eBook ISBN 978-1-84709-412-4

Typeset by Fakenham Prepress Solutions, Fakenham, Norfolk NR21 8NN
First printed in Great Britain by Ashford Colour Press
Subsequently digitally reprinted in Great Britain

eBook by Fakenham Prepress Solutions, Fakenham, Norfolk NR21 8NN

Produced on paper from sustainable forests